VISUAL QUICKPRO GUIDE

ASP.NET

DEVELOPMENT WITH MACROMEDIA DREAMWEAVER MX

Ryan Parnell
Joel Martinez

 Peachpit Press

Visual QuickPro Guide
ASP.NET Development with Macromedia DreamweaverMX
Ryan Parnell and Joel Martinez

Peachpit Press
1249 Eighth Street
Berkeley, CA 94710
510/524-2178
800/283-9444
510/524-2221 (fax)

Find us on the World Wide Web at: http://www.peachpit.com
To report errors, please send a note to errata@peachpit.com
Published by Peachpit Press in association with Macromedia Press
Peachpit Press is a division of Pearson Education

Macromedia Press Editor: Angela C. Kozlowski
Editor: Jill Marts Lodwig
Technical Editor: Alexander Hearnz
Production Coordinator: David Van Ness
Copyeditor: Sally Zahner
Compositor: Christi Payne
Indexer: Joy Dean Lee
Cover design: The Visual Group

ISBN 0-321-14642-5

9 8 7 6 5 4 3 2 1

Printed and bound in the United States of America

Dedication

Ryan Parnell

To Marlee, Derek, and Eric—your support has been off the chart. And to Mark—may you surpass me a thousandfold.

Joel Martinez

To my wife, Tabbitha, and daughter, Layla—thank you for being such a huge blessing in my life.

Acknowledgements

We'd like to thank our editor, Jill Marts Lodwig, most of all. Her tact, patience, guidance, and support in creating this book is an inspiration. In addition, we'd like to thank Alexander Hearnz, who made sure we kept the technical information as accurate as possible, and Sally Zahner, who helped make the material consistent and readable. Many thanks also to David Van Ness and Christi Payne, who made a book with a lot of code come together visually, and Angela Kozlowski, who got the initial ball rolling. Many more people behind the scenes at Peachpit Press, whom we didn't have the opportunity to meet, also made this book possible. We thank you all.

Ryan Parnell

I would like to thank my love, Marlee Eckard, for her support, cheerleading, and distraction—all perfectly timed. Thanks also to Derek Parnell and Eric Schaberg for giving me the time to work on this book and being behind me in the process. Most of all, I'd like to thank God for the opportunity to grow and learn. I hope I honored Him in this endeavor.

Joel Martinez

I'd like to thank God for blessing Ryan and I with this opportunity. My wife, Tabbitha, and daughter, Layla, for just being who they are. Massimo Foti for sending this project my way. Ray West for convincing me to use Dreamweaver instead of Notepad. My parents for always being supportive. And last but not least, my high school English teacher, Ms. Jones, for inspiring her students to make the best of themselves.

TABLE OF CONTENTS

INTRODUCTION

ASP.NET deviates dramatically from previous Web technologies. Fortunately, Macromedia's Dreamweaver MX, while retaining its power as an elegant design tool, smooths the transition to ASP.NET by providing tools that simplify the automation of a Web application. By combining the power of the ASP.NET with Dreamweaver MX, developers are sure to master ASP.NET in no time.

With ASP.NET, developers gain a long list of programming languages from which to choose for developing Web content. These languages are fully object oriented, making the code easier to reuse and maintain over time. Some of the languages are brand new, like C#, and some are rebuilds of familiar oldies, like Visual Basic.NET. In this book, we use C#, because with a new technology like ASP.NET, we felt it was best to start with a clean slate.

ASP.NET also introduces the separation of program code from the markup code. This is a significant advantage to teams of designers and developers: Designers don't have to look at—and potentially break—any program code, and developers won't accidentally destroy a beautiful layout. Another advantage of code separation is that a tool such as Dreamweaver can produce a more accurate WYSIWYG (What You See Is What You Get) representation of Web pages because the programming code isn't interfering with the layout.

Dreamweaver MX is the best editor (better than Visual Studio.NET) for building Web applications that have attractive layouts. Building on the great design tools that Dreamweaver has become famous for, Macromedia engineers have integrated .NET functionalities, such as programmable controls, database support, and validation controls, making Dreamweaver MX a fantastic Rapid Application Development (RAD) tool.

Because the dynamic capabilities of ASP.NET require the use of a lot of code, you'll find plenty of code in this book as well. But Dreamweaver has lots of preprogrammed buttons, wizards, and dialog boxes to do a great deal of the work for you. In then end, we're confident that with the momentum ASP.NET is gaining, along with the skills you'll learn using Dreamweaver, you'll become a Web page developer in high demand if you aren't already.

Chapter 13

Who should use this book?

This book is for people who want to start making their Web pages dynamic using ASP.NET with Dreamweaver MX. We're assuming you have a fair knowledge of Dreamweaver 3, 4 or MX and some experience with building Web pages. You don't need to know how to make pages dynamic with ASP.NET's predecessor, ASP, or any other technology. Your experience using other people's dynamic pages on the Web is sufficient.

This book also assumes you have some knowledge of programming. Because we present a lot of code, you'll need to read it fairly often. The syntax of C#, the language we've chosen to use in writing this book, is similar to other languages such as Java, JavaScript, and C++, so familiarity with one of these languages will make C# a quick study. If you're not familiar with any of these languages, you may have to study a few examples before the syntax really starts to gel for you. But fortunately, a lot of thought went into making C# a solid programming language, so you should find it very logical and consistent.

What's in this book?

We get things underway by introducing you to the .NET Framework and helping you set up your computer to use it. Once you're ready for action, we delve into ASP.NET concepts, so that you gain an intuitive grasp of how to accomplish generic tasks. We feel this approach works better than providing you with a reference guide or case-study like approach, because by understanding basic concepts for making your pages dynamic, you can customize the generic ASP.NET solution we've presented to best fit the problem you're trying to solve.

An example of this approach is the creation of custom validation controls that we cover in Chapter 6. The custom validation control we create in that chapter requires that a date be entered into a form field only when certain criteria are met. While your specific issue may not involve requiring a date in a form field under certain situations, surely you have instances in which you want to require certain data some, but not all, of the time. You can adapt the solution we provide for the creation of a custom validation control in these kinds of situations.

The concepts in this book build in complexity. The list below gives you a general idea of the flow:

◆ Chapters 1 through 3 introduce you to the .NET Framework, help you install it, and provide a quick overview of Dreamweaver MX, in case you're new to it.

◆ Chapters 4 through 6 cover ASP.NET Web Forms and their different components.

◆ Chapters 7 and 8 let you create and work with a database using Dreamweaver MX and ASP.NET.

◆ Chapter 9 discusses how to control access to your ASP.NET Web pages.

◆ Chapters 10 and 11 show you how to create your own ASP.NET controls.

◆ Chapter 12 exposes you to the world of Web Services and teaches you how to create and consume them.

◆ Chapter 13 explores the extensibility of Dreamweaver and ASP.NET.

How to use this book

Because of ASP.NET's new approach to Web development, we recommend reading this book in sequence rather than jumping around from chapter to chapter. Each chapter builds on concepts developed in the previous chapters, so this strategy will save you the trouble of going back to review something you may have missed if you jumped around.

Throughout this book you'll encounter stepped lists that show you how to do certain things. These tasks are meant to give you hands on experience using ASP.NET in Dreamweaver MX. The graphics that accompany the stepped lists illustrate what you should see on your computer while working through the task.

Any code you see is presented in `code` font to make it easy to recognize. Tips scattered throughout the book provide a hint, shortcut, or suggestion to help you accomplish your task. And sidebars, which are set off with a grey background, provide more in-depth or supplemental information where needed.

The Companion Web Site

The code used to develop all of the pages we created in the stepped lists of the book is available on our companion Web site at http://www.peachpit.com/vqp/asp.net/dreamweaver.

We're totally dedicated to providing you accurate information, so please submit any questions or concerns via the submission form on the site. Other resources such as links to downloads and supplemental information will be available at the site as well, so please be sure to check back now and then.

ASP.NET AND THE .NET FRAMEWORK

The .NET Framework is a programming environment made up of rules, definitions, prepackaged code libraries, and reusable software components. As with all things .NET, ASP.NET is built on top of that framework. If you want to master ASP.NET, you need to understand the underpinnings of the .NET Framework. This chapter is meant to help you gain that understanding.

The name ASP.NET sounds very much like the old ASP technology, and both ASP.NET and ASP can be used to make Web pages dynamic. But that's where their similarity ends. In the first half of this chapter, we discuss the major differences between ASP.NET and other dynamic Web page technologies, including traditional ASP. Then we introduce the different parts of the .NET Framework to better acquaint you with your new environment. And finally, because .NET languages are object-oriented technologies, we go over some of the major concepts behind using object-oriented programming languages and techniques.

A New Paradigm

ASP and other traditional dynamic Web page technologies are very different from ASP.NET because they're built using interpreted languages, such as VBScript and JavaScript, whereas ASP.NET is built using compiled languages. Using interpreted languages produces Web pages in which the program code and content code are joined. Compiled languages, on the other hand, keep program code and HTML separate. To understand this difference, first you've got to make sure you've got a solid grasp of how traditional technologies like ASP work.

Dynamic Web pages that are built using traditional technologies, including ASP, usually contain a few lines of code followed by a few lines of HTML, followed by still more lines of code (**Script 1.1**).

When code is intermingled with the content in this way, the Web server is forced to do what is called *context switching*. For each line in the page, the server must interpret whether it's code or content. Then it must compile and run the line if it's code, or output the line to the client's browser if it's content.

If you think code interspersed with HTML content is difficult for the server to deal with, consider the developer who has to write the code. This form of compilation forces developers to write code that's not easily structured and is difficult to reuse. Not only developers, but designers, Web servers, and even development and design tools like Dreamweaver also have a difficult time dealing with the confusion that makes up the page.

Script 1.1 This ASP page, written in JavaScript, contains program code between the HTML <body> and </body> tags. As a result, the server has to switch from processing HTML to processing code.

```
                    script
 1  <%@LANGUAGE="JAVASCRIPT"%>
 2  <%
 3  function hello()
 4  {
 5    Response.Write("Hello from ASP");
 6  }
 7  %>
 8  <html>
 9  <head>
10  <title>Untitled Document</title>
11  <meta http-equiv="Content-Type" content=
    "text/html; charset=iso-8859-1">
12  </head>
13  <body>
14  <% hello() %>
15  </body>
16  </html>
```

Script 1.2 This page, written in ASP.NET using C#, keeps the program code separate from the markup code. The program code occurs between the <script> tags, while the markup code is contained between the <body> tags. Some of the markup code, however, is actually ASP.NET markup code, as is the case with the markup describing the "lblHello" control in the page's body.

```
script
1  <%@ Page Language="C#" ContentType="text/html"
   ResponseEncoding="iso-8859-1" %>
2  <html>
3  <head>
4  <title>Untitled Document</title>
5  <meta http-equiv="Content-Type" content=
   "text/html; charset=iso-8859-1">
6  <script runat="server">
7  protected void Page_Load(Object Src,
   EventArgs E)
8  {
9    if( ! IsPostBack )
10   {
11     lblHello.Text = "Hello from ASP.NET";
12   }
13 }
14 </script>
15 </head>
16 <body>
17 <asp:label id="lblHello" runat="server" />
18 </body>
19 </html>
```

In contrast, with Microsoft's newest programming language for the .NET Framework, C# (pronounced C-Sharp), developers produce program code that's kept separate from the content on the page. **Script 1.2** shows a Web page written in ASP.NET. In this example, all the server-side code is found within the **<script>** tags.

When code is separated in this way, a number of advantages emerge:

♦ The Web server knows exactly which portion is the code and which is the content, so it can compile the code in its entirety once, rather than one line at a time, significantly reducing execution time.

♦ The designer doesn't have to look at all the developer's code while laying out the page.

♦ The developer won't accidentally alter the design when writing the code.

♦ Development and design tools like Dreamweaver can better serve their users by focusing on the two components of a dynamic page—program code and HTML—separately.

A final perk of ASP.NET pages is the fact that you can even place the code in a separate file called a *code-behind* file. By relocating program code to the code-behind files, your Web page can comprise only content. This full separation of markup and program code makes it easier to reuse both program code and the markup. However, we won't delve into any more detail on code-behind files in this book because Dreamweaver doesn't easily work with them.

A NEW PARADIGM

New Features of ASP.NET

Besides the complete change in separation between code and content and the resulting way in which the code is compiled, ASP.NET has some significant new features that aren't a part of standard ASP or other traditional Web development environments.

Server controls

ASP.NET server controls comprise programmable, prepackaged server-side program code written to perform dynamic functions. These server controls are referenced by tags using a special syntax, `<asp:tagname…>`, and are then placed within your Web pages, where they execute. When subsequently executed by ASP.NET, these tags are converted into HTML and content to be rendered by the user's browser. For example, a simple control, "asp:label," represents a server control that displays text using HTML `<span…>` tags.

Server controls vary in the functionality they provide. Standard ASP.NET server controls such as "asp:button" and "asp:textbox" are designed to be used in place of their more traditional counterparts (the HTML `<input>` form elements of type button and text). They look the same in Dreamweaver's Design view and will appear the same in the browser (**Figure 1.1**). However, notice in **Script 1.3** that although they look the same in Design view, the markup is vastly different. Using server controls in place of the traditional HTML controls lets you take advantage of ASP.NET features, such as being able to dynamically set the control's attributes at run time.

Script 1.3 Even though the asp:textbox and asp:label controls look the same in Dreamweaver's Design view, their markup is quite different.

```
                          script
 1  <%@ Page Language="C#" ContentType=
    "text/html" ResponseEncoding="iso-8859-1" %>
 2  <html>
 3  <head>
 4  <title>Untitled Document</title>
 5  <meta http-equiv="Content-Type" content=
    "text/html; charset=iso-8859-1">
 6  </head>
 7  <body>
 8  <form runat="server">
 9  <p>
10    <asp:textbox ID="txtSampleTextBox" runat=
      "server" />
11  </p>
12  <p>
13    <asp:button ID="btnSampleButton" runat=
      "server" Text="Sample Button" />
14  </p>
15  </form>
16  </body>
17  </html>
```

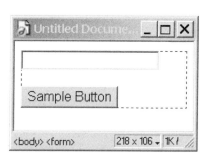

Figure 1.1 Standard ASP.NET server controls such as asp:button and asp:textbox look the same in Dreamweaver's Design view as their more traditional counterparts (in this case, the HTML `<input>` form elements of type button and text), and will also appear the same in the browser.

Script 1.4 In addition to replacements for traditional HTML elements like the asp:button, ASP.NET adds new elements such as the asp:RequiredFieldValidator and alters old ones like the hidden form field.

```
                      script
 1 <%@ Page Language="C#" ContentType="text/html"
   ResponseEncoding="iso-8859-1" %>
 2 <html>
 3 <head>
 4 <title>Untitled Document</title>
 5 <meta http-equiv="Content-Type" content=
   "text/html; charset=iso-8859-1">
 6 </head>
 7 <body>
 8 <form runat="server">
 9 <input type="hidden" id=
   "hdnSampleHiddenElement" runat="server" />
10 <p>
11   <asp:textbox ID="txtSampleTextBox" runat=
     "server" />
12   <asp:requiredfieldvalidator
13     ControlToValidate="txtSampleTextBox"
14     Display="Dynamic"
15     ID="rfvSampleValidator"
16     runat="server"
17     Text="This textbox is required." />
18 </p>
19 <p>
20   <asp:button ID="btnSampleButton" runat=
     "server" Text="Sample Button" />
21 </p>
22 </form>
23 </body>
24 </html>
```

Validation controls

Validation controls are used to validate the data an end user enters, or possibly fails to enter, into form elements. For example, a validation control can be used to make a field in an entry form a required field. In addition to requiring form fields to be filled, validation controls in ASP.NET can be used to validate the user's input against a range of values or to compare two values. **Script 1.4** uses the Required Field Validator control to force the user to enter data into the "txtSampleTextBox" control before the form will submit.

List controls and rich controls

ASP.NET list controls are used to iterate, process, and display dynamic data. To associate a list control with data, we bind (link) dynamic data, such as database query results, to a list control. Performing the binding operation automatically populates a List control with data from a data source such as an array or a database.

Rich controls are complex components that can be placed directly into an ASP.NET Web page. Examples of rich controls include the Calendar and Ad Rotator controls, which display a calendar and a rotating advertisement respectively. In ASP.NET, these two controls are easy to add to Web pages, whereas those same controls are difficult to add in ASP.

HTML server controls

HTML server controls look the same as normal HTML elements, except that they have an extra attribute, "runat," which is set to the value "server." You'll find an example of an HTML server control in Script 1.4. It's the hidden form element in Line 9, just before the first <p> tag in Line 10.

By adding the `runat="server"` attribute to make our hidden element a server control, the control is processed on the server and we gain programmatic accessto this hidden element in the code we write. Such access was not possible before ASP.NET and is not possible for plain HTML elements that lack the `runat` attribute setting.

User and custom controls

There are two types of controls we can create ourselves. The first is called a *user control,* which can be thought of as a mini-ASP.NET Web page because it may contain many of the same elements as ASP.NET pages, such as HTML, content, and server controls. User controls replace server-side include files used in traditional Web development platforms, but unlike include files, they are completely accessible and customizable at run time.

You create user controls the same way you create ASP.NET Web pages, and you can use them in ASP.NET Web pages the same way you use other controls such as asp:button or asp:textbox.

Custom controls, on the other hand, are controls that you can create that are more powerful and complex than user controls. They must be written entirely in programming code, such as C# or Visual Basic, and are precompiled prior to execution for faster turnaround.

Web services integration

Another new feature of ASP.NET is the complete integration of Web services. A *Web service* is, in a sense, a small program available over the Internet to which you can call functions and get results.

For example, the U.S. Postal Service might write a Web service that provides a list of all zip codes. From within your Web page, you could call this Web service to get the list of zip codes and add that data to a drop-down list box. Visitors to your Web site would then be able to select from that list. If the Postal Service updated the list, your page would automatically be updated as well, since the information isn't being stored locally.

Web services are going to become more and more valuable to Web developers, because they let the people who are experts in something (and let's face it, the U.S. Postal Service is an expert in zip codes) provide their expertise to others, like an up-to-date list of zip codes we could use in our Web page.

Web services work by transferring data encoded in XML over a transportation technology, such as HTTP. It takes some know-how to use them, and writing to them from scratch is even more complicated.

Fortunately, by leveraging ASP.NET's integration with Web services, Dreamweaver has made it fairly easy to create and use Web services. So we're sure you'll be using them in your Web pages and even creating your own for others to use.

Similarities to ASP

A great benefit to those who have previously built ASP-driven Web sites and are seeking to migrate to ASP.NET is that ASP pages may coexist with ASP.NET pages in the same site. This fact makes transitioning ASP Web sites into ASP.NET Web sites more feasible. However, ASP.NET pages can't share the same application and session information with ASP pages, so any data shared between an ASP.NET page and an ASP page must be done by sharing form elements, attaching data to hyperlinks, or using a shared database.

Script 1.5 This page, written in ASP.NET using C#, demonstrates how code doesn't have to be separated from content in ASP.NET.

```
 1 <%@ Page Language="C#" ContentType="text/html"
   ResponseEncoding="iso-8859-1" %>
 2 <html>
 3 <head>
 4 <title>Untitled Document</title>
 5 <meta http-equiv="Content-Type" content=
   "text/html; charset=iso-8859-1">
 6 <script runat="server">
 7 void hello()
 8 {
 9   Response.Write("Hello from ASP.NET");
10 }
11 </script>
12 </head>
13 <body>
14 <% hello(); %>
15 </body>
16 </html>
```

In making the transition from ASP to ASP.NET, you'll also find some of ASP's familiar features still available in ASP.NET.

For example, the Response and Request objects are still around, although they've changed a bit. If you forget what these objects do, they reflect all the information that's been submitted with a request for a Web page (the Request object) and all the information that's returned in the response (the Response object).

The Request object contains useful information about the request being made, including any form or Querystring data that's submitted with the request, while the Response object contains the information that's to be returned to the browser. Response and Request information is automatically tracked for you by the Web server as a byproduct of processing a request for a Web page.

Another familiar ASP feature you'll notice is that you can still intermingle your code with the content, although we don't recommend it. It's an acknowledged industry best practice to separate code from content for various reasons, including the fact that the page is much easier to maintain this way. Take a look at **Script 1.5**. It's written in ASP.NET using C#, but you see there's little difference between it and Script 1.1, which was written in ASP using JavaScript. This is because ASP.NET still allows you to develop using the prior ASP framework. You just won't be getting the benefits that ASP.NET provides in code and markup separation if you do.

Components of the .NET Framework

This section discusses the three major components on the .NET Framework: the common language runtime (CLR), the common type system, and the class library. Together they provide the rules, definitions, class libraries, and software components of the environment in which we'll be programming.

Common language runtime

The common language runtime (CLR) is the virtual machine in which all .NET programs run. If you're unfamiliar with the concept of a *virtual machine*, think of it as a program that runs other programs. We refer to it as a virtual machine because it's invisible in a sense—the programs that are running inside it have no awareness of it. They respond as if they were running directly on the operating system, just like other programs do.

However, there are some major differences between programs running in the CLR and programs running on the operating system. One of the main differences is that when running in the CLR, programs don't need to monitor memory and remedy errors like they do when they're running on their own. The CLR handles it all. It automatically manages the process of freeing up unused memory on a periodic basis. Another task the CLR performs is to intercept errors and report them in a standard format to the programs running within it. Capturing these errors early on provides an opportunity to trap and remedy errors programmatically before the user ever knows they're there.

Another difference between programs that run in the CLR and those that run directly on the operating system is the way in which they're compiled.

In general, before programs are able to execute, they must be compiled into *binary files*, which are simply files containing language the computer understands.

When we compile a .NET program, however, it's first converted into an intermediate virtual-machine-readable language, called the Microsoft Intermediate Language (MSIL). MSIL is then later compiled the rest of the way into a computer readable language, or binary file, when it executes.

This technique of creating the computer readable file just prior to execution is called just-in-time (JIT) compilation. With JIT compilation in ASP.NET, programs are compiled all at once and the resulting binary file is stored and available for reuse for the duration of the program's execution, without any additional compilation.

Interpreted languages such as JavaScript, on the other hand, require that each line of code get interpreted every time they are executed. As a result, a line of code that is part of a repeatedly called function will end up being interpreted and compiled several times.

Common type system

The common type system (CTS) is the glue that makes all the .NET languages such as C# .NET, Visual Basic .NET (VB .NET), and COBOL .NET work together. The CTS defines a standard set of types that must be supported by all .NET languages. These types can be value types, which are used for simple variables, or reference types, which are used with objects.

To get a sense of how a common definition helps these languages interact, think about the relationship between Visual Basic and C++. The seeming ubiquitousness of VB is due in large part to the fact that it doesn't require programmers to have an intimate knowledge of memory management or other low-level details in the same way that other languages like C++ require. As a result, a large percentage of programs available today have been written using VB. However, most of the Windows operating system was written in C++, and VB and C++ do not share common data type and value definitions. So developers writing VB programs to run on Windows have their work cut out for them.

When VB developers need access to some of the lower-level operating system functions (written in C++), they write program code to approximate the data types being passed during the function calls. This is standard practice, despite the fact that poor approximations sometimes cause errors during the function calls. If making a data type approximation isn't possible, the call to the operating system's function from Visual Basic can not be made, causing the program to fail.

In contrast, when the CTS defines a common set of data types, programs written in different .NET languages don't run into the same problem. This is because as the language types are being passed from one function to another, the CLR performs a safety check on them. If the CLR detects type-related problems, it suspends the compilation of the program, giving the developer time to correct the problem. As a result, the programmers don't have to approximate the other languages's types.

To supplement the common data type definitions, the CTS includes the common language specification (CLS), which defines the naming conventions that publicly available functions and interfaces must follow in .NET languages. By having a defined naming convention, programs written in different languages can call functions written in other languages without accidentally calling the wrong one or passing the wrong information.

With all these commonalities between the different languages defined, and with the CLR hosting the languages and running them as MSIL, they can interoperate seamlessly. In fact, the CLR, CTS, and CLS even make it possible for one part of a program to be written in one language and another part to be written in a different language! You most likely wouldn't want to do this, however, because it's harder to program in more than one language. But the CLR certainly wouldn't prevent you from doing it if you wanted to.

The class library

Because all .NET languages conform to the common type system and compile in the CLR as the same MSIL language, they also can use the same class libraries.

Let's look a little more closely at the concept of class libraries. In object-oriented programming, a *class* is an object that can be thought of as a template used to define something— for example, a circle—that you want to represent in code. The template stores the information about that object as *properties* and contains functions, called *methods*, that run based on those properties. (We discuss the concept of object-oriented programming in more detail in the next section, "Writing Code in .NET.")

A *class library* is a collection of predefined code packaged as classes that are available for general use. For developers, the trick lies in finding the right library to suit your needs. All too often, developers end up creating the classes they need from scratch, when a library of those same objects is already available. All of the .NET classes can be found on the branches of the System namespace.

If you're unfamiliar with the concept of *namespaces,* they are a hierarchical naming convention used to uniquely identify and group classes. For instance, say you need a class to store data in tabular format. If you look in the System.Data namespace, you'll find a class called DataTable. Or perhaps you need to write HTML out to a client visiting your Web site. If you look in the System.Web namespace, you'll find the HttpResponse class for that sort of work.

Classes can be named separately, without including their corresponding namespace, as seen in the examples in the previous paragraph, or you can affix the namespace to the beginning of the class. For example, the DataTable class might be referred to as System.Data.DataTable, and the HttpResponse class might be called System.Web.HttpResponse. Leaving the namespace off the class name is OK as long as it's clear which namespace it's associated with. Setting the namespace context and then referencing the class name separate from its namespace is what's normally done, because it reduces the amount of typing required. Having namespaces included in the class name groups classes together and gives them more specialized, unique names that avoid naming conflicts later on. For example, two classes named DataSet might exist: One DataSet class might reside in the System.Data namespace, while another might exist in the fictitious System.OtherData namespace. However, if the classes are named System.Data.DataSet and System.OtherData.DataSet respectively, there's no confusion as to which is which, so you won't end up using the wrong DataSet class.

The following is a list of common namespaces that can be found within the .NET Framework Class Library.

- **System:** This is the root .NET namespace. It contains the definitions of all data types—from Int32, commonly known as int or integer, to Object, the root class of all classes in .NET.

- **System.Data:** This namespace is where all classes having to do with data are defined.

- **System.Xml:** All classes having to do with reading, writing and manipulating XML (Extensible Markup Language) reside in this namespace.

- **System.Net:** Classes that support the transporting of data over a network are defined here.

- **System.Text:** The classes that handle character and string manipulation will be found in this namespace.

- **System.Security:** This namespace contains all the classes that have to do with security.

- **System.Web:** All classes that pertain to ASP.NET and Web Services will be found here.

Writing Code in .NET

Now that you have some understanding of the components that make up the .NET Framework, we want to introduce you to the C# language and some object-oriented programming concepts. We chose C# over the other .NET programming languages, such as Visual Basic.NET (VB .NET), because we believe using a brand new language will keep old, traditional Web development and ASP coding techniques from showing up in your new ASP.NET Web pages. This might happen if we chose VB .NET because of its similarity to Visual Basic, whereas C# is quite different from C++.

Let's start by introducing some vocabulary. Following each definition will be a C# code example to help you recognize what the code looks like for each of the concepts described.

- **Class:** See the previous section, "The class library," for a definition of class. An example of a class you could create yourself might be called Car. Your Car class should probably store information about how much gas it has. Then one of its methods might be Drive.

```
// The start of our class definition
public class Car {
}
```

- **Object:** An object is an instance of a class. In other words, while the class represents the blueprint for an object, the object is the physical representation of the class that your program creates in memory and references using a variable. Note that the two words *object* and *class* are sometimes used interchangeably to refer to the same thing.

  When we create an object in memory while a program is running, we call that *instantiation* because we're creating an instance of the class.

```
public class Car {
}
// variable c being assigned an
// object instance of our Car class
Car c = new Car();
```

- **Member variable:** These are the variables within an object that store data about that object. Using the Car class example, Gas would be a member variable of our class.

```
public class Car {
  // our integer member variable
  private int Gas;
}
```

- **Method:** This is the object-oriented vernacular for function. Methods are called to run by name and take zero or more parameters. They will return zero or one value when execution is complete. Here we've started our Drive method. It takes no parameters and doesn't return anything.

```
public class Car {
  private int Gas;
  public void Drive() {
    // write code to decrease Gas
  }
}
```

- **Property:** A property of a class is a specialized method. They are specifically meant to set (store) or get (retrieve) values of member variables. The reasoning is that member variables should never be directly accessible from outside the object to ensure the member variable's data integrity.

```
public class Car {
  private int Gas;
  public int Gasoline {
    get {
      // let them find out how much
      // is left in the tank
```

continues on next page

```
      return Gas;
  }
  set {
    // allow them to fill up
    Gas = value;
  }
}
public void Drive() {
  // write code to decrease Gas
}
}
```

♦ **Overloading:** This is the term given to a class's ability to define more than one method with the same name, but with a different set of parameters. For overloading to occur, the two methods must be uniquely identifiable by their parameter lists. If their parameter lists are the same but their return data types differ, that doesn't count as uniquely identifiable and the methods will not qualify for overloading.

The following example simplifies our Car class to just have two methods and no member variables or properties. The two methods are both called Drive. One doesn't have parameters and assumes you want to go forward. The second takes a parameter that indicates a direction. Often methods are overloaded to reuse method names and their associated code, and have them perform differently based on the parameter set being used.

We took this approach in making the Drive function with no parameters call the one that takes parameters. This makes the call easier for our caller, but saves us from having to write the same or similar code twice.

```
public class Car {
  public void Drive() {
    Drive( "forward" );
  }
  public void Drive(string direction)
```

```
  {
    // write code to drive in the
    // specified direction
  }
}
```

♦ **Inheritance.** This is the most complex and powerful concept of object-oriented programming. To explain it we'll go back to our Car class example. Suppose for a moment that our program has been working fine using the Car class, but now we need to add the ability to work not only with our un-specialized Car class, but with a specialized hatch-back type car. We could write a new class to satisfy our need for a hatch-back type car, but it would be almost exactly like our current Car class, just with the ability to open the hatch-back door.

To keep from having to duplicate code when defining our HatchBack class, we can inherit the definition of the Car class and specialize only what we need to. See what we mean in the following code.

```
public class Car {
  // Gas, Gasoline, Drive and
  // Drive(direction) definitions
  // go here
}
public class HatchBack : Car {
  public void OpenHatch() {
    // write code to open the hatch
  }
}
HatchBack hb = new HatchBack();
// hd inherits all of car's methods
hb.Drive();
```

Not only does inheritance save us from having to define everything in the Car class again, but if we add a method or property to the Car class later, our HatchBack class will automatically inherit the new addition as well.

GETTING
STARTED WITH .NET

Now that you have some understanding of .NET components, you're probably eager to get started with it. But before you can begin using .NET in your projects, you'll need to set up a few things first.

This chapter walks you through the installation and configuration of Microsoft's standard Web server software, Internet Information Server (IIS); Microsoft Data Access Components (MDAC); and the .NET Framework Software Development Kit (SDK). We discuss each of these applications and the part they play in the development of ASP.NET pages. If you already have them installed and know how to manage Web sites, feel free to skip this chapter. However, you may want to skim through it anyway—for the nuggets about security and to gain a better understanding of how each application is used.

Installing .NET

A lot of talk about the upcoming release of Microsoft's .NET Enterprise Servers has made some developers nervous that .NET's development requirements will be steep. But not to worry—most scenarios don't require anything more than the .NET Framework SDK. The SDK includes such components as compilers, assembly code tools, lots of prepackaged code that can be extended to create your own ASP.NET Web applications, and a global assembly cache tool. It also includes the .NET Framework discussed in Chapter 1.

Since this book focuses on ASP.NET, the compilers and prepackaged code are really all we'll need of the SDK. However, an additional requirement of ASP.NET is a .NET-capable Web server to serve those pages. As of this writing, IIS is the only .NET-capable Web server.

The .NET Framework must be installed on the target of deployment, such as the Web server. You shouldn't assume the target of deployment will already have it installed. However, Microsoft does have plans to include the Framework in a host of upcoming product releases, with the .NET Enterprise Servers being one of them. And Internet Explorer (IE) will soon include the .NET Framework as a standard component as well, which takes care of the majority of end-user computers. Thankfully, since all .NET code is executed on the server for ASP.NET pages, we won't have to wait for end users to upgrade to the latest version of IE. We only have to be concerned about what's loaded on the Web server.

Another concern of developers is the fact that .NET code can be easily changed back into readable source code after being compiled. As a result, you could end up having a lot of your code stolen.

.NET Framework SDK Requirements

According to Microsoft, you must have at least one of the following to run the .NET Framework SDK:

- Windows NT 4 with Service Pack 6a
- Windows 2000 with Service Pack 2
- Windows XP Professional

However, ASP.NET requires IIS 5.0 or later, which in turn requires Windows 2000 or XP. As a result, Windows NT isn't really an option, unless you're using a remote server to host your development pages.

In addition, Microsoft lists the following requirements:

- Internet Explorer 5.01 or later
- Microsoft Windows Installer 2.0

Order of Installation

We recommend that you follow the order of installation outlined in this chapter. It's especially important to install IIS *before* the .NET Framework SDK, since there's no easy way to add ASP.NET to IIS without reinstalling the whole .NET Framework.

Compounding this concern is the fact that .NET lets you store data (called metadata) within the assembled code module that makes code more readable when it's decompiled and viewed with a decompile tool. Some developers worry about the security risk this poses.

Fortunately, ASP.NET pages are usually kept on a secure Web server and aren't distributed, so they're protected.

For the instances when you do distribute your code widely, either fully or partially compiled, the best solution for preventing code theft is to use an obfuscator to make the code unreadable after it's been decompiled. An *obfuscator*—*obfuscate* means to confuse—is a tool that alters the code so that it's confusing to read but still functions exactly the same with no speed trade-off.

Dotfuscator is one such tool from PreEmptive Solutions (www.preemptive.com) that is specially made for .NET, though many similar products are available. If you're in doubt about your code's security, try using a decompiler and an obfuscator to compare the before and after effects of the obfuscator.

Now that you have an underlying knowledge of .NET, let's get to the installations.

INSTALLING .NET

To install IIS:

Although installing IIS 5.0 is straightforward, you must use the Windows Install CD-ROM to do it.

1. Open Windows' Add/Remove Programs control panel.

2. Choose the Add/Remove Windows Components button on the left side of the new window.

   The Windows Components Wizard appears (**Figure 2.1**).

3. Check the box next to Internet Information Server. If you want to learn more about the components that make up IIS, click the Details button.

4. To start the installation, click Next.

   The installation displays a status window throughout the process (**Figure 2.2**).

   The installation program will prompt you for the CD-ROM during this process if it's not already in the CD-ROM drive.

5. Click Finish when the Windows Component Wizard prompts you upon completion of the install (**Figure 2.3**). No restart is required.

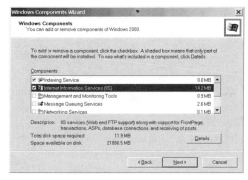

Figure 2.1 The Windows Components Wizard allows you to install IIS as well as other Windows software components.

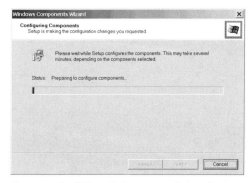

Figure 2.2 The IIS installation status window displays the installation process' level of completion.

Figure 2.3 Click Finish when the IIS installation is complete.

INSTALLING .NET

Microsoft Data Access Components

You must also install and use the Microsoft Data Access Components (MDAC) version 2.6 or later with the .NET Framework. We agree with Microsoft's recommendation that you use the current release, which is version 2.7. Before discussing what MDAC is, let's look at the previous data access technology: ODBC.

ODBC—Open Database Connectivity—has been around for years. Defined by Microsoft, it became a standard generic driver for connecting to a variety of different database management systems (DBMSs). It's such an entrenched standard that you can assume any DBMS you work with will be ODBC compliant. And if you're careful not to use vendor-specific extensions to the interface, you'll be able to easily switch database vendors down the road.

Microsoft, however, has taken data access to the next level with its Universal Data Access strategy. The company recognized that much useful data resides in locations other than databases, such as email servers, spreadsheets, and even data sources not yet recognized or even invented. Universal Data Access lets you access the data directly in its native environment instead of having to copy it over to an ODBC-compliant database. This strategy is implemented in the MDAC.

MDAC uses what are called data providers to reach that data. A *data provider* permits access to a type of data store. One type of data provider, the OLE (Object Linking and Embedding) DB provider, is a system-level programming interface to individual relational and nonrelational data sources. Data providers abstract any features specific to one source type and format the data into a common format called a *rowset*.

MDAC also uses two provider-neutral application-level programming interfaces: ADO and ADO.NET (ADO.NET extends ADO by adding support for disconnected datasets and XML). Using ADO or ADO.NET, programmers can utilize any OLE DB compliant driver at a higher level to connect to databases. This frees programmers from having to manage memory and other low-level operations, but doesn't remove the ability for those programmers who want that power.

Finally, MDAC implements ODBC to ensure access to data sources that aren't OLE DB compliant.

INSTALLING .NET

To install the latest MDAC:

1. Download a file from Microsoft called MDAC_typ.exe.

   You can find a link to the (5 MB) download file at www.microsoft.com/data/download_270RTM.htm.

2. Run the file to start the installation.

3. You'll be greeted by a standard Microsoft End User License Agreement, or EULA (**Figure 2.4**). You must accept Microsoft's terms to continue.

4. Ignore the warning to shut down any tasks you have running in order to avoid having to reboot after the install—the fact is, you'll have to reboot in any case (**Figure 2.5**). Just click Next to proceed to the installation.

5. Click the Finish button to start the install (**Figure 2.6**).

6. The installer lets you choose when to restart (**Figure 2.7**). Click the radio button of your choice, and then click the Finish button at the bottom of the screen.

   In either case, you'll need to reboot before continuing on to the .NET Framework SDK installation.

Figure 2.4 Read and accept the Microsoft End User License Agreement.

Figure 2.5 The Task shutdown warning displays any programs currently running that will need to be restarted after the installation process.

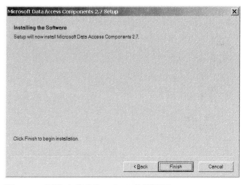

Figure 2.6 Click Finish to install MDAC.

Figure 2.7 Choose how to restart the computer after the MDAC installation program has completed.

.NET Framework SDK

In Chapter 1, we presented a basic overview of what makes up the .NET Framework. Here, we discuss the high-level parts of a program that has been built with the .NET Framework SDK. We also discuss some tools in the SDK you may find useful.

This section provides only the basics you need in order to become familiar with the parts of .NET you'll use in the ASP.NET arena. If you want more information about .NET technology, you'll find many books that go into great detail.

Assemblies

Assemblies are a newer format of executable files. ASP.NET Web pages are automatically made into assemblies by IIS and the ASP.NET Application Server to help increase their execution speed.

Like the previous version of compiled executable files, these files are still named with .dll and .exe extensions, but beyond that they're quite different. They execute in the CLR (common language runtime), which provides a run-time environment and access to all the resources .NET programs require. In addition, they contain *metadata,* or data about data (see the next section for more information on metadata).

We will be building assemblies with the .dll extension later in Chapter 11.

Metadata

We like to think of metadata as "data about data"—specifically, information that further explains and describes the parts of an executable file and how it should run. This information is used by the CLR and even by other programs that are inspecting the executable at run time.

In short, metadata provides the information about the locations of class definitions in the file, how to load those classes, and any defined attributes describing how the program should behave at run time. Metadata also contains additional information, making it a powerful tool for those who know how to use that information; but most of it is way beyond the scope of this book.

Global Assembly Cache

When you build an assembly, you have the option of building it to be flexible enough for reuse in other projects. The Global Assembly Cache (GAC) is a centralized location for assemblies that can be used by many programs, including ASP.NET Web sites, without requiring a copy of the assembly for each program.

For a developer to register an assembly in the GAC, the assembly needs what's called a Strong Name, generated by the sn.exe tool. For more information on this subject, search for "strong named assemblies" at http://msdn.microsoft.com. The results of the search will point to several articles providing good explanations of the concepts and steps involved in registering an assembly in the GAC.

INSTALLING .NET

The .NET Framework Configuration tool

The .NET Framework Configuration tool, a Microsoft Management Console (MMC) plug-in called mscorcfg.msc, helps manage the Global Assembly Cache, the security policy for the .NET Framework, and the applications that use *remoting services* (services to facilitate communicating with other applications). Becoming familiar with the .NET Framework Configuration tool will give you valuable insight into how security and scalability work in .NET.

We recommend you get to know this tool. The .NET Framework Configuration tool is divided into sections for those functional areas mentioned above, plus a few more minor ones. Read the descriptions of each functional area of the tool in the documentation that comes with the .NET Framework SDK to learn what's possible. Then, if you don't fully understand a portion of the tool, http://msdn.microsoft.com is the next place to look for more information.

Other tools and such

Tools and other files that are part of the .NET Framework SDK can be found in the following directory: %windir%\Microsoft.NET\ Framework\v1.0.*x* directory. The *x* variable in this path represents the build you're using. The build number is simply part of the version number given to software. As many of you know, the smaller the increment, the less that has changed. In .NET, the version number consists of *<major version>.<minor version>.<build number>.<revision>*

By default, the highest version number installed is the one your system uses to run .NET programs. Storing .NET in a directory named by its version number means you can have multiple versions on your system. .NET allows more than one version to run simultaneously, because in rare cases you may need to tell your program to use an earlier version than the default one to make your program work properly.

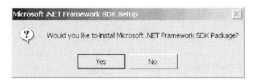

Figure 2.8 The .NET Framework SDK installation verifies that you want to install the development kit.

Figure 2.9 The .NET Framework SDK Setup wizard alerts you that ASP.NET will be installed if IIS is already on the system.

Figure 2.10 Install all of the development kit's components.

To install the .NET Framework SDK:

1. First you need to download the program for installing the .NET Framework SDK. You can do this by visiting www.microsoft.com/net.

2. Execute the file you downloaded by double-clicking it. A dialog box opens to confirm that you want to install the SDK.

3. Click Yes when the install program prompts you to confirm that you want to install the .NET Framework SDK (**Figure 2.8**).

   Note: After all the files have been extracted, you may be alerted that your Windows Installer program needs to be upgraded. If so, the program does it automatically for you.

   The .NET Framework SDK Setup wizard appears (**Figure 2.9**). It starts the actual installation process and alerts you that ASP.NET will automatically be installed if IIS 5.0 exists on the system. We installed IIS first for this very reason.

4. Before continuing you must read through and accept yet another End User License Agreement.

5. Now select your installation options (**Figure 2.10**). We recommend accepting the default settings; you need the SDK, and you'll find the samples handy when reviewing the documentation. Click Next to continue.

continues on next page

INSTALLING .NET

6. Next, you need to indicate where you want the SDK installed (**Figure 2.11**).

We also recommend that you check the box next to Register Environment Variables. This lets the installer register the Environment Variables for you. Setting them later may be more difficult—it's hard to find help in the documentation for this.

7. In the same window, click Next.

The Installing Components window appears, and the program begins copying files to your computer (**Figure 2.12**). What the installer is actually doing is registering the components that make up the Framework and SDK, copying the documentation and samples, and deleting all those temporary files. This process can take a while—about 15 minutes—so sit back and relax!

8. When the installation concludes, you'll be prompted to restart you computer. Restart to continue preparing your computer for working with .NET.

Figure 2.11 Set the installation folder and have the wizard register the environment variables for you.

Figure 2.12 The SDK installation status is displayed throughout the process.

INSTALLING .NET

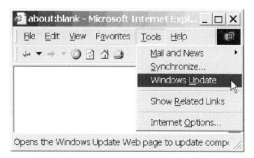

Figure 2.13 Choose Windows Update from Internet Explorer's Tools menu to update Windows.

Service packs and security patches

Microsoft highly recommends updating its software to the highest service pack available and installing all hot fixes because they often remedy security issues. We agree with this recommendation: Not doing it is putting your applications unnecessarily at risk.

At the time of this writing, Service Pack 2 for the .NET Framework is the latest version available. You can always get the latest service pack at www.microsoft.com/net.

✔ Tip

■ Because you never know exactly what side effects a patch will have, we recommend that you back up your system before applying the service packs.

Microsoft has also provided an easy way for you to stay patched via Internet Explorer. The Microsoft Windows Critical Update Notification plug-in works in tandem with the Windows Update tool described in the "Keeping Patched" sidebar. To install the plug-in, follow the directions below.

To install Critical Update:

1. Open Internet Explorer.

2. From the Tools drop-down menu, choose Windows Update (**Figure 2.13**).

3. You'll be taken to a section of Microsoft's Web site that asks your permission to automatically install the tool.

   Once it's installed, Windows will alert you of critical updates. You'll have the option of installing noncritical updates using that tool as well.

INSTALLING .NET

Keeping Patched

Another patching tool you may want to consider is HFNetCheck, a command line tool that helps you view which hot fixes haven't yet been applied to your system. In addition, some other vendors offer extended interfaces for finding and downloading the fixes—something the command line tool doesn't do. But if you don't want to add any of the extended interfaces, you can use the article number that HFNetCheck provides to search for the fixes yourself.

HFNetCheck works like this: It inspects the computers on your network and determines the status of the ones running Windows NT 4.0, Windows 2000, and Windows XP. While inspecting those operating systems, it also inspects IE 5.01 or later, IIS 4.0 or later, and SQL Server 7.0 or later, including Microsoft Data Engine (MSDE). The result of the overall investigation is a list of which patches and fixes haven't been applied to which computers. It includes the numbers of the articles in which the fixes can be found.

HFNetCheck is available from http://support.microsoft.com. Just search for 'HFNetCheck' and you'll find the page to download it from.

Another option you have is the Windows Update tool. However, it inspects only the operating system, IE, and IIS for available updates—not SQL Server or MSDE. Also, it inspects only the computer on which it's installed.

For a similar investigation of all Microsoft Office products, you'd need to use another tool called Office Product Updates, available via a button labeled Office Update at the top of the same Windows Update Web page you opened in Step 2 of "To install Critical Update."

Hosting ASP.NET Web Sites

Now that you have IIS, MDAC, and the .NET Framework SDK installed, you're ready not only to build ASP.NET Web sites, but to host them as well. Fortunately, Dreamweaver MX does most of the work of setting up a new Web site for you when you create a Dreamweaver site. The Site Definition wizard walks you through everything you need to build and host basic Web sites. Chapter 3 delves more deeply into the Site Definition wizard; however, you'll need to know a few things about Web sites in general, and ASP.NET Web sites specifically, to host them effectively.

Web sites as applications

Web sites have evolved from being a collection of static, informational pages to being dynamic, goal-oriented applications. For this reason, they've come to need their own settings, memory spaces, and even supplemental executable files such as the .dll file Dreamweaver provides for use in ASP.NET Web sites.

Because Web sites are now so dynamic, Microsoft has tools to manage those settings and memory spaces. In addition, ASP.NET Web sites have certain files you can use to better handle any application-specific settings that you may need.

We'll start by looking at the application settings you can configure in IIS using one of Microsoft's more useful tools. Then we'll see how the flexibility of those settings in IIS can help you manage a Web site's architecture and how this affects .NET Web applications. Finally, we'll walk through how to create a more complex directory structure for your Web site—which can be useful for you as a developer.

But first, let's get familiar with that useful tool Microsoft provides: an administrative tool called Computer Management.

To open Computer Management:

1. Open the Computer Management tool by clicking the Start button on your Windows taskbar and choosing Programs and then Administrative Tools.

2. Expand the Services and Applications section of Computer Management by clicking on the + (plus sign) next to that heading.

3. Expand the Internet Information Services section by clicking on its plus sign (**Figure 2.14**).

This tool provides quick access to many often-used utilities such as the Event Viewer, which lets you see many different event logs; Services, for easily starting and stopping your computer's different services; and of course Internet Information Services, for managing your Web sites. We'll only be working with Internet Information Services in this chapter, but you'll doubtless come back to this tool often for your management needs because it's so convenient.

Now on to looking at the application settings you can configure on your Web site within IIS.

Figure 2.14 Expand the Internet Information Services section of the Computer Management tool by clicking the + (plus sign).

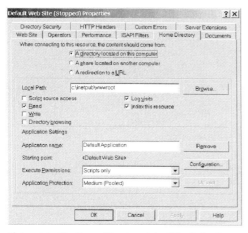

Figure 2.15 The Home Directory tab of the Default Web Site Properties dialog box allows you to set the path to the Web site's directory, access rights and application settings.

To review the Default Web Site's application settings:

1. Open the Computer Management tool as described in "To open Computer Management."

2. Right-click Default Web Site, and click Properties from the context menu that appears.

3. In the Default Web Site Properties dialog box that opens, click the Home Directory tab found at the top (**Figure 2.15**).

4. Locate the Application Settings area in the bottom third of the tab.

5. Explore the different settings available to an application.

Now that you've seen exactly what settings are available for a Web application, let's talk about what those settings do and how you can use them.

As you probably already know, a Web site is a physical entity representing a directory structure on the host computer that contains your Web pages. Settings that map the host computer's Internet Protocol (IP) address and the location of the directory containing your Web pages can be configured within IIS. You specify these settings using the various tabs of the Properties dialog box we just reviewed.

When Web sites are created using IIS, they assume default settings derived from the settings for the application that the site is associated with. In IIS, a Web site is its own application (with its own settings), or it's created as part of an existing application and therefore it inherits the default settings for that application.

HOSTING ASP.NET WEB SITES

For an application, settings for security and memory space can be configured. Two settings you'll see often are the Execute Permissions setting, which grants or denies visitors access to run scripts and executables contained in the application, and the Application Protection setting, which lets administrators control how separate the different applications' memory spaces are. The setting ranges from low separation of memory spaces to high separation. High separation means that if one Web application goes awry, it won't affect the others.

Applications in Web sites

By default, when a new Web site is created in IIS, the settings applied are those from the default application created during IIS's installation for the Default Web Site. The default application's settings cascade down the directory structure, affecting all contained directories and files, so that settings remain consistent throughout the site.

However, you have the option of overriding the site's default application settings by configuring settings on every directory. Configurable Web site settings provide a way to organize sites with their own group of settings. This can be useful in ASP.NET because of how ASP.NET Web applications work, as we'll explain in more detail in the next few paragraphs.

But before diving into how application settings affect ASP.NET Web applications, let's create an application on a subdirectory of the Default Web Site to see what is involved.

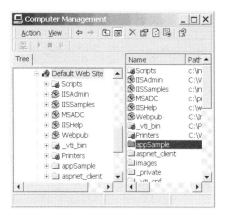

Figure 2.16 Here is the new appSample directory under the Default Web Site.

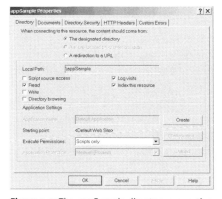

Figure 2.17 The appSample directory properties allow far fewer settings than applications do.

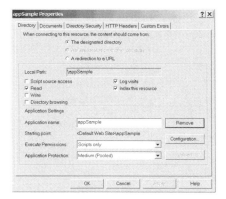

Figure 2.18 Here is the appSample application properties with all its settings available.

To create an application:

1. Open the Computer Management tool by following the steps in "To open Computer Management."

    In the fully expanded left pane of the Computer Management tool, you'll find the Default Web Site.

2. Leave the Computer Management tool for now, and open the Default Web Site's folder on the computer's hard drive. The default location is C:\Inetpub\wwwroot.

3. Create a directory called "appSample" (the directory must already exist when you create a new application—IIS won't create it for you).

4. Now go back to IIS in the Computer Management tool. You may have to refresh the screen to see the new appSample directory (**Figure 2.16**).

5. Right-click the appSample directory from within the Computer Management tool, and choose Properties.

    The appSample Properties dialog box appears (**Figure 2.17**).

6. Review the appSample directory properties to get a feel for what can be done with a normal directory under IIS. Then click the Create button to create a new application.

    A few of the gray, inactive fields will become active, and the Create button will rename itself to Remove (**Figure 2.18**).

HOSTING ASP.NET WEB SITES

Now that we have the appSample directory set up as an application within the Default Web Site, we can configure it to manage security and memory and all the other settings available for applications however we wish. Those settings may be completely different than the ones set for the application at the root of the Default Web Site. However, now that appSample has been defined as an application, those settings configured at the root will no longer cascade down into the appSample directory.

This, however, raises an issue for an ASP.NET Web application. There are two files in which ASP.NET Web application–specific settings may reside. If those files and their settings were defined at the root of the Default Web Site, those settings would not cascade down into the appSample directory now that it's been defined as its own application.

This may sound like a bad side effect, but it's actually quite beneficial. This is the way you can separate a Web site into many ASP.NET Web applications, each with it's own configuration.

Configuring ASP.NET Web applications

The first of the ASP.NET configuration files is global.asax. It's where ASP.NET looks for variables associated with the application, as well as variables associated with individual user sessions.

Generally, *application variables* are used for static types of variables that need to be available across all the application's Web pages. Because the variables are for static data, they're not normally updated during the course of the application. Should they need to be updated, special consideration should be taken to ensure that only one user updates the data at a time.

A database connection string might be a good candidate for being stored in an application variable because it's fairly static and available to all application Web pages. (The database connection string referred to here defines the information required to access a database, including it's location, login and driver software.)

Session variables, on the other hand, are associated with each individual Web application user and are thus safely read from and written to for each user. A common use for a session variable is storing the user's identification information so it's readily available from page to page after they log in. You see the distinction between *application* and *session* here. The application is the whole application, including all users; sessions are created uniquely for each user. Keeping this distinction in mind, developers may define functions in the global.asax file to run at the start and/or end of the application as well as each session. Those optional functions are useful for initializing or cleaning up the application or sessions, respectively.

The second of the ASP.NET configuration files is web.config. Web.config is an XML-formatted file where debugging, tracing, application, and even custom settings you create yourself may be set. This file is so flexible and well designed, it's often used to store application-level variables in ASP.NET instead of the global.asax file. In fact, Dreamweaver uses this file for storing settings such as the database connection information used by the Dreamweaver server behaviors.

Supplemental Files in Applications

Often in ASP.NET Web applications, .dll files are used to supplement the functions defined in the ASP.NET Web pages. In fact, Dreamweaver has one such file you'll need to make available to your Web applications when working with Dreamweaver's server behaviors. Its name is DreamweaverCtrls.dll, and it defaults to the location C:\Program Files\Macromedia\ Dreamweaver MX\Configuration\ ServerBehaviors\Shared\ASP.Net\Scripts.

Normally, supplemental .dll files are placed within the bin directory of the Web site; but when you create multiple applications, a new bin directory with the necessary .dll files will need to be created within that application directory, too.

In addition, ASP.NET can use what are called *validators* on form elements. The client-side JavaScript functions for validating are available in the aspnet_client directory that is automatically placed under your Default Web Site when the .NET Framework SDK is installed, if IIS is already on the computer. As with the bin directory, you'll need to copy this aspnet_client directory into any new application directories if you plan to use the validator functions in that application. You'll receive an error from IIS if you forget.

As noted before, the settings specified in these two configuration files start anew when an application is created in a directory within a Web site. They aren't inherited from the higher application, if there is one. This means that the root of a Web site may have a database connection string defined in the web.config file, but that connection string will need to be redefined within a separate web.config file in each new application created within that Web site. Fortunately, in most scenarios you wouldn't create a new application if it needed the same settings, such as the same database connection string as the existing application. However, this separation does provide great flexibility when you do need to start with a completely blank slate.

Hiding your directory structure

When you visit a Web site, it often looks like a ton of subdirectories exist within the site. Would you believe the Web site's directory structure may not be set up that way at all? Often Web sites use aliases called *virtual directories* to make the Web site look like one big consistent directory structure, but in reality the site may be spread out across a computer's hard drives or even across several computers. Usually this is done in production Web sites to help with security and scalability, but virtual directories can help you as a developer by providing a way for you to have your projects in different directories throughout your computer, while keeping them available from the http://localhost URL.

HOSTING ASP.NET WEB SITES

31

To create a virtual directory:

1. Open the Computer Management tool by following the steps in "To open Computer Management."

   In the fully expanded left pane of the Computer Management tool, you'll find the Default Web Site.

2. Right-click the Default Web Site, and from the New submenu choose Virtual Directory.

   There's nothing to set in the window that pops up. It simply states that you are using the Virtual Directory Creation wizard.

3. Click the Next button.

4. Type in a name for your new virtual directory (**Figure 2.19**). This is what will appear as a subdirectory of your site in the site's URL. Click Next.

   For example, if your site's URL is http://localhost/, you would navigate to a virtual directory called ProjectX by going to http://localhost/ProjectX.

5. Specify a pre-existing directory where you want your Web files to reside (**Figure 2.20**). This directory can be anywhere, even on other computers, but the wizard won't create the specified directory for you. Click Next.

   Continuing the ProjectX example, this would potentially be the D:\projects\ProjectX directory.

6. Assign the access rights you want the virtual directory's Web visitors to have. The defaults should be sufficient (**Figure 2.21**). Click Next.

   For information on what the various rights mean, see the sidebar "Too Much Access."

7. Click Finish on the last screen of the wizard to complete the process.

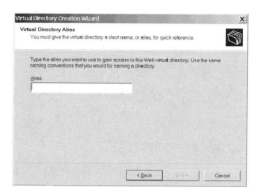

Figure 2.19 The Virtual Directory Creation wizard alias screen prompts you to create an alias for your new virtual directory.

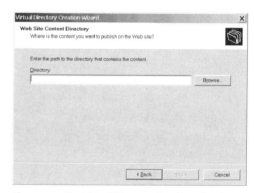

Figure 2.20 The Virtual Directory Creation wizard directory location screen prompts you to enter the location of your Web content.

Figure 2.21 You can set access rights for the virtual directory you're creating right in the Virtual Directory Creation wizard.

An important thing about virtual directories is that the wizard creates a new application for them. That's another reason why virtual directories are so useful for grouping disparate Web application projects under one Web site. As you use virtual directories, you'll learn when you can use them and when they simply won't work for your situation. Keep experimenting and learning about your Web server and what's available to you. This chapter has only scratched the surface, but the information will come in handy when we try to answer some questions that will arise as you get to know ASP.NET.

Now that you've set up your computer to build and host ASP.NET Web applications, let's move on to the next chapter to learn more about Dreamweaver MX, the tool you'll be using to build those ASP.NET Web applications.

Too Much Access

Be sure not to grant Web users more clearance than they absolutely need. The default access permissions of Read and Run Scripts are usually enough.

The Execute permission is necessary only if you have an executable program, such as an .exe or .dll file, the visitors will need to run. But typically you should avoid this, as visitors could hack in and run their own program. In case you're wondering, this permission is not needed for the assemblies IIS automatically creates for you or for assemblies used by your ASP.NET files. It's only required for the older-style CGI programs that you probably won't ever use again.

The Write permission is obviously too much to grant visitors, since it gives them the ability to upload anything they want to your Web site.

Browse also is not typically set, because it allows visitors to look at all the files on the site. They might find things you don't want them to find, such as testing files. Worse, they might find a file they know has hacking potential. The less information you provide, the better.

HOSTING ASP.NET WEB SITES

DREAMWEAVER MX OVERVIEW

Dreamweaver MX is the next-generation version of both Dreamweaver 4 and Dreamweaver UltraDev 4, combining the functionality of both products into one very functional and cohesive application development tool. The two products were merged in the MX release, and in the process both got significant upgrades. Not only did the application development side (UltraDev) improve with new server models and improved code generation capabilities, but the design tools within Dreamweaver received many fixes and upgrades to make them compliant with evolving Web standards such as XHTML. Most important, however, especially if you're reading this book, is the fact that ASP.NET is now one of the supported server models in Dreamweaver MX.

But not all Web developers greet these improvements with enthusiasm. For every Web developer who's hooked on programs like Dreamweaver, there are others who swear against the use of any rapid application development tool out there, including visual Web editors like Dreamweaver. The consensus of those that eschew these tools is that "*real* developers use Notepad." Dreamweaver converts, on the other hand, argue that, unlike using a simple text editor such as Notepad, using a visual Web editor keeps you from having to reinvent the wheel every time you create a new site. We believe the sentiments of a well-rounded developer should lie somewhere in between on this matter.

It's probably all too easy for new developers just getting into the field of Web applications to look to Dreamweaver as an easy way out. Instead of learning HTML, they'll simply learn how to use the visual tools that have made the program so famous. While those developers may be able to go a long way without knowing HTML, there will always be situations that call for hand editing of the code Dreamweaver generates. On those occasions, any developer who doesn't understand the underlying technology behind HTML will be in trouble.

Once you accept the idea that as a Web developer you need a good grasp of the basic underpinnings of HTML, using a visual Web editor like Dreamweaver actually gives you an advantage over developers who don't use one. For instance, Dreamweaver displays what the end result of a developers' changes will look like, which free developers to focus on visualizing their Web masterpieces while they work, instead of having to constantly verify that each change they've made to their HTML code looks the way they think it will in the browser. Other Dreamweaver tools, such as those found on the Tables tab of the Insert bar, can insert HTML tags such as the tags that define the different parts of a table, saving developers a lot of time.

For those of you who are new to Dreamweaver, this chapter shows you enough of Dreamweaver's design, development, and management tools to give you a jump start. We take a look at how to configure Dreamweaver to best fit your workflow, how to create and manage your Web sites using Dreamweaver's site management tools, and how to use some of its tools.

A more comprehensive look at Dreamweaver is beyond the scope of this book. If you want to improve your knowledge of more advanced Dreamweaver topics, you can find many good books or resources (such as Macromedia's web site, www.macromedia.com) dedicated solely to Dreamweaver.

DREAMWEAVER MX OVERVIEW

The Dreamweaver Interface

For the most part, Dreamweaver simply translates a text file into what it will probably look like in a browser. Of course, this often amounts to a rough approximation, given all the different browsers that are out there. But this feature does go a long way toward helping you design your page.

You'll find that most tasks you want to accomplish in Dreamweaver can be executed using the point-and-click tools available on the main user interface. From inserting common HTML elements to making rollover image effects to validating your page markup, you'll rarely have to use any tool other than Dreamweaver.

Despite the apparent simplicity of its point-and-click tools, Dreamweaver gives you full access to the code it generates, so that on those occasions when you want to customize that code, you can. You can view code through the program's built-in Code view windows or through the code editor of your choice (Dreamweaver lets you specify this).

Choosing a workspace configuration

Dreamweaver's interface is also highly configurable, so you can customize it to fit your workflow. You can choose from three main configurations: the Dreamweaver 4 Workspace, the Dreamweaver MX Workspace, and the HomeSite/Coder-Style Workspace. Your choice depends on which of the configurations best meets your needs.

The Dreamweaver 4 Workspace configuration is characterized by a separate floating panel for each document you work on, with a corresponding entry in your Site window for easy access. Panel groups, such as Design and Code can be docked together although not docked into an all-encompassing application window.

If you're lucky enough to have a dual-monitor setup, the Dreamweaver 4 Workspace might be a good option for you. You can use one of the monitors to view the page you're working on, while placing all of your floating windows in the other monitor. This makes for a useful layout. However, if you're using Dreamweaver MX, Macromedia recommends the Dreamweaver 4 Workspace configuration only if you're comfortable working within the Dreamweaver 4 interface.

The new workspace in Dreamweaver MX is the Multiple Document Interface (MDI), so it's much easier to manage if you don't have a dual-monitor setup. MDI allows you to have any number of child windows displayed within a main window. We recommend this layout because of its ease of use. You can dock all the tools you use, and they'll remain in the location of your choosing. And the new paneling system in Dreamweaver MX lets you show and hide information quickly. These panel improvements, combined with the MDI technology, allow you to make the most of the space you have.

THE DREAMWEAVER INTERFACE

The HomeSite/Coder-Style Workspace is similar to the Dreamweaver MX Workspace, except that the panel groups appear on the left side of the screen by default. As the name suggests, this configuration is available for developers who are migrating to Dreamweaver from Macromedia's HomeSite (another Web editor) or ColdFusion Studio (a Web development tool derived from HomeSite), and for developers who primarily will be writing their own code.

The Dreamweaver MX and HomeSite/Coder-Style workspaces are both very configurable. Although each workspace contains everything inside one main application window—unlike the Dreamweaver 4 workspace—all the panel groups can be moved to different locations (**Figure 3.1**). In addition, each panel group can be renamed. You can even rearrange which panels go with which panel groups.

When Dreamweaver starts up for the first time, it gives you the option of choosing between these configurations. Because Dreamweaver MX and HomeSite/Coder-Style workspaces are so similar, you must first select the Dreamweaver MX Workspace and then click the HomeSite/Coder-Style check box below it if you want to use the HomeSite/Coder-Style workspace.

If you change your mind about which interface you want to use, you can edit your workspace configuration later via the Preferences dialog box.

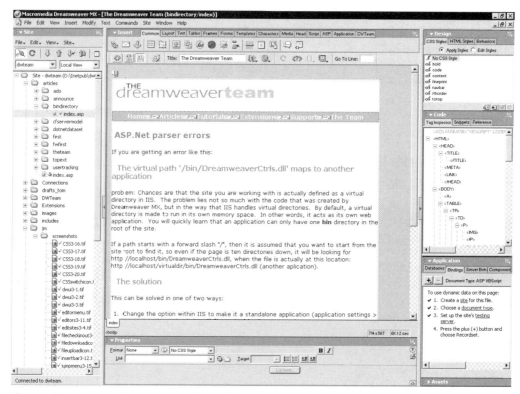

Figure 3.1 You can customize Dreamweaver's interface by moving panel groups to new locations.

THE DREAMWEAVER INTERFACE

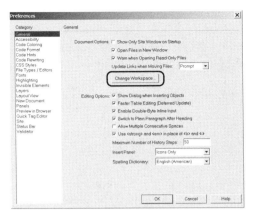

Figure 3.2 The Preferences panel allows you to customize Dreamweaver to suit your workflow.

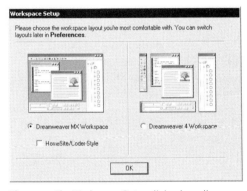

Figure 3.3 The Workspace Setup dialog box allows you to choose your preferred workspace.

To edit your workspace configuration:

1. On the menu bar at the top of Dreamweaver, click Edit and choose Preferences. The Preferences dialog box will appear.

2. In the list of categories on the left side of the Preferences dialog box, click General (**Figure 3.2**).

3. On the right side of the Preferences dialog box, click the Change Workspace button near the middle of the screen. The Workspace Setup dialog box appears (**Figure 3.3**).

4. Choose your configuration and click OK. If you want to use HomeSite/Coder-Style, you must first click the Dreamweaver MX Workspace radio button, and then select the HomeSite/Coder-Style check box.

5. Restart Dreamweaver.

THE DREAMWEAVER INTERFACE

Defining a Site

Not many developers are fortunate enough to be in a position where they don't have to worry about the design of a Web site. In fact, lots of developers don't even have the advantage of working in a team environment, so they're left to deal with every aspect of the site themselves. From design to coding to maintenance—and even to administration—many developers are their own sole point of support.

The Web has been described as "the great equalizer" because it allows anyone to enter the market and compete with larger competitors. In a way, Dreamweaver can be regarded as "the developer's great equalizer" (you heard it here first), because it makes it easier for the solitary developer to manage every aspect of a site and keep everything organized.

One of the first tasks you'll undertake when starting a Web development project using Dreamweaver MX is the creation of a site. A site in Dreamweaver represents a grouping of the resources that make up a Web site. Those resources can include HTML pages, dynamic code modules, style sheets, images, and so on.

Sites also contain various configurable definition settings that allow you to describe the characteristics of the Web site being created. These settings include the location of files, dynamic development environment settings, and the URL (Web address) for locating site resources via the Web.

Site Definition settings also allow you to define your development environment and the connectivity between your local system and the server that hosts your Web site. Your Site Definition configuration is accessible via the Site panel.

Figure 3.4 The Site panel is where you handle file-related operations, among other things.

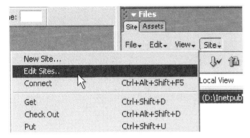

Figure 3.5 The Site drop-down menu is where you can find all site-management–related options.

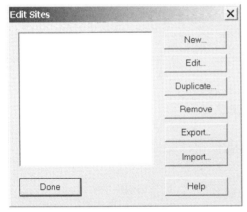

Figure 3.6 You can manage your site settings at a high level from the Edit Sites dialog box.

To define a site for your local server:

1. From the Files panel group, open the Site panel (**Figure 3.4**). If the Site panel isn't visible, press the F8 key.

2. From the menu bar on the Site panel, choose Site, and then Edit Sites (**Figure 3.5**).

    The Edit Sites dialog box appears (**Figure 3.6**).

3. Click New.

    The Site Definition wizard appears (**Figure 3.7**).

4. Make sure you're in Basic mode by clicking the Basic tab at the top left of the wizard. We'll use Basic mode because it will easily guide us through the settings required to create a site.

continues on next page

Figure 3.7 This is the first step of the Site Definition wizard.

DEFINING A SITE

5. Give your site a name, such as "FirstSite" at the prompt.

Notice how the title of the wizard at the top of your screen changed to match your new name.

6. Click Next.

The Editing Files, Part 2 dialog box of the Site Definition wizard appears (**Figure 3.8**). Here you'll specify which server technology you'll be using.

7. Click the radio button beside "Yes, I want to use a server technology." Then choose ASP.NET C# in the field directly below, and click Next.

The Editing Files, Part 3 dialog box appears (**Figure 3.9**). This box asks you to specify how you want to work with your files during development.

8. Choose "Edit and test locally (my testing server is on this computer)."

As you recall, we set up a local Web server on your computer in Chapter 2, so this is the correct choice.

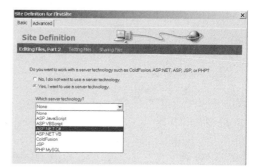

Figure 3.8 At the time of this writing, only C# and VB .NET are supported by Dreamweaver as it relates to ASP.NET.

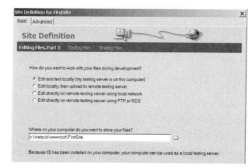

Figure 3.9 There are several different options for working with your files, depending on your server setup.

Figure 3.10 Enter the URL of your testing server so that Dreamweaver can communicate with it via HTTP.

Figure 3.11 You can choose to either develop just on your local machine or upload files to a remote testing or production server when you're finished editing.

9. In the same dialog box, define the path for where your Web files will be located, and click Next.

Note: Make sure that the directory exists. The folder icon to the right of the text box enables you to browse your file system to locate and verify the directory for this Web site.

The Testing Files dialog box of the Site Definition wizard appears, asking you to verify the URL of the testing Web site (**Figure 3.10**).

10. Check the URL in the field below the prompt "What URL would you use to browse to the root of your site?" Correct it if necessary. Click the Test URL button to make sure Dreamweaver can find the Web site. Then click Next to continue.

A new Testing Files window appears (**Figure 3.11**). (If you're having trouble, review Chapter 2 to make sure your computer is ready for your new site.)

continues on next page

DEFINING A SITE

11. Click the "No" radio button to indicate that you don't want to connect to a remote server. Then click Next.

The Summary dialog box appears (**Figure 3.12**).

Note: We don't require a connection to a remote server for the purposes of this exercise, so we've selected "No" at the prompt. However, should you need to access Web pages stored on a remote server, then you'll need to select "Yes, I want to use a remote server." By selecting this option, you'll then be prompted to define the settings that describe how you will connect to the remote server.

12. Review your settings, go back and change them if necessary, and then click Done.

Your new site will be created with the settings you specified.

As you may have noticed going through the site definition process, many settings are available from the Site Definition wizard, making it useful to environments of all kinds. Because every environment is unique, we recommend that you walk through the wizard, selecting the options that will fit your needs when defining your site. If you need further explanation of the different Site Definition settings, Dreamweaver's Help is the first place to look.

Figure 3.12 Look over your settings to make sure you didn't miss anything.

Figure 3.13 Select a site to edit from the Edit Sites dialog box.

Figure 3.14 The Advanced tab lets you edit all of the options presented in the Site Definition wizard, plus a few more.

Advanced mode

During the life of your projects, you may need to revisit your site settings to change them. Because you'll likely need to change only one or two settings, the Advanced mode of the Site Definition tool will help you side-step much of the process. Using Advanced mode lets you access a setting directly, without first having to navigate through several screens. Advanced mode may also be more useful once you've become familiar with the settings needed to define a site.

During the following exploration of Advanced mode, you'll find even more settings available that weren't configurable in Basic mode.

To edit site definitions in Advanced mode:

1. Repeat Steps 1 and 2 of the previous task to open the Edit Sites dialog box.

2. Select FirstSite —the site we created previously—from the list in the Edit Sites dialog box, and click Edit (**Figure 3.13**). The Site Definition wizard for FirstSite appears (**Figure 3.14**).

3. Select the Advanced tab in the upper left of the screen to switch to Advanced mode.

4. Explore the different sections of the site definition that are listed on the left. One useful site setting that can be configured while in Advanced Mode, for example, is what data columns to display when viewing site settings. And don't be afraid to click the Help button to find a better explanation of all that's available to you.

5. Click OK at the bottom of the wizard when you're ready to save your changes. The Edit Sites dialog box is visible again.

6. Click Done in the Edit Sites dialog box.

DEFINING A SITE

Defining remote-server sites

Most likely, you won't be hosting your finished Web site using your local computer, so you'll need to set up your local site to communicate with the production server that will host your finished site. This will enable you to upload the completed site to the production server when it's done. The following list will help you navigate the Site Definition wizard for that setup.

Keep in mind that this is simply a walk-through of the most often used settings. Some of them may not apply to your particular situation. When you're in doubt, review Dreamweaver's Help on this subject.

To define a remote server for our site:

1. From the Site panel, click the Site pull-down menu and select Edit Sites. Then select the site, FirstSite, and then select Edit to view its settings.
   The Edit Sites dialog box appears.

2. Using the Basic tab of the Site Definition dialog box, scroll through the screens.

3. When prompted to use a remote server, select "Yes, I want to use a remote server." Click Next to continue to the Sharing Files, Part 2 dialog box (**Figure 3.15**).

4. In the Sharing Files, Part 2 dialog box, type in the connection information for the remote server you'll be using (**Figure 3.16**).

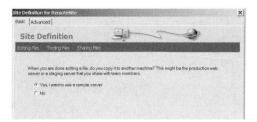

Figure 3.15 Using a remote server allows you to publish your site on the Internet.

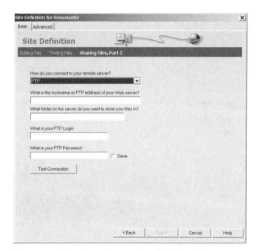

Figure 3.16 Most people use FTP (File Transfer Protocol), but there are other options for connecting to your server.

Figure 3.17 File check in and check out will be covered later in the chapter.

5. Click Test Connection to verify that Dreamweaver can communicate with your remote server using the settings you've provided. Then click Next, which is enabled as soon as you have entered your settings.

The Sharing Files, Part 3 dialog box appears (**Figure 3.17**).

6. Now you need to choose whether you want to control file synchronization issues. Select "No, do not enable check in and check out." Then click Next.

We discuss check in and check out options in more detail in "Using site integrity features" later in this chapter.

7. Review your settings and click Done.

Now that you have a remote server set up, you'll find that some features of a site that are specific to working with remote servers become available that are not applicable when you're using only a local site. The rest of this chapter will cover each one of the remote site specific settings and how to configure them.

Uploading Files

When working with a remote server, you'll need to upload the files you create on your local computer to that server. Dreamweaver sites have an easy way to accomplish this. Let's create a file, and then upload it.

To create a new file:

1. Make FirstSite the active site for editing files by following Step 1 of the previous list.

2. On the menu bar at the top of the Dreamweaver interface, select File > New File.

   The New Document wizard appears (**Figure 3.18**).

3. In the Category box on the left side of the screen, highlight Basic Page to define the type of page you want to create.

4. In the Basic Page box, select HTML, and click Create. For the purposes of this exercise, we can leave the "Make Document XHTML Compliant" check box unchecked.

   A new file will open, containing basic HTML tags where you can add your content.

   Type "This is a test page" into the document.

5. From the File drop-down menu, choose Save As to open a standard File dialog box. Name the document "FirstPage," and click Save.

   The file will automatically be appended with the .htm suffix.

✔ Tip

- When a new HTML file is created, it's given the name Untitled-1.htm by default. You'll be able to change the name to something more meaningful when you save the file.

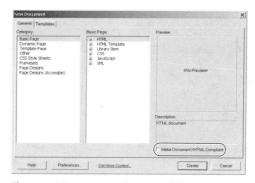

Figure 3.18 Dreamweaver has many different file types to choose from.

Figure 3.19 Start a new document by clicking the New icon on the Standard toolbar.

Figure 3.20 Upload your files to the remote server by clicking the Put File(s) icon.

Dreamweaver provides a variety of ways to initiate many of the features you'll use. For example, you can open the New Document wizard by doing any of the following:

◆ From the File drop-down menu at the top of the Dreamweaver interface, choose New.

◆ On the Standard toolbar, click the New icon (**Figure 3.19**).

◆ From the Site panel, right-click a folder and choose New File from the context menu that appears. This will automatically add a file named Untitled.html in the selected folder

◆ From the Site panel, choose File, and from the drop-down menu that appears, choose New File..

Now that we have our new file, let's upload it to the remote server.

To upload files to a remote server:

1. From the Site panel, select the FirstPage.htm that we created in the previous list.

2. With the file that you want to upload highlighted, click the Put File(s) icon at the top of the screen (**Figure 3.20**).

Dreamweaver connects to your remote server via the connectivity protocol you set for your site (To review how to define connectivity settings, see Step 4 in "To define a remote server for our site" earlier in this chapter) and uploads the file.

You can upload files manually every time you're ready to put your files onto the remote server, like we've done here, or you can configure Dreamweaver to automatically upload your files when you save them.

UPLOADING FILES

To automatically upload your files:

1. Make FirstSite the active site for editing files by following Step 1 of "To define a remote server for our site" earlier in this chapter.

   The Edit Sites dialog box appears.

2. Select the Advanced mode of the Site Definition wizard (see "To edit site definitions in Advanced mode" for more information).

3. Select Remote Info from the Category list on the left of the wizard (**Figure 3.21**).

4. You'll see your site's remote settings appear on the right. Put a check next to "Automatically upload files to server on save."

5. Click the OK button at the bottom of the wizard, and then in the Edit Sites dialog box, click Done.

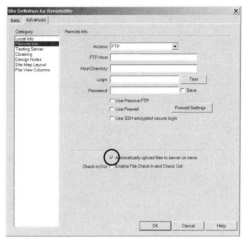

Figure 3.21 Choose to automatically upload your files to relieve yourself of this repetitive task.

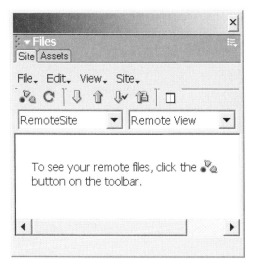

Figure 3.22 You can work directly with remote sites to make sure you're working with the latest version.

Downloading Files

Obviously, no remote server would be useful if you couldn't download files from it.

To avoid file synchronization problems, Dreamweaver alerts you when the remote version of the file is more recent than your local copy. It does this by displaying a warning before it downloads the remote copy. You'll need to confirm that you want to replace your local files with more current remote files in order to proceed.

To download a file:

1. Go to the Site panel, and highlight the file you wish to download by clicking it.

2. Click the Get File(s) icon at the top of the Site panel ⬇.

   You'll be prompted to overwrite your local copy of the file.

3. Click OK.

   The file will begin to download.

You may choose to work directly on remote files. To do this you need to change some things in the Site panel.

To work directly on remote files:

1. With your remote site open in the Site panel, choose Remote View from the right drop-down list box (**Figure 3.22**).

2. When prompted to connect to the remote server, click the Connects to Remote Host icon 🔌.

   From now on, when you double-click a file in the Site panel, you'll be automatically downloading the file from the remote server.

Using Site Integrity Features

One of the hardest things to do with files of any kind is to maintain a consistent level of version control. A common scenario: After making changes to a file at work, you go home and work on it for a few hours more. Just seconds after you upload your final changes to the server, you realize you forgot to download the most recent file before you started, so the version you've just completed has overwritten some important changes you made that day at work. Argh!

You can prevent file synchronization issues such as this in one of two ways. Either you can enable file check in and check out so that the file must be downloaded every time, or you can synchronize your site every time you begin to work, whether you know or not that the files have remained untouched by anyone but yourself. Obviously, the first choice, file check in and check out, is perfect for developers working as a team on one Web site; but as you've seen, it's equally useful for developers working alone. Let's take a look at how to do both.

To enable file check in and check out:

1. Go to the Site panel and double-click FirstSite in the drop-down menu. The Site Definition wizard for your site appears in Advanced mode.

2. Click Remote Info from the Category list on the left (**Figure 3.23**).

3. Check the option to Enable File Check In and Check Out.

4. Enter your name and email address in the fields that appear below.

5. Click OK at the bottom of the wizard to save your changes.

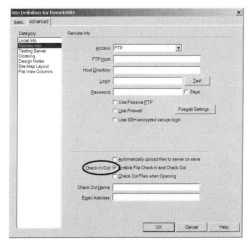

Figure 3.23 File check in and check out makes sure you don't overwrite someone else's (or even your own) work.

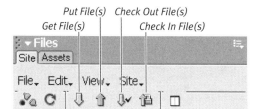

Figure 3.24 Upload and download files from a remote server, optionally checking them out.

From now on, instead of using Get File(s) and Put File(s) icons, you should use the Check Out File(s) and Check In File(s) icons (**Figure 3.24**).

When you have a file checked out, your name and email address will appear next to the file-name in the Site panel so that anyone else who's connected to the site will see it. If they try to edit the file, they will get a message telling them who has the file checked out. Of course, this solution isn't foolproof. Anyone can overwrite files using a tool other than Dreamweaver. However, it does go a long way toward preventing accidental overwrites.

In the next set of stepped instructions, we'll illustrate how to synchronize local and remote files manually.

Other Site Management Options

If you're serious about keeping your files in order, you'll be grateful for Dreamweaver's excellent integration with some of the third-party source-control software. If you don't already have this software, you should look into one of the two following packages. Not only do they augment the file check in and check out capability within Dreamweaver, but they also automatically maintain versions so you have a history of the changes you make to your documents.

Visual SourceSafe
Available from Microsoft (http://msdn.microsoft.com/ssafe/), SourceSafe offers great integration with other Microsoft products such as Visual Studio .NET. A good choice if you're in a predominantly Microsoft shop.

CVS (Concurrent Versions System)
Available at www.cvshome.org/, this source-control server can be run on Windows or Linux operating systems. Its open source model make it an attractive choice for small businesses (or large ones, too) looking to keep costs under control.

To synchronize your site:

1. From the Site panel, select Site > Synchronize.

   The Synchronize Files dialog box appears **(Figure 3.25)**.

2. In the Synchronize drop-down list box, specify whether to synchronize only selected files or the entire site.

3. In the Direction drop-down list, you have several options:

   ▲ *Put newer files to remote*. Uploads any files that you've made changes to.

   ▲ *Get newer files from remote*. If any files have been updated (say on another machine), this will download the latest version so that you won't overwrite anything on upload.

   ▲ *Get and Put newer files*. This combines the functions of both previous options. You should do this every time you start working if there's a chance the files might not be synchronized.

4. When you've finished making your synchronization choices, click Preview to view what synchronization actions need to occur. You may be informed that there's nothing to do.

5. If you need synchronization, a list of files and the action needed to achieve synchronicity will appear. Click OK to proceed with the synchronization **(Figure 3.26)**.

✔ Tip

■ You can synchronize from any view of a site. For instance, if your testing server's files are out of synch with your local files, you can switch to the Testing Server view and then initiate synchronization. This may be necessary, as some files aren't automatically copied to the testing server when they're saved.

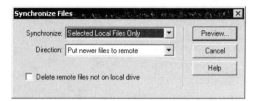

Figure 3.25 Synchronizing your site is a good idea if more than one person is involved in the site development.

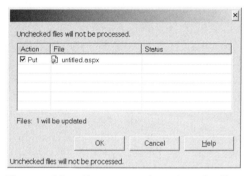

Figure 3.26 Once Dreamweaver determines what files need to be synchronized, it gives you a report so that you can approve which files to synchronize.

Other .NET Editors

There are many .NET editors on the market, some free, some not. Some even have the ability to compile .NET code. Although you can use the command line utility to compile .NET assemblies (.dll), it's much easier to simply press a button and have it built for you. Here are some to choose from:

SharpDevelop
www.icsharpcode.net/

Primalscript
www.sapien.com/

Antechinus
www.c-point.com/

Microsoft ASP.NET Web Matrix
www.asp.net/

Choosing the Right Editor

Although Dreamweaver MX has advanced leaps and bounds when it comes to code editing, many developers still prefer to use a dedicated code editor. Luckily, Dreamweaver makes it easy to use one. All it takes is a brief setup process, and you're ready to go.

If you don't already know, Dreamweaver MX comes bundled with HomeSite+. So if you don't have an editor preference but you want to use a dedicated text editor, you could try this one.

Dreamweaver has an area within its Preferences dialog box that allows you to assign file types to external programs.

To add a new external editor:

1. Go to the Edit menu at the top of Dreamweaver and click Preferences.

   The Preferences dialog box opens.

2. From the Category list on the left, click File Types / Editors (**Figure 3.27**).

3. In the Extensions list box on the right, select the file type you want to be edited by a different editor.

   You can also add or remove a file type using the plus and minus buttons found above the Extensions list.

4. With the file type selected, click the plus button above the Editors list box to add the external editor of your choice.

   This opens a standard File dialog box.

5. Locate the .exe file of the program you want to use and click OK.

   The Standard File dialog box closes, so that you can return to the Preferences dialog box.

6. If you want your new editor to be the primary editor for that file type, click the Make Primary button above the Editors list box.

7. When you're finished changing your preferences, click OK.

   This saves the changes and closes the Preferences dialog box.

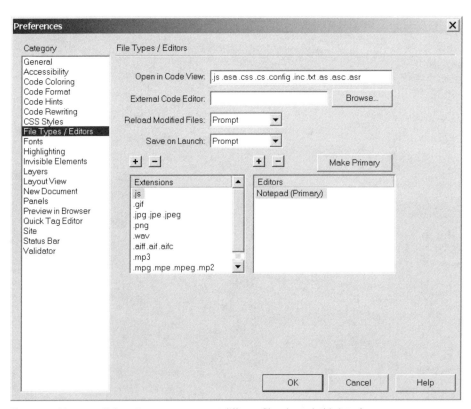

Figure 3.27 You can edit how Dreamweaver treats different files through this interface.

Figure 3.28 Browse for an alternate program to open a file by right clicking the file in the Site panel.

A good example of how using an external editor within Dreamweaver might be useful is if you use Microsoft Word frequently. Dreamweaver doesn't associate .doc files with Microsoft Word by default and can't open them by itself (it will tell you so in a warning message). But by adding the .doc extension in the Preferences dialog box, you'll be able to easily open a Word document by double-clicking on a .doc file from the Site panel. If you have more than one editor set up for a file type, you may choose the secondary editor by right-clicking the file in the Site panel and finding your editor in the Open With submenu. If you don't have one defined, you can browse for a second application in the same way (**Figure 3.28**)

In the context of ASP.NET, editor assignment can be especially useful because you can assign an alternate editor, such as Antechinus, to some of the specialized files you can create in ASP.NET.

Adding Basic Design Elements

Although this book focuses on ASP.NET development, we thought it would be wise to include a small overview of how to use the design tools in Dreamweaver. This way, readers who are migrating from ASP to ASP.NET and are looking to learn Dreamweaver at the same time can get at least a basic understanding of the visual design tools in Dreamweaver MX. For a more in-depth look at Dreamweaver, you'll want to consult books designed for this purpose, like J. Tarin Towers' *Macromedia Dreamweaver MX: Visual QuickStart Guide* from Peachpit Press.

In the introduction to this chapter, we mentioned that some "old guard" developers don't trust or like using visual Web editors. This may be because early versions sometimes produced less than stellar code. Fortunately, this isn't true with Dreamweaver. In fact, Dreamweaver MX gives you the option of making the code that it generates XHTML-compliant, which enforces a stricter syntax standard on code

By generating XHTML-compliant code, you know your code follows sound coding practices and is "well formed," eliminating some of the inconsistent coding practices in HTML. This is because XHTML is based on XML and imposes stricter guidelines on HTML code, such as the requirement to have a closing tag for every opening tag. Along with a multitude of HTML *validators* that inform you automatically when HTML syntax rules are violated, you have the tools in place to guarantee fail-safe code.

Of course, that's not to say the code generated by the visual design tools will always be exactly what you want. You still have to keep an eye on the HTML and validate as you go by viewing the results to make sure that everything works as you intended.

The following section shows you many of the basic tools you'll need to create your Web pages. You'll still need to edit the code now and again to make it fit your specific requirements; however, these design tools do a great job for most scenarios.

Using structural design objects

The most basic HTML that Dreamweaver generates for you is paragraph and line break tags. As you type text in Design view, pressing Enter will wrap your paragraph in <p> tags, then start a new paragraph (a new set of <p> tags). If you press Shift + Enter, a line break (<br>) will be inserted instead of a new paragraph. You'll find that this is similar to what occurs in a variety of popular word processing programs . Of course, this capability is available only in Design view. Dreamweaver doesn't alter code entered in the Code view window.

Regardless of which view you use, you'll find most design tools that generate code available on Dreamweaver's Insert bar (**Figure 3.29**).

The Common tab on the Insert bar has one of the most useful objects in your arsenal— the Insert Table dialog box.

To insert a table:

1. From the Insert bar, click on the Common tab.

2. Click the Insert Table icon 🖼️ . This opens the corresponding dialog box (**Figure 3.30**).

3. Set the parameters for your table from this dialog box, including the number of rows and columns your table should have.

4. Click OK to insert the table into your page and have the table's HTML code automatically generated for you.

If you prefer to draw your tables directly onto the page, you may change to the Layout view of your page. Drawing tables can be useful for creating complex table structures, such as tables that contain other tables, because the HTML can become unwieldy.

Figure 3.29 The Insert bar has many different tabs, each containing different elements that can be inserted into your page.

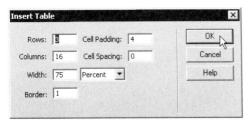

Figure 3.30 The Insert Table dialog box allows you to set the properties of your table without requiring you to write HTML.

ADDING BASIC DESIGN ELEMENTS

To work in Layout view:

1. From the Insert panel, click on the Layout tab (**Figure 3.31**).

2. To switch from standard view to Layout view, click on Layout View.

   Note: You won't be able to switch to Layout view if you're in the page's Code view.

3. Use the Draw Layout Table 🖼 and Draw Layout Cell 🖼 icons in the Layout tab to specify what you're about to draw on the page.

4. Then use your mouse to draw the table or cell.

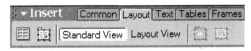

Figure 3.31 Changing to Layout view is useful when you're designing complex pages.

Inserting form elements

HTML form elements, such as text boxes, are central to most Web applications, and in Dreamweaver most of your form needs can be handled right from the Forms tab on the Insert bar.

When you first try to insert a form element, Dreamweaver will detect whether it's contained within <form> tags. If it's not, Dreamweaver will prompt you as to whether it should automatically add the tags.

Most of the form elements, such as text boxes, buttons, text areas, and check boxes, will be embedded in your page as HTML code when selected. So all you need to do is click the appropriate icon after positioning your cursor where you want the element inserted into the page. If desired, you can click and drag the selected icon onto the page instead.

Some form elements, however, offer a bit more functionality. A radio group object, for example, provides an interface to automate the creation of multiple radio button elements.

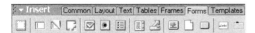

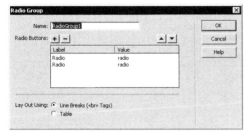

Figure 3.32 The Forms tab of the Insert bar is where you'll find HTML form elements.

Figure 3.33 Radio buttons are meant to be used in groups. This dialog box allows you to generate multiple radio buttons without writing HTML code yourself.

To insert a radio button group:

1. Place the cursor wherever you want your radio buttons to be inserted into the page.

2. From the Insert bar, click on the Forms tab (**Figure 3.32**).

3. Click on the Radio Group icon ▦ .
   This opens the Radio Group dialog box (**Figure 3.33**).

4. In the dialog box, give the group a name.

5. Use the plus and minus buttons above the Radio Buttons list box to increase and decrease the number of radio button options within the group.
   You may also reorder the radio buttons using the up and down arrows at the top right of the Radio Buttons list.

6. To set the Label and Value of each of the radio buttons, click their default values in the list and type in the new values.

7. Determine whether the list should be displayed within a table or simply formatted with line break (<br>) tags.

8. Click OK to save your changes and close the dialog box.
   Once you click OK, the necessary HTML will be inserted into your page so that only one radio button in the group may be selected at a time.

ADDING BASIC DESIGN ELEMENTS

Another useful form element is the jump menu. The *jump menu* uses an HTML drop-down control (called a *select* control) to create a list of URLs that can be linked to. An optional feature of the jump menu is the ability to link to the target page automatically without the user having to click on a Submit button. Not only does this object insert HTML, but it also inserts a client-side JavaScript function into your page that redirects the browser to whatever location you specify. For example, you can use a jump menu to have users select a preferred Web search engine from drop-down list, which will a automatically direct them to that page.

Figure 3.34 The Jump Menu object hides the complexity of this functionality by inserting all of the necessary HTML and JavaScript.

To insert a jump menu:

1. Place the cursor on your page wherever you want your jump menu to be inserted.

2. From the Insert bar, click on the Forms tab.

3. Click on the jump menu icon 🖼.
   The Insert Jump Menu dialog box opens (**Figure 3.34**).

4. In the dialog box, use the + (plus) and – (minus) buttons to increase or decrease the number of menu items in the Menu Items list box.

5. For each menu item in the list, click it and set its Text and URL properties.

6. In the text box labeled Open URLs In, define which window of the browser the URL should open in.

7. In the Menu Name text box, give the jump menu a name.

8. Specify whether the jump menu should be activated by a Go button. Then specify whether the first item should be selected after a URL change (which means you use a selection prompt like Choose One).

9. Click OK to save your changes and close the dialog box.

Applying styles with CSS

Cascading Style Sheets (CSS) have been around for quite a while now, and although the early implementations left much to be desired, this technology has come a long way. CSS allows you to control your page's style attributes, such as font, font face, borders, and so on. You can use CSS to save an entire site's style characteristics in a file that you can then access from any page in the Web site. Using a linked style sheet helps you manage your site, because you can make a change in one file that defines your site's style, and have the change reflected throughout the entire site.

Although CSS is still going through many revisions, much is being done in the browser arena to support the standard correctly. CSS support in Dreamweaver MX has been greatly improved from the last release, not only in the way the Design view interprets CSS, but in the way it lets you edit and apply your CSS styles.

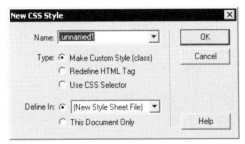

Figure 3.35 CSS allows you to efficiently modify many display properties of your Web site.

To make a new style sheet:

1. From the Text drop-down menu at the top of Dreamweaver select CSS Style > New CSS Style.

   The New CSS Style dialog box appears (**Figure 3.35**).

2. Since the type of style you use influences the name you assign, you need to set the style type first. You have several options to choose from:

   ▲ *Make Custom Style (class)*. A class, whose name begins with a period, may be assigned to any HTML element you wish. It only needs to be specified (without the period) in the class attribute of the desired element.

   ▲ *Redefine HTML Tag*. This option applies the style to all HTML elements of the selected type. There's no need to add an extra attribute to that element, as you must with a custom class.

   ▲ *Use CSS Selector*. A CSS Selector will let you define the style for several of the HTML link states (active, hover, visited, and so on).

3. Once you've selected the type, do one of the following:

   ▲ If you chose Make Custom Style (class), give your class a name starting with a period. For example, ".highlight" could be a class name assigned to a CSS custom style used specifically to make screen objects stand out.

   ▲ If you chose Redefine HTML Tag, select that tag from the Tag drop-down list box that appears at the top of the dialog box.

   ▲ If you chose Use CSS Selector, choose your link state from the new drop-down list box at the top of the dialog box.

continues on next page

4. From the Define In drop-down menu, choose New Style Sheet File to create your new style sheet.

5. Click OK.

This opens the Save Style Sheet File As dialog box, which helps you define certain settings for your new style sheet. Give your new file a name, and click Save to accept the default settings (**Figure 3.36**).

The CSS Style Definition wizard appears (**Figure 3.37**).

6. Using the wizard, you can define many different attributes for your style, such as the font, size, style, line height, and so on. Set the desired attributes and click OK.

Most style settings will work in most current versions of modern browsers.

✔ Tip

■ It's still up to you to test your sites in all target browsers. It's always wise to validate your CSS with an online validator such as the one found at http://jigsaw.w3.org/css-validator/.

Figure 3.36 Saving your style sheet in a separate file allows you to consolidate your styles in a common repository.

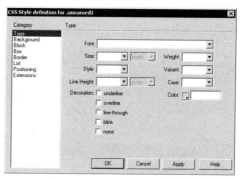

Figure 3.37 The CSS Style Definition dialog box gives you an interface to define almost every known CSS property.

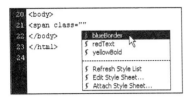

Figure 3.38 Code Insight lets you see a list of all defined CSS classes available to that page.

Figure 3.39 You can apply styles to your pages from the Design panel group's CSS Styles tab, as well as create new styles and delete old ones.

To apply a style:

1. Highlight the text to be formatted on your Web page.

2. Choose from one of the following to apply your style:

   ▲ From the Text drop-down menu at the top of Dreamweaver interface, select the style from the CSS Styles submenu.

   ▲ Using Dreamweaver's Code Insight functionality available in Code view, add the class attribute to most any HTML tag, and a list of defined classes will conveniently appear (**Figure 3.38**).

   ▲ Select your class from the CSS Styles panel (**Figure 3.39**).

   ▲ Select your class from the class list on the Property inspector. (The Property inspector is the panel labeled Properties, residing directly below the document window.) Remember to click the Toggle CSS/HTML Mode icon ⒶL beside the Format drop-down list box if you don't see the class list on the Property inspector.

Once you get the hang of using CSS, you'll find that you can better control the way your Web pages look. Moreover, you'll gain the benefit of knowing that your pages will be forward compatible as technology progresses.

ADDING BASIC DESIGN ELEMENTS

Final word on Dreamweaver

As you undoubtedly know, we've only skimmed the surface in discussing Dreamweaver's capabilities. As we mentioned earlier in the chapter, for a more in-depth discussion or tutorial, try one of the many Dreamweaver resource books that are available on the topic.

From this point forward, we'll assume that you know how to use the basics of the program. We'll now move on to a more ASP.NET-centric discussion.

INTRODUCTION TO ASP.NET WEB FORM CONTROLS

Chapter 3 introduced Dreamweaver and many of its editing tools. It also showed you how to create a site. In this chapter we'll dive into ASP.NET Web Forms and the controls used in them. We'll start out by discussing what Web Forms are and how controls can turn them into dynamic pages. Then we'll create a Web Form and then add controls to see how they perform. Later in the chapter, we'll get into more advanced stuff, so that by the end of the chapter we'll be writing code to programmatically alter the contents of our Web Form.

Preparing Our Web Site

A Web Form is a potentially dynamic Web page. It doesn't have to contain dynamically created content, but it usually does. One use of a dynamic Web Form is a Web page that displays up-to-date items from a sales catalog. Web Forms are similar to HTML pages in that they contain HTML code and JavaScript. However, instead of ending with the .html extension, they end in the .aspx extension. More important, they serve as containers for most other parts of ASP.NET, such as controls. Controls are the building blocks of dynamic content, and that's what we'll be adding to the Web Form we create in this chapter. To process the logic that drives the dynamic content, we'll include blocks of code, another differentiating factor from plain HTML Web pages, which don't contain these code blocks.

Let's start fresh by creating a new site in Dreamweaver to feature our Web Forms. Since we learned in detail how to create a new site in Chapter 3, we'll use the Site Definition wizard to speed the process here.

To create a site:

1. From the Site drop-down menu at the top of the Dreamweaver interface, choose New Site (**Figure 4.1**).

    This opens the Site Definition wizard. Make sure it's in Basic mode (**Figure 4.2**).

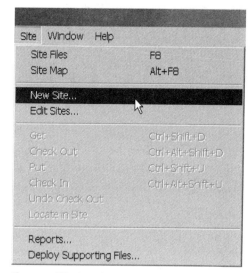

Figure 4.1 Site drop-down menu.

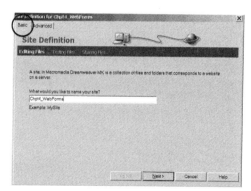

Figure 4.2 In Step 1 of the Site Definition wizard, you name your site.

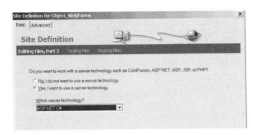

Figure 4.3 In Step 2 of the Site Definition wizard, you pick ASP.NET C# as your server technology.

2. Name the site "Chpt4_WebForms" and click Next.

The wizard will present some new questions about your server technology preference (**Figure 4.3**).

3. Click the second radio button to indicate that you want to use a server technology. For this book, we'll use ASP.NET C#, so pick that as your server technology. Click Next to proceed to the next questions.

4. Accept the default answers for the rest of the screens the wizard presents.

At the conclusion, the wizard will show a summary of the settings you've chosen (**Figure 4.4**).

5. Confirm your entries, then click Done.

This will create the site according to the settings you've specified.

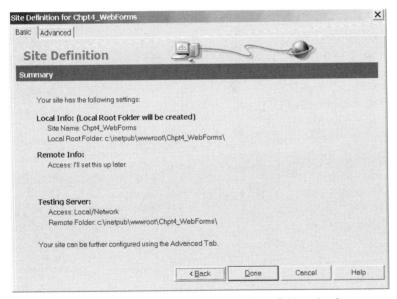

Figure 4.4 A summary of the settings you chose in the Site Definition wizard.

Building a Web Form

To start working with a Web Form and the controls it contains, we'll need to create one first.

To create a new Web Form:

1. Choose New from the File drop-down menu at the top of Dreamweaver.

   The New Document dialog box opens (**Figure 4.5**).

2. In the left pane of the dialog box's General tab, click Dynamic Page.

3. In the right pane, click ASP.NET C#.

4. Click the Create button to make the new .aspx file.

   For simplicity, we're not checking the box to make the new document XHTML compliant.

5. Save the file with its default name.

Now that we have a Web Form, let's start working with it. Switch your view to show Code and Design views simultaneously by clicking the Show Code and Design Views icon on the Document tool bar (**Figure 4.6**). This will help you see what's unique about a Web Form and its controls (**Figure 4.7**).

The only real difference we see between this page and an HTML page so far is in the code of the page. At the top is a command, commonly referred to as a Page Directive, that tells the Web server that the page is a C# Web Form:

```
<%@ Page Language="C#" ContentType=
"text/html" ResponseEncoding=
"iso-8859-1" %>
```

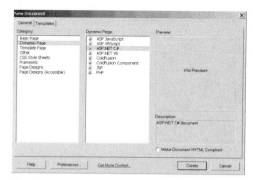

Figure 4.5 Create a new ASP.NET C# Web Form with the New Document dialog box.

Figure 4.6 The Show Code and Design Views icon is located on the Common tab of the Insert bar.

Figure 4.7 A newly created Web Form in split view, with Code view on the top and Design view on the bottom.

Figure 4.8 You know the Insert bar is open in Dreamweaver when you see a check next to its listing in the Window drop-down menu.

Figure 4.9 You click the Form icon on the Insert bar's Forms tab to insert a form element.

Figure 4.10 A Web Form with a form element in split Code/Design view.

The Page Directive also specifies that the resulting content should be HTML. Then it states that the resulting page should be encoded using iso-8859-1, which in English is Western (Latin 1). This coding is the default; the only time you might need to change it is if you're writing pages for other languages.

To embed controls in the Web Form, we'll need to first define the form layout. Doing so involves inserting form tags, and then adding form elements, which is very similar to how you define the form layout for an HTML document—with one exception, as you'll see in Step 4 in the following instructions.

To add a form element:

1. Start by making sure the Insert bar is open.

   You can verify this by looking at the Window drop-down menu found at the top of Dreamweaver. There should be a check mark next to the word *Insert* (**Figure 4.8**).

   The Insert bar's default location is across the top of Dreamweaver, just below the menu bar where you found the Window drop-down menu.

2. Click on the Web Form in Design view, and then from the Insert bar, select the Forms tab and click on the Form icon (**Figure 4.9**).

   This automatically inserts a form element onto your page (**Figure 4.10**).

   You'll see the new HTML code for the form element in the Code view of the Web Form. Below that, in Design view, you'll see a red dotted line representing the boundaries of the form.

   Note: The Tag Editor starts if your cursor is in Code view when you click the Form icon to add a form to your Web page.

3. In the code of the Web Form, click just in front of the form element's name attribute.

   continues on next page

BUILDING A WEB FORM

4. Now go to the Insert bar and click on the ASP.NET tab (**Figure 4.11**). Then click the Runat Server icon ![icon].

This inserts the command that tells the Web server that the form element should be available for server-side processing. It looks like this:

```
<form runat="server" name="form1"
method="post" action="">
```

This last step in the creation of a form element for an ASP.NET Web Form is critical. Controls need the `runat="server"` attribute setting to inform the Web server to process them as ASP.NET controls. We'll see exactly what that means in a moment. But for now, know that the most common error you'll likely make when building Web Forms is forgetting to add the `runat="server"` attribute setting to a control.

At long last we'll add a control to our Web Form. In the next exercise, we'll add an asp:label control that's handy for displaying text. It won't do anything dynamic right now, but it will make clear what distinguishes a control from a normal HTML tag.

To add a Label control:

1. Using the same Web Form we've been working with so far, click inside the red dotted area found in the Design view of the Web Form.

2. Click the asp:label icon ![icon] found in the ASP.NET tab of the Insert bar.

This will start the Tag Editor for a label control (**Figure 4.12**).

3. In the Tag Editor, set the label's ID to "lblMessage" and its Text to "Hello from ASP.NET." Click OK.

The Tag Editor closes and writes the code for you (**Figure 4.13**).

Figure 4.11 The ASP.NET tab of the Insert bar displays the Runat Server icon.

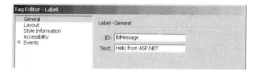

Figure 4.12 The Tag Editor for the lblMessage control.

Figure 4.13 The result of adding the lblMessage control with the Tag Editor.

4. Preview the Web Form in your default browser by saving the document and pressing the F12 key.

Your browser should open and display the text "Hello from ASP.NET."

Let's review what we just completed. After adding an asp:label control to the Web Form, we just previewed the text "Hello from ASP.NET" in Design view. That makes perfect sense, since this control is called a Label. In the code, however, you'll notice a new tag that doesn't look quite like HTML but is very close in syntax.

ASP.NET controls are defined using XML (eXtensible Markup Language) coding standards, as is XHTML (or eXtensible HTML). We chose earlier not to force the document to be XHTML compliant, but that doesn't mean it can't contain XML. To understand what XML is, all you have to know is that it is text that must follow a strict format for describing information. Here, ASP.NET controls describe the programmable objects the Web server should create when processing the page.

Now, to see the new tag the asp:label control created, go back to the browser you previewed your page with in Step 4 and view the page's source code. You don't see the asp:label control anywhere, do you? In its place you'll find the following code:

```
<span id="lblMessage">Hello from
ASP.NET</span>
```

ASP.NET converted the asp:label control into the appropriate HTML—in this case the `<span>` tags—so that it could be rendered by a browser.

It's time to start looking into just what makes up a control. We'll also discuss why we'd want to use one instead of simply writing the resulting HTML in the first place.

BUILDING A WEB FORM

Building Dynamic Pages Using Controls

There are lots of common uses for dynamic pages. One might be to have an online catalog for your products that dynamically checks the current price and quantity in your warehouse every time one of your customers visits the page. This is just one example; the list of possibilities is endless. You probably already have an idea of what you want to achieve since you're reading this book.

You may remember from Chapter 1 that historically, dynamic pages mixed the programming code with the HTML markup code, which has a number of disadvantages (see "A New Paradigm" in Chapter 1 for more information). ASP.NET uses controls like the asp:label control we presented earlier to allow programmable elements to be intermixed with the HTML markup code without mixing actual programming code with the HTML. Tools like Dreamweaver MX then simply have to be configured to know which HTML element each of these controls represents in order to present them graphically in Design view.

The `runat="server"` attribute setting in our controls tells the Web server that the control is a candidate for the programming code to manipulate. Then, once the Web server is done running all the programming code, it sends to the browser the HTML markup that the controls represent. Since the program might have manipulated the controls, the HTML sent to the browser could have different values than the controls had prior to execution.

To see this in action, let's take the Web Form we were just working on and make a dynamic page. The element that makes the page dynamic will involve the entry of a message into a textbox that will display in the label control when the user clicks on a button.

Figure 4.14 The Tag Editor for the txtNewMessage control.

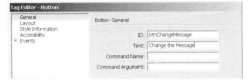

Figure 4.15 The Tag Editor for the btnChangeMessage control.

Figure 4.16 The code that results from adding three common controls: asp:label, asp:textbox, and asp:button.

To create a dynamic page:

1. In the Web Form, click beside the text "Hello from ASP.NET" in Design view.

2. From the Insert bar, click on the ASP.NET tab, and then click the asp:textbox icon ⎇.

   The Tag Editor for the asp:textbox control opens (**Figure 4.14**).

3. In the Tag Editor, set the ID to "txtNewMessage" and the Text to "New Message," and click OK.

   The Tag Editor closes and writes the code for you.

4. Click beside the new text box in Design view.

5. Then from the ASP.NET tab of the Insert bar, click the asp:button icon ⌐.

   The Tag Editor for the asp:button control opens (**Figure 4.15**).

6. This time in the Tag Editor, set the ID to "btnChangeMessage" and the Text to "Change the Message," and click OK.

   The resulting page will have three commonly used controls. The code for them will be in the Web Form's Code view, and the visual representation of them will be in Design view (**Figure 4.16**).

7. We still have some additional code to write in order to change the lblMessage control's text to what we enter into the txtNewMessage control. In Code view, click just before the </head> tag.

continues on next page

8. From the Insert bar's ASP.NET tab, click the Page_Load icon ▣ to automatically add the `Page_Load` function to the page. It'll look like this:

```
<script runat="server">
protected void Page_Load(Object Src,
EventArgs E)
{
    if (!IsPostBack) DataBind();
}
</script>
```

You don't have to understand this right now—we're about to change it.

9. Change the contents of the `Page_Load` function to the following:

```
if( IsPostBack )lblMessage.Text =
txtNewMessage.Text;
```

You can view the results in Code view (**Figure 4.17**).

10. Finally, save the document and press F12 to view your page in your default browser.

11. Try clicking the "Change the Message" button. You'll see the text displayed by the asp:label control change to read "New Message." To change the text again, you can change the value of the asp:textbox control and click the button.

Now, admittedly, this Web Form doesn't do a great deal, but this shows how easy it is to make a page dynamic.

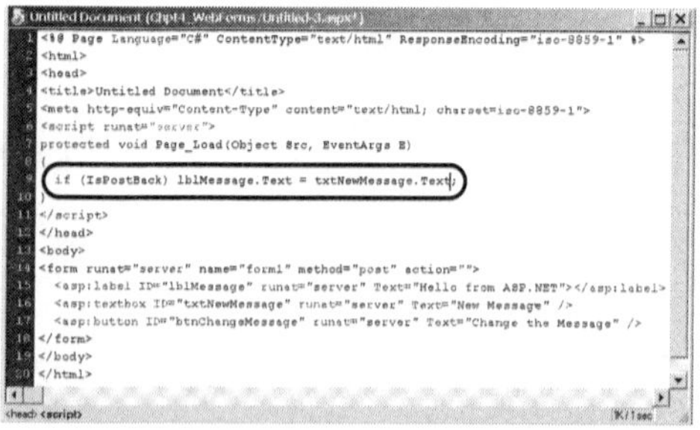

Figure 4.17 The result of changing the `Page_Load` function.

Now, let's dive into the guts of the Web Form to learn what's really going on. As mentioned earlier, the Web server looks at the page to see if there are any elements on which it needs to run code. It also runs any code contained in the page. In our Web Form, for instance, we used a built-in function called `Page_Load`. Notice that this function resides in a script block that also contains the `runat="server"` attribute. This attribute tells the Web server to process the function before sending the page to the client. Script blocks without this attribute are assumed to be executed on the client and are ignored by the server.

The `Page_Load` function is automatically called by the Web server when the page is loaded for processing. The first line, `if( IsPostBack )`, checks if the page is in post-back mode. A Web Form is considered to be in post-back mode when it has already been sent to the client's computer and the client has then done something to cause the form to post back to the server. Therefore, the first time the visitor opens the Web Form, it's not a post back. The next section, "Handling Post Back," discusses this in more detail.

So the `Page_Load` function does nothing the first time the page is visited; then when the visitor clicks the button labeled Change the Message, the form is submitted back to the server. This time the Web server runs the same `Page_Load` function, but it's in post-back mode. Therefore, the Text property of the asp:label control is set to the value of the asp:textbox's Text property. Notice that now we called Text a property, not an attribute. The reason we call Text a property in the function and an attribute in the markup is that in the function we're dealing with a programmable object and in the markup we're dealing with the XML markup describing that object.

Handling Post Back

One of the biggest differences between ASP and ASP.NET is that in ASP.NET, a Web Form must post back to itself rather than post to a different page.

Historically, developers posted to a different page by setting the form's action attribute. Posting to a separate page used to be a good idea because it made for a cleaner separation of code from HTML. Now, because ASP.NET handles events in the same Web Form in which they're raised, the form must post back to the same page. Even if you set the action attribute of the form to a different page, the Web server finds the `runat="server"` attribute setting and overrides your action value.

The changes required to handle post back in the same Web Form instead of a different page are minimal. One of the nice things about posting to the same page is that it takes less code to process the data elements such as the Querystring or form fields. (See the sidebar "Form vs. Querystring Fields.") You saw that demonstrated in the previous exercise, "To create a dynamic page." There was no need to look in the Request.Form collection, as ASP developers would have had to do to access the form data being passed from the form. However, if you're stuck on using the Request.Form collection, you can still use it.

Form vs. Querystring Fields

Passing data back to the server is commonly done in one of two ways: via form field or Querystring.

We're all familiar with forms, because we've all had to enter information like our name into text boxes when purchasing something online. Those text boxes are placed in between opening and closing <form> tags in HTML, which makes them form fields. If you want to pass the data about these text boxes back to the server, you'd need to make sure you set the form's method attribute to its default value of post. Using method="post" means the form field values will be retrieved from the Response.Form collection.

The technique of posting fields in a Response.Form collection is sometimes called the "put" method. For example, say there was a text box named txtFirstName inside of a form, with the form's method attribute set to post. Then in the code of the page to which the form posted, the value entered into the txtFirstName text box would be available by referencing the Response.Form["txtFirstName"] field.

On the other hand, we could have set the form's method attribute to get. This attribute will still pass the data about the text boxes back to the server; however, in the code of the page to which the form posted, the value entered into the txtFirstName field will be available by referencing the Response.Querystring collection, rather than the Response.Form collection. It would look something like this: Response.Querystring["txtFirstName"].

Posting fields in the Response.Querystring collection is usually referred to as the "get" method. The main difference between the two posting methods is that form fields can't be seen in a URL, while Querystring fields can. Most of the time you'll want to "put" fields, because then the field values won't be seen in the URL.This might be important, for example, if you need to pass sensitive information, such as social security numbers.

However, if you want to make a hyperlink pass information on to the page it links to without using a form at all, the "get" method of sending data to a page would be the perfect choice. For example, you might want to list summary information about products and provide links to a detail page for users to obtain more information about each product. Once a link is clicked, the detail page is passed data that indicates which product was selected via the Querystring. You won't need <form> tags around your data when passing it in this way.

The URL would look something like this:

```
http://localhost/detail.aspx?ProductID=002411027
```

In the above example, we have a Web Form called detail.aspx and the Querystring field, ProductID, is set to a value of 002411027.

The code for the URL can just be a normal hyperlink, followed by a question mark ('?') and then the field name set to equal a value, just as we showed in the previous example:

```
<a href="http://localhost/detail.aspx?ProductID=002411027" > 002411027</a>
```

To use the Request.Form collection:

1. Once again, open up the same Web Form you've been working with.

2. Click beside the button in the Design view of the Web Form to set your insertion point.

3. On the ASP.NET tab, click the asp:label icon `abc`.

   This opens its Tag Editor (**Figure 4.18**).

4. In the Tag Editor, set the ID to "lblOldWay" but leave the Text field blank. Click OK to close the Tag Editor and create the control.

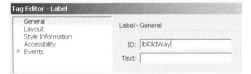

Figure 4.18 The Tag Editor for the lblOldWay control.

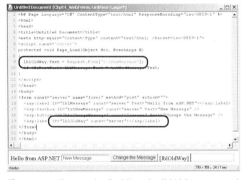

Figure 4.19 The result of adding the lblOldWay control and setting its Text to the Request.Form collection's txtNewMessage field.

5. Now add the following line of code to the `Page_Load` function, just above the code you entered in the last list, "To create a dynamic page."

   ```
   lblOldWay.Text = Request.Form
   ["txtNewMessage"];

   if ( IsPostBack )lblMessage.Text =
   txtNewMessage.Text;
   ```

   Note that the label has a visible place-holder in Design view (**Figure 4.19**).

6. Save the document and press the F12 key to view your changes.

   The lblOldWay element isn't shown, because it has no default value; but when you click the button, it changes to the text box's value, too.

✔ Tip

- If a Request.Form variable doesn't exist, it will be `null`, rather than an empty string, as it is the case in ASP.

If you looked at the source code of the page generated by the Web server while you were moving through the steps, you might have noticed a hidden form field called `__VIEWSTATE`. Don't bother to look for it now if you didn't see it before. It's really just a bunch of encoded stuff only the server understands. But what it's doing is keeping track of all your form field values so that they maintain state between post backs to the server. To remind you of what *maintaining state* means, remember that each time you visit a Web page, the server has no good idea who you are or what you were doing last. This *statelessness* is intrinsic to the Web and something programmers have always had to write code to get around. ASP.NET's `__VIEWSTATE` variable makes your life easier by not requiring you to write program code to maintain state anymore. It does it for you.

Moving Between Pages

So how do you help your visitors navigate to other pages on your site if you're always posting back to the same Web Form? The answer is the Response.Redirect command. First, handle the post back in your Web Form. Then give the Response.Redirect command the URL of the next page you want the visitor to go to, like this:

```
Response.Redirect("NextPage.aspx");
```

To increase performance there's a second, optional parameter you can add to the command. It determines whether the server should halt processing the current page and transfer immediately or whether it should finish the page first. The Boolean value of true halts processing and transfers immediately. That would look like this:

```
Response.Redirect("NextPage.aspx", true);
```

Transferring to a new page is when we really have to start worrying about maintaining state. The reason is that we won't have that handy __VIEWSTATE hidden form element doing the work for us. It's not available when transferring between pages using the Response.Redirect command.

In the past, when programmers posted to a different page, hidden form fields were often used to keep track of things such as the current visitor's ID number. Other options for maintaining state are common as well. For example, it's still possible to post a form that lacks the runat="server" attribute to your next page and gather those form values in the same way we described in the previous list, "To use the Request.Form collection." However, a better way to maintain state in ASP.NET is to use session variables.

Session variables are a great way to store data that only concerns an individual user for the duration of time the user is interacting with the Web site. Session variables are commonly used in E-commerce sites for the "shopping cart" feature, which stores items the visitor wants to buy. Don't let what you may have heard in the past about session variables put you off of ASP.NET's version; they're flexible and they let you easily overcome or minimize most of the problems associated with session variables, such as accessibility and performance. We'll start by using them in a simple way.

In the next list, we'll illustrate how to create and reference a session variable. Two Web Forms will be created: the first we'll use to create a session variable to store a text value and the second we'll use to retrieve and display the session variable's contents.

To use a session variable:

1. Create a Web Form as outlined earlier in this chapter in "To create a new Web Form," and name it "SetSession.aspx." Make sure the page shows both Code and Design views by clicking the Show Code and Design Views icon ▦.

2. Add a form element to it. Make sure to set the runat="server" attribute as we did in "To add a form element."

3. Now click inside the form's red dotted line to set your insertion point.

4. On the ASP.NET tab, click the asp:button icon ▭.
   Its Tag Editor opens (**Figure 4.20**).

5. In the Tag Editor, set the ID to "btnSetSessionVariable" and Text to "Set Session Variable."

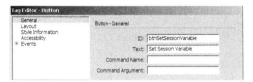

Figure 4.20 The Tag Editor for the btnSetSessionVariable control.

Figure 4.21 The code setting the SampleVariable session variable and redirecting to the ReadSession Web Form.

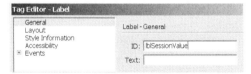

Figure 4.22 The Tag Editor for the lblSessionValue control.

6. In the page's code, add the Page_Load function by clicking the Page_Load icon 🖼 like we did in "To create a dynamic page." This time, replace the Page_Load function's contents with code to set a session variable called "SampleVariable" to the value "Session Variable Sample," as follows:

```
protected void Page_Load(Object Src,
EventArgs E)
{
   Session["SampleVariable"] =
   "Session Variable Sample";
}
```

7. On the line that follows the code we just added, add the command to redirect to a page called ReadSession.aspx (**Figure 4.21**).

```
Response.Redirect("ReadSession.aspx");
```

8. Now create the Web Form you'll be redirecting to. Do it the same way you did in Step 1, but name it "ReadSession.aspx."

9. In the ReadSession Web Form you just created, add an asp:label, setting its ID to "lblSessionValue" (**Figure 4.22**). This time a form element is not necessary.

10. Add the Page_Load function with code that sets lblSessionValue's Text property to the session variable.

```
protected void Page_Load(Object Src,
EventArgs E)
{
   lblSessionValue.Text =
   Session["SampleVariable"].ToString();
}
```

continues on next page

MOVING BETWEEN PAGES

Make sure to change the session variable to a string using the `ToString()` method, since that's what Text properties expect (**Figure 4.23**).

11. Finally, save the files and preview the SetSession Web Form in your default browser.

12. To test, click the button in the SetSession Web Form.

This will cause the page to post back to the server, set the session variable, and redirect to the ReadSession Web Form.

You learned from "To use the Request.Form collection" earlier in this chapter that if the lblSessionValue control hadn't been set in the ReadSession page's `Page_Load` function, the page would have been blank.

These instructions present a generic scenario for using a session variable. Session variables can be used to store almost anything the programmer needs. However, Web sites usually store things like the identifier for the logged in user, the number of the products the user is looking for more details about, and so on. Typically, it's best to try to store just a small number of temporary but reusable things that require little memory. This is because session variables are stored in the server's memory by default. You easily can change this default, however, by specifying that the server store the session variables in a database.

Then, also by default, an in-memory cookie on the visitor's computer tells the server which session variables belong to which visitors. You can also change how this session identifier is stored: Instead of the server placing a cookie on the visitor's computer, you can have the server automatically tack it onto the URL of every page the user visits (for both hyperlinks and redirect commands) using a Querystring variable.

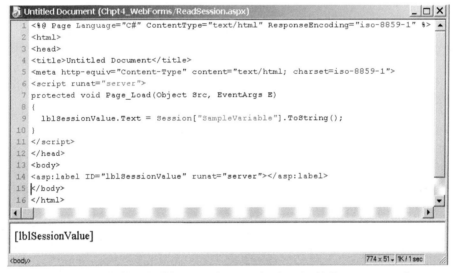

```
1  <%@ Page Language="C#" ContentType="text/html" ResponseEncoding="iso-8859-1" %>
2  <html>
3  <head>
4  <title>Untitled Document</title>
5  <meta http-equiv="Content-Type" content="text/html; charset=iso-8859-1">
6  <script runat="server">
7  protected void Page_Load(Object Src, EventArgs E)
8  {
9     lblSessionValue.Text = Session["SampleVariable"].ToString();
10 }
11 </script>
12 </head>
13 <body>
14 <asp:label ID="lblSessionValue" runat="server"></asp:label>
15 </body>
16 </html>
```

[lblSessionValue]

Figure 4.23 The result of adding the lblSessionValue control and setting it's Text property to the SampleVariable Session variable.

Working with Lists

The last type of control we'll work with in this chapter is the list control. Most anyone who's ever filled out their address on a Web page has likely encountered either a list of countries or a list of state in the United States. Because those lists are rather long, we'll make our own short list.

There are actually many types of lists. The two examples above are usually shown as drop-down lists, but we can have check box lists, radio button lists, or just plain list boxes. Since drop-down lists are the most common, we'll use that type in the following list. We encourage you to try some of the other types as well.

The following instructions create an asp:dropdownlist control and add list items to it in two different ways.

To make a drop-down list:

1. Create a new Web Form, and then add a form element, making sure to add the runat="server" attribute setting.

   If you need to refresh your memory, see "To create a new Web Form" and "To add a form element" earlier in this chapter.

2. Click inside the form element in Design view to set your insertion point.

3. Then from the Insert bar's ASP.NET tab, click the asp:dropdownlist icon 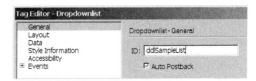.

   This opens the Tag Editor (**Figure 4.24**).

4. In the Tag Editor, set the ID to "ddlSampleList" and click OK.

   Never mind the faded check in the box next to Auto Postback. The default is to not post back automatically when the user's dropdownlist control selection changes, which is what we want right now.

5. Between the <asp:dropdownlist> and </asp:dropdownlist> tags, type the following code:

   ```
   <asp:dropdownlist ID="ddlSampleList"
   runat="server">
     <asp:listitem>
       List Item 1
     </asp:listitem>
   </asp:dropdownlist>
   ```

6. Once again, add the Page_Load function and change its contents to the following:

   ```
   protected void Page_Load(Object Src,
   EventArgs E)
   {
     ddlSampleList.Items.Add(
     "List Item 2" );
   }
   ```

7. Review your Web Form and try to guess what the results will be (**Figure 4.25**).

8. Save the page and view it by pressing the F12 key to see if your guess was correct.

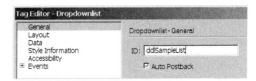

Figure 4.24 The Tag Editor for the ddlSampleList control.

Figure 4.25 Adding list items to the ddlSampleList control through two different methods: code and markup.

Inheritance

.NET is built using object-oriented design, and the .NET languages are object oriented (OO). OO programming is a huge subject in itself, but one key concept in it is called *inheritance*. In OO languages you can create what is called a Class. A *Class* defines an Object—specifying what data is part of the Object, as well as what functions you can run on it. ListControl is one such Class.

Inheritance is when you create a second Class, say a DropDownList, and then specify in its definition that it should inherit all the functions and properties from another Class, such as the ListControl. You could then customize some of those functions to better fit your new Class. If several Classes inherit from the same Class, they will all inherit those same functions.

For a deeper discussion of this subject, refer to Chapter 11.

You see from the resulting page that both ways of adding items to the drop-down list work well. Step 5 was not a dynamic approach because you just typed the item directly within the drop-down list. That's actually a good way to do it for lists that are short and won't change, such as a list of gender choices.

Step 6 uses a more programmatic approach to adding a list item by working with the list control's Items collection. All list type controls have an Items collection so they all have the Add function. In fact they have a slew of common functions because they all inherit from the ListControl class (see the "Inheritance" sidebar).

There is a completely different way to dynamically add list items, however. It's called *data binding*, and it's handy for building dynamic pages. Data binding is the process of associating data from a database table or an array, for example, to a control at runtime. Data binding isn't limited to lists—many of the standard controls can also be bound to data. The stepped instructions that follow use two different syntaxes for achieving data binding; you'll see both regularly. You just have to know that the two styles exist and that sometimes one will be more useful than the other.

To bind data to a control:

1. Using the same Web Form you used in the previous exercise, "To make a drop-down list," remove both the programming code and the markup code that added list items to ddlSampleList.

2. Click beside the ddlSampleList control in Design view to set your insertion point.

3. Then on the ASP.NET tab, click the asp:textbox icon .

   The Tag Editor opens (**Figure 4.26**).

4. In the Tag Editor, set the ID to "txtDataString" and Text to "str." Click OK.

5. Back in the code of the Web Form, highlight the value of "str" assigned to txtDataString. Don't include its surrounding quotes in the highlighting.

6. Then on the ASP.NET tab, click the Bound Data icon . This will change the value of the Text attribute to <%# str %>.

   Note: You'll run into situations where the bound data syntax will need to use quotation marks. Because of the outer double quotation marks of the Text attribute, you would need to use the single quotation marks inside.

7. Now up above the Page_Load function, create a String variable called str like the following:

```
<script runat="server">
String str = "Sample String";

protected void Page_Load(Object Src,
EventArgs E)
```

Figure 4.26 The Tag Editor for the txtDataString control.

8. Inside the `Page_Load` function, create a String array called `dataList` and set it to be ddlSampleList's data source. Also set the Page object to execute the `BindData` command (**Figure 4.27**).

```
protected void Page_Load(Object Src,
EventArgs E)
{
  String[] dataList = new
  String[2]
      {"List Item 1", "List Item
      2"};
  ddlSampleList.DataSource =
      dataList;
  Page.BindData();
}
```

9. Save the Web Form, and press F12 to view it in your default browser.

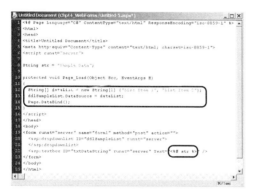

Figure 4.27 The two techniques for binding data to controls.

First we set the text box's Text attribute to a dynamic value by using the `<%# %>` bound data syntax. At first glance this may seem to be the same as the old ASP way of inserting dynamic data into HTML. However, the syntax is where the similarity stops. The biggest difference is that the data doesn't get bound until you call the `BindData` function. We did so in the `Page_Load` function by calling the Page object's `BindData` function. We could have called the `BindData` function for ddlSampleList and txtDataString separately; however, the call cascades down to all contained objects, so calling it on the Page object requires less code.

The second style of binding data we used was to set the `DataSource` attribute of ddlSampleList to the array of strings. This style of code is less clear in describing exactly what will happen, but the style better separates the programming code from the markup code, which can be beneficial.

We'll thoroughly explore the subject of binding data in Chapter 8, but next we'll take a closer look at the programmability of Web Forms in Chapter 5, "Effectively Using Web Form Controls."

EFFECTIVELY USING WEB FORM CONTROLS

In Chapter 4 we discussed the concepts around Web Forms and embedding ASP.NET controls to provide server-side functionality. Now that you've gained some experience with them, we can delve into examining their controls in a little more detail.

ASP.NET Web Forms can be difficult to implement for developers who are migrating from any of the older server-side scripting languages. This is because ASP.NET is event-based and object-oriented, whereas most older scripting languages such as ASP use eventless, procedural code. Event processing in ASP.NET is similar to the type of event processing found in other Microsoft applications like Excel and Word. Here, events are raised by user actions, such as a mouse click, and associated event handlers are triggered to process the event.

To better understand the difference in approach, let's look a little closer at the way older scripting languages process code. When a page is run in ASP, for example, all of the code on the page is executed in the order in which it appears, from top to bottom. Of course, you can write most ASP code into functions to make the code more organized and controllable, but the Web server still needs some code in addition to those functions to know which functions to call and when.

In contrast, ASP.NET allows you to assign functions (called *event handlers*) to events, which may or may not be initiated by the user. One event might be the loading of the page; another could be the clicking of a button. When the event occurs—and only then—the Web server will run the code in the handler assigned to that event. This allows programmers to keep all code inside functions and not worry about when to call them. The Web server will do that automatically when the assigned event occurs.

In this chapter, we'll show you how to use these events and their handlers to add functionality to common controls. We'll also take a look at some useful complex controls that have functionality built right in.

Using Events to Interact With Controls

First, let's review events. Most of you have experienced an image rollover effect on a Web page. A *rollover* effect is when an image changes as users place a mouse pointer over it. Rollover effects are most often used for navigation buttons, to let users know when the button can be clicked. With rollover effects that are initiated by the user, the code that actually changes the image is written in client-side JavaScript. That JavaScript code is linked to the image's Mouseover event so that when the mouse pointer moves over the image, the Web browser runs the code.

Events can range from Mouseovers and button clicks to the loading or pre-rendering of a page. Events are merely messages sent out by objects. Software that's programmed to detect those messages, such as a Web browser, executes any code registered for that event. So in the case of the Mouseover event, the Web browser detects the event and executes any code registered to run when that event is triggered.

Using ASP.NET, however, you can register functions with the Web server so that they'll be executed when the *server* detects an event. The only difference between this scenario and the Mouseover event described in the previous paragraph is which software is responsible for detecting the event, the Web browser or the Web server. Client-side code, which comprises mainly HTML and script blocks of JavaScript or VBScript code, runs when the Web browser detects the event; whereas server-side code, which comprises dynamic processing logic, runs when the Web server intercepts the event.

Page-level events

As we mentioned in the introduction to this chapter, some events, like a button click, may be initiated by the user. Other events, like the Page Load event, may be initiated in a more indirect way. We call these Page-level events.

The Page Load event, for example, is triggered every time a user visits a Web page. It is loaded by the server, so it's not the direct result of a user's action, but rather a side effect of one. The "Order of Events" sidebar discusses many of the page-level events that are automatically triggered by ASP.NET at specific intervals in the page processing life cycle.

Here we'll focus on the Page Load event because it's the most often utilized event in ASP.NET Web Forms. Dreamweaver even has an icon on the ASP.NET tab of the Insert bar that automatically inserts the Page_Load event handler function into your page (**Figure 5.1**).

Figure 5.1 The Page_Load function has its own icon on the Insert bar's ASP.NET tab.

Order of Events

The Web Form triggers 11 events every time it's loaded. You'll probably only use about three of them in your day-to-day dealings with ASP.NET, but they're all listed here in the order in which they're triggered. The ones you'll most often need to work with have their function names next to them.

1. Initialization (`Page_Init`)
2. Load View State
3. Post Back Data Processing
4. Page Load (`Page_Load`)
5. Post Back Change Notification
6. Post Back Event Processing
7. Pre-rendering (`Page_PreRender`)
8. Save View State
9. Rendering
10. Disposing
11. Unload

Custom controls follow this event sequence as well. (Custom controls are similar to ASP.NET provided controls, except that they're user defined.) However, they execute after the main page's events with the exception of `Page_Init`, which executes before the control's initialization. Any other events, such as `OnClick`, are raised after the `Page_Load` event. We discuss custom controls in more detail in Chapter 10.

As you've seen in Chapter 4, the following code is what Dreamweaver inserts when the icon is clicked.

```
<script runat="server">
Protected void Page_Load(Object Src,
EventArgs E)
{
   if (!IsPostBack) DataBind();
}
</script>
```

Normally you need to register event handlers to handle specific events so that the Web server knows which functions handle which events. But because the Page Load event handler is so common, you don't have to register it. We still show you how to register events in the "Control events" section later in this chapter, however, because all the other event handlers do need to be registered.

To illustrate the Page Load event, we'll create a Web Form that checks the current time when the page is loaded. The result will determine what message to display to the user.

You'll notice as you work through the steps below that a lot of the code is automatically added for you as you type in your code. This is because Dreamweaver MX's wonderfully helpful Code Insight functionality makes an educated guess as to what you'll type next. It positions a drop-down list at your cursor location, allowing you to select the code you want, so that you don't have to type it in yourself.

To utilize the Page Load event:

1. Create a new Web Form(If you need help with this, see "To create a new Web Form" in Chapter 4.) Make sure the page is in Code view by pressing the Show Code View icon (**Figure 5.2**).

2. Start by adding two asp:panel controls to the body of the page. Give the first one the ID of "pnlOpen" and the second one the ID of "pnlClosed."

The result will look like this:

```
<asp:panel id="pnlOpen" runat=
"server"></asp:panel>

<asp:panel id="pnlClosed" runat=
"server"></asp:panel>
```

If you're not familiar with asp:panel controls, we discuss them in more detail at the end of these steps.

3. Inside the body of the pnlOpen asp:panel control, add the following code to let the visitor know they may call the fictitious office:

```
<p>Call us at (555) 555-5555.</p>
```

The result will look like this:

```
<asp:panel id="pnlOpen" runat=
"server">
<p>Call us at (555) 555-5555.</p>
</asp:panel>
```

4. Similarly, add the following code into the pnlClosed asp:panel to inform the visitor they'll have to try again during business hours.

```
<asp:panel id="pnlClosed" runat=
"server">
<p>
We are not open at this moment.<br />
Call back between 9 a.m. and 5 p.m.
</p>
</asp:panel>
```

Don't worry, in a moment we'll add some code to make sure that both this message and the message in Step 3 won't display at the same time.

5. Higher up in the page, click just before the closing </head> tag. This sets the insertion point for our Page_Load function.

6. To insert the default Page_Load event handler, go to the Insert bar, click on the ASP.NET tab, and then click the Page_Load icon ▦ .

7. Replace the code Dreamweaver adds to the Page_Load function by default with the following:

```
DateTime open = new DateTime(
DateTime.Now.Year,
DateTime.Now.Month,
DateTime.Now.Day, 9, 1, 1);

DateTime closed = new DateTime(
DateTime.Now.Year,
DateTime.Now.Month,
DateTime.Now.Day, 17, 1, 1);

DateTime now = DateTime.Now;
```

This code creates and initializes the three variables we'll use to determine which asp:panel control to make visible.

The first, open, is set to 9 a.m. The second, closed, is set to 5 p.m., though it's in military format. The last is set to the current time, which will be the time the function is run.

Now that our variables are set, we can start working with them.

Figure 5.2 Click the Show Code View icon to view the page's code.

Script 5.1 This code displays different asp:panels depending on the time.

```
                      script
1 <%@ Page Language="C#" ContentType="text/html"
  ResponseEncoding="iso-8859-1" %>
2 <html>
3 <head>
4 <title>Untitled Document</title>
5 <meta http-equiv="Content-Type" content=
  "text/html; charset=iso-8859-1">
6 <script runat="server">
7 protected void Page_Load(Object Src,
  EventArgs E)
8 {
9   DateTime open = new DateTime(DateTime.Now.
    Year,DateTime.Now.Month,DateTime.Now.Day,
    9,1,1);
10  DateTime closed = new DateTime(DateTime.
    Now.Year,DateTime.Now.Month,DateTime.Now.
    Day,17,1,1);
11  DateTime now = DateTime.Now;

12  if ( (now >= open) && (now <= closed) )
13  {
14    // open for business
15    pnlOpen.Visible = true;
16    pnlClosed.Visible = false;
17  }
18  else
19  {
20    // we're closed
21    pnlOpen.Visible = false;
22    pnlClosed.Visible = true;
23  }
24 }
25 </script>
26 </head>
27 <body>
28 <asp:panel id="pnlOpen" runat="server">
29   <p>
30     Call us at (555) 555-5555.
31   </p>
32 </asp:panel>
33 <asp:panel id="pnlClosed" runat="server">
34   <p>
35     We are not open at this moment.<br />
36     Call back between 9 a.m. and 5 p.m.
37   </p>
38 </asp:panel>
39 </body>
40 </html>
```

8. Add the following `if` statement to determine whether the store is open:

```
if((now >= open) && (now <= closed))
{
  // open for business
  pnlOpen.Visible = true;
  pnlClosed.Visible = false;
}
```

This code simply checks to see if the current time, now, is between the opening time of 9 a.m. and the closing time of 5 p.m. If this evaluates to true, pnlOpen is made visible and pnlClosed is made invisible.

9. To deal with the scenario of the office being closed, add the following code immediately after the closing bracket of the `if` statement:

```
else
{
  // we're closed
  pnlOpen.Visible = false;
  pnlClosed.Visible = true;
}
```

This additional code runs when the `if` statement evaluates to false. In this case, it makes pnlOpen invisible and pnlClosed visible.

Now we're ready to test our Web Form. You may want to compare your code against **Script 5.1** to check for mistakes before testing.

10. Press the F12 key to run your page in the default browser.

You'll find that your page displays a different message depending on what time you try it. To see if it actually changes messages, change the time on your computer and run it again. Just remember to change your computer's clock back to the correct time.

Now that you know the Web server is listening for events and the `Page_Load` function is automatically registered to handle the Page Load event, things are probably making more sense. In previous chapters we've referred to the `Page_Load` function, but you just had to take it for granted that somehow it was being called. Now you know exactly what's happening. When the user first requests the page, the Web server finds the page and starts to process it. This triggers the Page Load event, and your code is run.

If you've been unfamiliar with asp:panel controls until now, you'll find they're immensely useful. Granted, they don't usually display anything themselves when translated into HTML; they're translated into `<div></div>` tags that wrap the asp:panel's contents, which usually isn't noticed on a Web page. But this is precisely why they're useful.

As you saw in the previous exercises, you can place page content into an asp:panel and then simply change that asp:panel's `Visible` property to change its visibility. Because Web Forms post back to themselves (as we discussed in Chapter 4), you can also use the result of the post to determine which panel on a page to display next.

This makes it easy to keep user feedback in the same page as the content the feedback is addressing. The asp:panel controls also allow you to control the appearance (font, color, border, and so on) for all controls contained inside the asp:panel control because you can assign styles to them.

Control events

We mentioned in the "Page-level events" section above that handlers for events like button clicks need to be registered so that the Web server knows which functions run for which events. The Web server doesn't care about the name of our functions, but it does care about the function signatures. Simply put, a function *signature* is the definition of its input parameter types and return type.

It's possible for each event to have many handlers, although this is rare. In order to keep track of all these possible handlers, Microsoft adds each handler to a list known as a *Delegate,* which propagates each event to the handlers in that list. Delegates act as listening devices for events, detecting that an event has occurred and then delegating responsibility for handling the event to its assigned handler.

Microsoft might not have had to make it this complicated if it weren't for the fact that different events expect different types of information. You saw in the `Page_Load` function that its return type is void, meaning that it doesn't return anything, and that it expects two parameters. The first parameter to the `Page_Load` function is of type Object, which represents the root object for the .NET object hierarchy; so the function can accept a reference to any type of object in this parameter. The object reference normally passed to this parameter is a reference to the object that caused the event. The second parameter is of type EventArgs and represents specific information about that event. This information can vary depending on the control and the event triggered.

Armed with this information about events and their handlers, let's extend the page we were working on by adding a button our visitors can click to contact the office via email, regardless of the time of day.

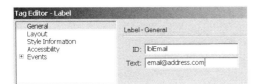

Figure 5.3 The General section of the Tag Editor for the lblEmail control.

To assign a handler to an asp:button:

1. Open the page we were working on in the last list. If you need to recreate it, make sure you refer to Script 5.1.

   Once the page is open, the first thing you'll need to do is add a form to the page.

2. Start the form just after the <body> tag by adding the following line:

   ```
   <form runat="server">
   ```

3. Then close the form by adding </form> just before the closing </body> tag.

   Remember that when dealing with scenarios where the page posts a form back to the server (often referred to as "postback"), we need a form with its runat attribute set to "server."

4. Now that we have our form set up, add the following asp:panel, which will contain our new controls below both asp:panels, but still inside the form:

   ```
   <asp:panel id="pnlEmail" runat=
   "server"></asp:panel>
   ```

5. With your cursor blinking in between the opening and closing <asp:panel> tags of the pnlEmail control, go to the Insert bar and click on the ASP.NET tab. Then click on the asp:label icon abc .

   The Tag Editor dialog box for an asp:label control will appear (**Figure 5.3**).

6. In the Tag Editor, set the ID to "lblEmail" and the Text to "email@address.com."

   continues on next page

7. Click Style Information on the left menu of the dialog box, and then deselect the Visible checkbox at the bottom (**Figure 5.4**).

   Clearing this checkbox will keep the email address invisible by default. However, because the lblEmail control resides outside of the pnlOpen and pnlClosed asp:panels, it's visibility may be set independent of their visibility settings.

8. Click OK to close the dialog box.

9. Back in the Code view of the page, click after the closing tag of the lblEmail control that we just added so we can insert an asp:button control to our page. Start the Tag Editor again, only this time by clicking the asp:button icon ⊟.

10. In the Tag Editor for an asp:button control, set the ID to "btnShowEmail" and the Text field to "Show Email" (**Figure 5.5**).

11. Then click the plus sign next to Events in the left of the Tag Editor and select OnClick from the expanded list that appears (**Figure 5.6**).

12. In the large text box on the right, type in the name of the function you want to have handle the On Click event. Let's call it something that is meaningful, like "btnShowEmail_OnClick".

13. Click OK to have the handler generate the markup for this control and close the dialog box.

    By setting the value of the OnClick attribute of the btnShowEmail control, we only told the ASP.NET server which function to run when the button is clicked. Now that we have the lblEmail and btnShowEmail controls, we have to write the function handler that will work with them.

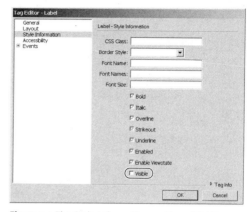

Figure 5.4 The Style Information section of the Tag Editor for the lblEmail control.

Figure 5.5 The General section of the Tag Editor for the btnShowEmail control.

Figure 5.6 The On Click Event of the Tag Editor for the btnShowEmail control.

Script.5.2 Here we're adding an event handler for the btnShowEmail control's On Click event.

```
                    script

1  <%@ Page Language="C#" ContentType="text/html"
   ResponseEncoding="iso-8859-1" %>
2  <html>
3  <head>
4  <title>Untitled Document</title>
5  <meta http-equiv="Content-Type" content=
   "text/html; charset=iso-8859-1">
6  <script runat="server">
7  protected void Page_Load(Object Src,
   EventArgs E)
8  {
9    DateTime open = new DateTime(DateTime.Now.
     Year,DateTime.Now.Month,DateTime.Now.Day,
     9,1,1);
10   DateTime closed = new DateTime(DateTime.
     Now.Year,DateTime.Now.Month,DateTime.Now.
     Day,17,1,1);
11   DateTime now = DateTime.Now;

12   if ( (now > open) && (now < closed) )
13   {
14     // open for business
15     pnlOpen.Visible = true;
16     pnlClosed.Visible = false;
17   }
18   else
19   {
20     // we're closed
21     pnlOpen.Visible = false;
22     pnlClosed.Visible = true;
23   }
24 }
25 void btnShowEmail_OnClick(Object Src,
   EventArgs E)
26 {
27   lblEmail.Visible = true;
28 }
29 </script>
30 </head>
31 <body>
32 <form runat="server">
33 <asp:panel id="pnlOpen" runat="server">
34   <p>
35     Call us at (555) 555-5555.
36   </p>
37 </asp:panel>
38 <asp:panel id="pnlClosed" runat="server">
39   <p>
```

(script continues on next page)

14. Click just before the closing `</script>` tag in the upper portion of the page, and type the following:

```
void btnShowEmail_OnClick(Object
Src, EventArgs E)
{
   lblEmail.Visible = true;
}
```

This function matches the signature expected by the OnClick Delegate. It will change the lblEmail control to be visible when the Delegate intercepts that event from btnShowEmail and passes it on to this function.

You may want to compare your file to **Script 5.2** to verify you don't have any mistakes

15. Finally, press the F12 key to test the page. The email address won't show until you click the Show Email button. However, when you do click it, your OnClick event handler will run and the email address will become visible.

✔ Tip

■ A good naming convention for event handlers is to start with the name of the control that triggers the event, followed by an underscore, and then the name of the event being handled. This convention was used in Step 12 above. However, this naming convention works just for functions called by only one object for only one event. When this is not the case, give the function a name that describes what it's accomplishing instead.

An important thing to note about control events is that they all start with the word *On* in their markup representation. Say you wanted to have some function run when the selection of your asp:dropdownlist control changed. You would simply define that function with the correct signature and set the `OnSelectedIndexChanged` attribute of your control to the name of that function. You can use Dreamweaver's Code Insight to see a list of available events for each control. Often, as in this case, the signature will be the same as for Page Load and On Click. If you run into trouble, use .NET documentation to find the correct signature for the event you're trying to handle.

Controls can be inserted either when the Web Form is created or dynamically at time of execution. We've just completed steps where we added the controls as the page was being created. In the next section, we'll try the alternative method of adding controls dynamically (or programmatically) as the Web Form executes.

Script 5.2 *continued*

```
40      We are not open at this moment.<br />
41      Call back between 9am and 5pm.
42    </p>
43  </asp:panel>
44  <asp:panel id="pnlEmail" runat="server">
45      <asp:label ID="lblEmail" runat=
        "server" Text="email@address.com" Visible=
        "false"></asp:label>
46      <asp:button ID="btnShowEmail" runat=
        "server" Text="Show Email" OnClick=
        "btnShowEmail_OnClick" />
47  </asp:panel>
48  </form>
49  </body>
50  </html>
```

Script 5.3 Instead of adding the button and label using markup, we're adding them with code.

```
           script

1 <%@ Page Language="C#" ContentType="text/html"
  ResponseEncoding="iso-8859-1" %>
2 <html>
3 <head>
4 <title>Untitled Document</title>
5 <meta http-equiv="Content-Type" content=
  "text/html; charset=iso-8859-1">
6 <script runat="server">
7 Button btnShowEmail = new Button();
8 Label lblEmail = new Label();

9 protected void Page_Load(Object Src,
  EventArgs E)
10 {
11   DateTime open = new DateTime(DateTime.Now.
     Year,DateTime.Now.Month,DateTime.Now.Day,
     9,1,1);
12   DateTime closed = new DateTime(DateTime.
     Now.Year,DateTime.Now.Month,DateTime.Now.
     Day,17,1,1);
13   DateTime now = DateTime.Now;

14   if ( (now > open) && (now < closed) )
15   {
16     // open for business
17     pnlOpen.Visible = true;
18     pnlClosed.Visible = false;
19   }
20   else
21   {
22     // we're closed
23     pnlOpen.Visible = false;
24     pnlClosed.Visible = true;
25   }

26   lblEmail.ID = "lblEmail";
27   lblEmail.Text = "email@address.com";
28   lblEmail.Visible = false;
29   pnlEmail.Controls.Add( lblEmail );

30   btnShowEmail.Text = "Show Email";
31   btnShowEmail.Click += new EventHandler(
     this.btnShowEmail_OnClick );
32   pnlEmail.Controls.Add( btnShowEmail );

33 }
34 void btnShowEmail_OnClick(Object Src,
   EventArgs E)
```

(script continues on next page)

To add controls and events programmatically:

1. Working with the same Web Form as the one we created in the last exercise, remove the button and label controls from within the pnlEmail control. See Script 5.2 if you need to reference the code we generated in the last exercise.

2. Aboves the `Page_Load` function but within the <script> block, add the following variables to the script:

   ```
   Button btnShowEmail = new Button();
   Label lblEmail = new Label();
   ```

   Now we need to add to the pnlEmail control programmatically.

3. To set our variable's values and add them to the pnlEmail control, add the following code after the last line in the current `Page_Load` function:

   ```
   lblEmail.ID = "lblEmail";
   lblEmail.Text = "email@address.com";
   lblEmail.Visible = false;
   pnlEmail.Controls.Add( lblEmail );
   btnShowEmail.Text = "Show Email";
   btnShowEmail.Click += new
   EventHandler( this.btnShowEmail_
   OnClick );
   pnlEmail.Controls.Add(btnShowEmail);
   ```

   As you can see, we're setting the same values in the same way as in the last exercise, except that now we're doing it in code instead of markup. Notice that the Click property doesn't start with the word *On* in code. Plus, the btnShowEmail uses the += instead of just = so that any preexisting event handlers assigned to the On Click event will not be overwritten.

4. Compare your file to **Script 5.3** to check for inconsistencies, and then save it. Then press F12 to view it in your browser. It should look and behave the same as Script 5.2 did.

You'll probably find many places to use this new technique in your projects. For example, it could come in very handy as a way to dynamically add controls to a Web Form, based on user responses.

In the following section, we present techniques you can use to improve your productivity even if you don't have extensive programming skills.

Script 5.3 *continued*

```
35 {
36    lblEmail.Visible = true;
37 }
38 </script>
39 </head>
40 <body>
41 <form runat="server">
42 <asp:panel id="pnlOpen" runat="server">
43    <p>
44      Call us at (555) 555-5555.
45    </p>
46 </asp:panel>
47 <asp:panel id="pnlClosed" runat="server">
48    <p>
49      We are not open at this moment.<br />
50      Call back between 9am and 5pm.
51    </p>
52 </asp:panel>
53 <asp:panel id="pnlEmail" runat="server">
54 </asp:panel>
55 </form>
56 </body>
57 </html>
```

Complex Controls

Complex controls, also called *rich controls* because they contain a lot of functionality, are the controls that accomplish tasks that until now have required additional ActiveX controls, or just lots of code. ASP.NET comes with several rich controls for performing Web page functions.

The controls we cover in this section address two fairly common Web tasks: advertisement rotation and the uploading of files from client computers. In addition to the controls included in ASP.NET, you can also create your own. We show you how in Chapters 10 and 11.

Rotating advertisements

Microsoft has long provided the ability to rotate images in banner advertisements automatically. But until now, you had to do it using a COM (Component Object Model) component that came with IIS. You would create a text file listing the images you wanted displayed, and then the COM component would display the next image in the list each time the page containing the component was visited. The result would be a different advertisement in the page every time the visitor returned to that page.

ASP.NET still offers that functionality, but now it's available in the asp:AdRotator control. The differences are that the control is readily available in your code so that you can affect it programmatically, and you now use an XML file instead of a plain text file to list which images the control should display. We'll need to create this XML file to practice using the asp:AdRotator control. But first, let's review the format of the XML file.

The advertisement file may contain any number of <Ad> elements, and each <Ad> must contain other elements that give the control the information it needs to display the advertisements. The format is as follows:

```
<Advertisements>
  <Ad>
    <ImageUrl />
    <NavigateUrl />
    <AlternateText />
    <Impressions />
    <Keyword />
  </Ad>
</Advertisements>
```

Here are the meanings of each element that makes up an <Ad>:

◆ <ImageUrl>

This element's value identifies the path of the image for the control. The image can be in either .jpg or .gif format. The path can be either a relative path to the file or a full URL that points to another server.

◆ <NavigateUrl>

This element indicates where the user will be taken if they click on the image.

◆ <AlternateText>

This element indicates what text will be read by text readers. It's displayed in place of the image in the browser when a user has images turned off or if an image is broken. Some browsers, however, by default display it in addition to the image when the mouse rests over the image.

◆ <Impressions>

The number in this element dictates how many times the ad is shown in relation to other ads. An example of this would be two ads, the first with a value of 25 and the second with a value of 75. The ad with a value of 75 will be shown three times as often as the other.

◆ <Keyword>

You can use the <keyword> attribute of the AdRotator component to filter in ads that contain the specified keyword. This way you can use the same advertisement file for many asp:AdRotator controls and have each control use different entries of the file.

One of the main drawbacks of this control is that it doesn't support Flash banner ads. But as with so many things .NET, you can always extend it or remake it to support them.

Note: The following instructions use two images found in Dreamweaver's sample code. You can find them in their default location at C:\Program Files\Macromedia\Dreamweaver MX\Samples\GettingStarted\Code\Assets \images. Or you may use your own images if you wish.

Figure 5.7 The New Document dialog box for creating an XML file.

To create the advertisement file:

1. From the File menu in Dreamweaver, choose New to open the New Document dialog box.

2. Click Basic Page from the Category pane (**Figure 5.7**).

3. In the Basic Page pane on the right, click XML.

4. Click the Create button to create your new XML file and save it as ads.xml.

   Your new file will have the standard XML file declaration at the top of it. That declaration looks like this:

   ```
   <?xml version="1.0" encoding=
   "iso-8859-1"?>
   ```

5. Just below this declaration, in line 2, type <Advertisements> to give your document the expected root element.

6. On the second line, open your first <Ad> element and iterate through its different elements, setting the values like this:

   ```
   <ImageUrl>
     btnHome.jpg
   </ImageUrl>
   <NavigateUrl>
     http://www.macromedia.com
   </NavigateUrl>
   <AlternateText>
     Home to Macromedia
   </AlternateText>
   <Impressions>
     50
   </Impressions>
   <Keyword>
     Macromedia
   </Keyword>
   ```

Script 5.4 This XML file holds the information about the advertisements that the asp:AdRotator control will display.

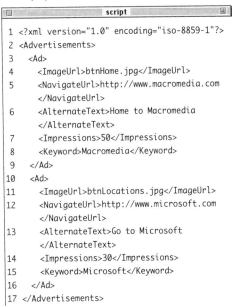

```
     script
 1 <?xml version="1.0" encoding="iso-8859-1"?>
 2 <Advertisements>
 3   <Ad>
 4     <ImageUrl>btnHome.jpg</ImageUrl>
 5     <NavigateUrl>http://www.macromedia.com
       </NavigateUrl>
 6     <AlternateText>Home to Macromedia
       </AlternateText>
 7     <Impressions>50</Impressions>
 8     <Keyword>Macromedia</Keyword>
 9   </Ad>
10   <Ad>
11     <ImageUrl>btnLocations.jpg</ImageUrl>
12     <NavigateUrl>http://www.microsoft.com
       </NavigateUrl>
13     <AlternateText>Go to Microsoft
       </AlternateText>
14     <Impressions>30</Impressions>
15     <Keyword>Microsoft</Keyword>
16   </Ad>
17 </Advertisements>
```

7. On the line following </Keyword>, close the <Ad> element you opened in Step 6 by typing </Ad>.

8. Now create a second <Ad> element after the first and set its elements as follows:

```
<ImageUrl>
  btnLocation.jpg
</ImageUrl>
<NavigateUrl>
  http://www.microsoft.com
</NavigateUrl>
<AlternateText>
  Go to Microsoft
</AlternateText>
<Impressions>
  30
</Impressions>
<Keyword>
  Microsoft
</Keyword>
```

9. On the line following </Keyword>, close the <Ad> element you opened in Step 8 by typing </Ad>.

10. Finally, close your root element by typing </Advertisements> at the end of the file.

11. Review your file using **Script 5.4** as a reference and save it. We'll make use of it when we practice using an asp:AdRotator control in the steps that follow.

COMPLEX CONTROLS

To use an asp:AdRotator control:

1. Create a new Web Form in the same way we've done in the previous exercises. Only this time, make sure you're in Code view.

2. Click just after the <body> tag. Then from Dreamweaver's Insert menu, click on the ASP.NET tab, and from the ASP.NET panel click the More Tags icon 🔲.

   The Tag Chooser dialog box appears.

3. Click the plus sign next to Markup Language Tags. Then click the plus sign next to ASP.NET Tags, and finally select Web Server Controls to get a list of ASP.NET tags (**Figure 5.8**).

   The right pane of the Tag Chooser becomes populated with ASP.NET tags.

4. From the list, select asp:AdRotator and click the Insert button.

   The Tag Editor for the asp:AdRotator appears (**Figure 5.9**).

5. Set the ID to "AdRotator" and the Advertisement File field to "ads.xml."

   If you wish, you can use the Browse button to browse for the file instead.

6. Click OK to close the Tag Editor and have the control's markup written to the file.

7. Then Close the Tag Chooser.

   You're done!

8. Use **Script 5.5** to make sure the script you're using is accurate, and then press F12 to open the page in your browser.

   You can refresh the page a few times to see the image change now and then. You'll find the btnHome image appears more often than the btnLocations image because of our <Impressions> setting.

Figure 5.8 The Tag Chooser ready to insert an asp:AdRotator control.

Figure 5.9 The Tag Editor for the asp:AdRotator.

Script 5.5 With all the advertisements defined in the ads.xml file and all the code provided by Microsoft, adding an asp:AdRotator control to a page is very simple.

```
1 <%@ Page Language="C#" ContentType="text/html"
   ResponseEncoding="iso-8859-1" %>
2 <html>
3 <head>
4 <title>Untitled Document</title>
5 <meta http-equiv="Content-Type" content=
   "text/html; charset=iso-8859-1">
6 </head>
7 <body>
8 <asp:adrotator AdvertisementFile=
   "ads.xml" ID="adRotator" runat="server" />
9 </body>
10 </html>
```

Uploading files

Every now and then we developers find ourselves in the situation of wanting to receive files from site visitors. This has proved problematic, because HTML was designed for displaying information on the client, not for sending complex information like a file from the client back to the server.

One workaround to this HTML limitation has been to set the HTML `<input>` tag to accept the type File, but you still need to write plenty of code to receive the file properly. If you don't want to write the code yourself, you have the option of using a third-party tool to do it for you. Unfortunately, these tools vary widely and are difficult to implement correctly.

Now, thanks to .NET, a Web control solves the problem.

This is the first time we've mentioned Web controls. Until now, all the controls we've talked about have been server controls, as Microsoft calls them. Server controls always start with "asp," followed by a colon and then the name of the control. The "asp" is a *namespace,* which simply means that it tells the Web server that the control is defined in a certain place. Using namespaces allows a way for there to be several things called "Button" without confusing the server; it will be able to tell them apart because they'll have different namespaces.

Web controls are another category of controls. The difference between these and server controls is that Web controls use the exact same markup as plain old HTML elements. They don't even use a namespace. What differentiates Web controls from their HTML counterparts is the addition of the `runat` attribute with the value of `"server"`.

Here is the markup of a plain old hidden input tag:

```
<input type="hidden" id="hdnHTML"
name="hdnHTML" />
```

and here is the Web control version:

```
<input type="hidden" id=" hdnASPNET"
name="hdnASPNET" runat="server" />
```

Notice the only difference is the `runat` attribute. But it is a big difference. The first one will not be available in your ASP.NET code, but the second one will be. This is because without the `runat="server"` attribute, the control is rendered by the browser. The `runat="server"` attribute specifies that the ASP.NET server process the tag. At run time in your code, you'll be able to manipulate the Web control version of this input element in exactly the same way as you could your server controls.

Let's see how to use the Web control version of the input form element of type File and how this change makes a difference in our code.

To upload and save a file:

1. Create a new Web Form, and set it to Code view.

2. To add a form, type the following just after the <body> tag:

```
<form runat="server"
enctype="multipart/form-data">
</form>
```

This form element sets the runat attribute as we've seen elsewhere, but it also sets the enctype attribute. This is necessary to provide the ability to upload files and is not new in ASP.NET.

2. Now click just after the </form> tag. Then go to the Insert bar and click on the ASP.Net tab. On the ASP.NET panel, click the More Tags icon 🔲 .

The Tag Chooser dialog box appears.

3. Click the plus sign next to Markup Language Tags. Then click the plus sign next to HTML Tags, and select Forms (**Figure 5.10**).

4. In the list of available form elements in the right pane of the Tag Chooser dialog box, double-click input type="File."

The Tag Editor dialog box appears.

5. In the Tag Editor, set the Name to "fileUpload," and click OK (**Figure 5.11**).

The Tag Editor closes.

6. Click the Close button in the Tag Chooser.

7. Back in the Code view of the page, alter the newly added input element by setting the attributes id="fileUpload" and runat="server".

Now, to enable the actual uploading of a file, we need to add a Submit button to the form.

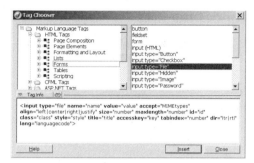

Figure 5.10 The Tag Chooser ready to insert an input from element of type File.

Figure 5.11 The Tag Editor for the input form element.

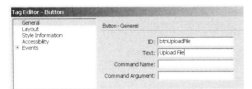

Figure 5.12 The General section of the Tag Editor for the btnUploadFile control.

Figure 5.13 The OnClick Event of the Tag Editor for the btnUploadFile control.

8. Click after the input Web control in the code. Then on the ASP.NET panel, click the asp:button icon ⬜.

The Tag Editor for an asp:button appears.

9. In the Tag Editor, set the asp:button's ID to "btnUploadFile" and the Text field to "Upload File" (**Figure 5.12**).

10. On the left of the Tag Editor dialog box, click the plus sign next to Events and then select OnClick. In the new box that appears on the right, type "btnUploadFile_OnClick" and click OK (**Figure 5.13**). (To review how to assign an event handler to a control's event, see "To assign a handler to an asp:button" earlier in this chapter.)

11. To implement the OnClick event handler for the btnUploadFile control, add the following code just before the </head> tag in the page:

```
<script runat="server">
void btnUploadFile_OnClick(
Object o, EventArgs e )
{
    fileUpload.PostedFile.SaveAs(
        Server.MapPath("upload.txt")
);
}
</script>
```

Note: In order for this code to work, however, the ASPNET user must have access to write to the directory containing this page. We recommend the use of a directory especially set aside for uploads in production Web sites for security reasons.

continues on next page

COMPLEX CONTROLS

12. Script 5.6 shows the resulting page. Use it to make sure you have no errors. Then press F12 to browse the file.

You'll find a Browse button next to a text box, both of which are automatically generated by the input Web control. Use the button to find a file to upload. In this exercise the code is expecting a text file, but it could be any type of file.

After you've selected a file, the text box will show the local path to that file. Click the Upload File button to start the upload, and then go see the new file in your Web directory called upload.txt. When you find it, make sure it's got the right contents.

In working with ASP.NET, you'll find that many of things you used to have to do that took lots of time and effort are made much simpler. In fact, in the next chapter we'll be inspecting Form Validators that almost completely take the work out of validating the data your visitors will enter into form elements. Read on to see just how simple it really has become.

Script 5.6 Instead of having to write lots of code or use a third-party product, ASP.NET Web controls and event handlers make quick work of uploading files from the visitor's computer.

```
1  <%@ Page Language="C#" ContentType="text/html"
   ResponseEncoding="iso-8859-1" %>
2  <html>
3  <head>
4  <title>Untitled Document</title>
5  <meta http-equiv="Content-Type"
   content="text/html; charset=iso-8859-1">
6  <script runat="server">
7  void btnUploadFile_OnClick( Object o,
   EventArgs e )
8  {
9    fileUpload.PostedFile.SaveAs(
     Server.MapPath("upload.txt") );
10 }
11 </script>
12 </head>
13 <body>
14 <form runat="server" enctype=
   "multipart/form-data">
15 <input name="fileUpload" type="file" id=
   "fileUpload" runat="server">
16 <asp:button ID="btnUploadFile"
   runat="server" Text="Upload File"
   OnClick="btnUploadFile_OnClick" />
17 </form>
18 </body>
19 </html>
```

WEB FORM VALIDATION

Ever since the form's inception, Web developers have had to validate the data entered into form fields because users often make mistakes, either by mistyping the data or by not paying attention to the type of data that the field requires. When bad data is fed to a program, one of two things happens: Either a program exception error occurs, or the data is ultimately saved to the database, causing program execution failures down the line.

By validating the data entered into form fields, you can vastly improve the quality of the data collected, reducing the likelihood of errors. Data validation enforces a firm's data requirements in terms of format, range of values, and data type (such as number versus character). Unfortunately, because validation code is time-consuming to write and not absolutely necessary for the program to work, developers tend to leave this task for last—or don't do it at all. But dispensing with data validation will likely produce program errors that could go undetected, even during the testing phase.

Form fields accept diverse types of data; most of the time, however, only a few of the available types are used. The data types most often gathered are text, for things such as name and street address, and number, for zip codes and order quantities. Because we collect the same sorts of data in forms so often, programmers have developed libraries of reusable validation functions. By reusing these functions, we can greatly reduce the time it takes to add validation to forms fields. However, since each programmer's function library is unique to his or her specific platform and development tools, those libraries can't be used by developers with dissimilar environments.

Thankfully, ASP.NET includes controls that automatically provide form field validation with little or no extra coding. This chapter will cover the different ways of using those validators. You'll even learn how to create a custom validator for those unique situations in which the preprogrammed ones don't do what you need. With what you learned in Chapter 5 for programming Web Forms, you'll be able to create data-validated submission forms with almost no work at all.

Preprogrammed Validators

ASP.NET contains many preprogrammed validation controls. The validation controls are designed to execute on the client as well as on the server.

On the client, the validation controls are preprogrammed using DHTML (Dynamic Hypertext Markup Language). DHTML uses a combination of JavaScript and Cascading Style Sheets to control and generate HTML dynamically. The JavaScript code used for performing client-side validation is already written for you—it's available in the aspnet_client directory of your Default Web Site as soon as you install .NET. But because not all browsers support JavaScript, client-side validation is not mandatory and may be disabled. To compensate for this possibility, the data is checked by default on the server as well.

Server-side validation for preprogrammed validation controls doesn't require any additional code to enable it, and it can't be disabled. A benefit to running server-side validation every time is that it keeps a malicious hacker from slipping bad data into your program by circumventing any client-side validation.

In most cases, you'll want to validate the data on both the client and the server each time. Validation on the client side offers advantages including a more intuitive interface (a pop-up window for error messages) and no round-trips to the server that increase network traffic. Server-side validation provides the added assurance that validation is active, because it's guaranteed to execute.

In addition to the controls that handle the actual validation of form field data, we can use a control specifically designed to display a summary of messages our validation process generates. This useful control is called asp:ValidationSummary, and we'll be using it often throughout the rest of the chapter.

However, we'll start with the most basic data validator, the one that makes sure a field that requires data isn't left blank: the asp:RequiredFieldValidator.

Required Field Validator

As we've all experienced, some form fields require the user to enter data before the form can be submitted for processing. An example is an email address field in a form used to sign up on an email list. The data collected from that field is obviously essential, so the form should not submit if the email address is left blank. ASP.NET provides a control called asp:RequiredFieldValidator that stops form submission if the form field representing the control to which it's assigned is left blank. It can also display an error message to explain why submission did not succeed, so that the user can correct the mistake.

But before we can start using the asp:Required FieldValidator control, we need to create the Web Form to which it will be added. Throughout the rest of this chapter, we'll build on this Web Form by adding various controls, so that when we're finished we'll have a fully developed submission form.

To create the form to be validated:

1. Create a Web Form as we did in the "To create a new Web Form" in Chapter 4. Click the Show Code and Design Views icon (**Figure 6.1**).

   Both the Code and Design views become visible.

2. Between the opening and closing \<body\> tags, add an HTML \<form\> tag with its runat attribute set so that we have a form to work in:

   ```
   <form runat="server">
   </form>
   ```

3. Click inside the red dotted line that represents the form in Design view. On the Insert bar, click on the Tables tab, and then click on the Insert Table icon (**Figure 6.2**).

   The Insert Table dialog box opens, allowing us to quickly add a table to make our resulting page easier to read.

continues on next page

PREPROGRAMMED VALIDATORS

Figure 6.1 Show both code and design to work most efficiently in your Web Form.

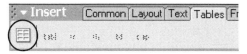

Figure 6.2 Click the Insert Table icon on the Tables tab of the Insert bar to start the Insert Tables dialog box.

4. In the dialog box, specify that the table should have two rows and two columns. Then clear the Width field, and set both the Cell Padding and the Cell Spacing fields to 5 (**Figure 6.3**).

5. Click OK.

The dialog box closes, and the HTML is automatically added to our page.

6. Still in Design view, highlight the two cells that make up the bottom row of our new table. Then in the Properties panel, click the Merge Cells icon (**Figure 6.4**). Change the newly merged cell's horizontal alignment to "center" in that panel as well.

7. In the left cell of the table's top row, enter "Email."

This will label the field into which the user will type an email address. It will also help the user know what sort of data to enter into the form field that we'll be adding to the cell next to this one.

8. Now click on the right cell of the table's top row. From the Insert bar, click on the ASP.NET tab, and then click on the asp:textbox icon (**Figure 6.5**).

The Tag Editor dialog box opens.

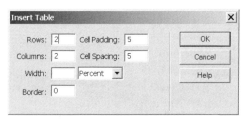

Figure 6.3 Use the Insert Table dialog box to define the type of table you want to insert.

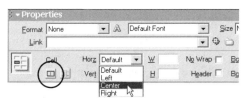

Figure 6.4 Use the Properties inspector to merge table cells using the Merge Cells icon and set cell alignment.

Figure 6.5 Click the asp:textbox icon on the ASP.NET tab to start the Tag Editor dialog box.

PREPROGRAMMED VALIDATORS

9. In the ID text box, enter "txtEmail" and click OK (**Figure 6.6**).

10. Next click in the bottom row of the table. On the ASP.NET tab, click on the asp:button icon ▣. In the Tag Editor dialog box that opens, enter "btnSubmit" in the ID text box and "Submit Form." in the Text text box. Click OK (**Figure 6.7**).

The button is added to the table (**Figure 6.8**).

We don't need to create a special OnClick event handler for this button in order to tell the server which function to run, because a button's default action is to submit the form in which it resides.

11. Verify that your code matches that in **Script 6.1,** and save your Web Form as validate.aspx.

We'll build on this template in upcoming steps, so there's no need to test the page in your browser at this time.

Now that we have a Web Form ready to accept data from a user, we'll need to add a validation control to make sure that the email address field contains data before submitting the form.

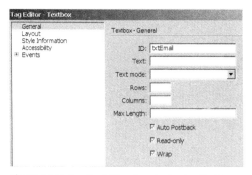

Figure 6.6 Define the txtEmail control using the Tag Editor.

Figure 6.7 Define the btnSubmit control using the Tag Editor.

Figure 6.8 Here is the finished Design view of the Web Form.

Script 6.1 The result of creating a form to validate is a simple Web Form with two controls in a table.

```
1  <%@ Page Language="C#" ContentType=
   "text/html" ResponseEncoding="iso-8859-1" %>
2  <html>
3  <head>
4  <title>Untitled Document</title>
5  <meta http-equiv="Content-Type" content=
   "text/html; charset=iso-8859-1">
6  </head>
7  <body>
8  <form runat="server">
9    <table border="0" cellspacing="5"
     cellpadding="5">
10     <tr>
11       <td>Email</td>
12       <td>
13         <asp:textbox ID="txtEmail" runat=
           "server" /></td>
14     </tr>
15     <tr align="center">
16       <td colspan="2">
17         <asp:button ID="btnSubmit" runat=
           "server" Text="Submit Form" /></td>
18     </tr>
19   </table>
20 </form>
21 </body>
22 </html>
```

To use the asp:RequiredFieldValidator control:

1. Open the validate.aspx Web Form we just created.

2. Click to the right of the txtEmail control but inside the table cell in Design view. From the Insert bar, click on the ASP.NET tab, and then click the More Tags icon (**Figure 6.9**).

   The Tag Chooser dialog box opens.

3. Click the + (plus) sign next to Markup Language Tags in the left pane of the Tag Chooser, and below that click the + sign next to ASP.NET Tags. Select Validation Server Controls.

   This populates the right pane of the dialog box with a list of available validation controls (**Figure 6.10**).

4. In the right pane of the Tag Chooser, double-click the asp:RequiredFieldValidator.

   The Tag Editor opens.

5. Using the Tag Editor, set the following values:

   ID: **rfvEmail**
   Text: *****
   Display: **Dynamic**
   Control to Validate: **txtEmail**
   Error Message: **Email is required.**

   Setting the values like this creates a validation control that appears only when there's an error (**Figure 6.11**). So the only way users will know there's a validation problem is if they leave the email field blank when submitting the form, in which case they'll see an asterisk (*) displayed next to the email field, indicating their error.

6. Click OK to create the control in your form. Then click Close to exit the Tag Chooser.

   In the next step we'll add an asp:ValidationSummary control so that the user will see an "Email is required" error message in addition to the asterisk next the errant form field.

Figure 6.9 Click the More Tags icon on the ASP.NET tab to start the Tag Chooser dialog box.

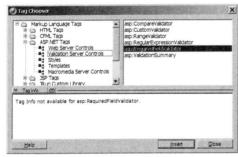

Figure 6.10 Select the asp:RequiredFieldValidator control from the Tag Chooser.

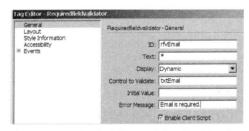

Figure 6.11 Use the Tag Editor to define the rfvEmail control.

Click here

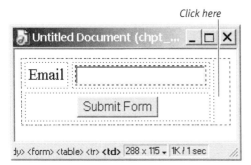

Figure 6.12 Click beside the email form's table to set your insertion point.

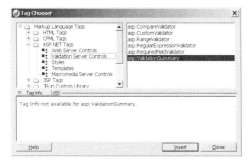

Figure 6.13 Select the asp:ValidationSummary control from the Tag Chooser.

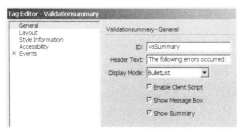

Figure 6.14 Use the Tag Editor to define the vsSummary control.

7. Back in the Web Form in Design view, position the cursor after the table (**Figure 6.12**). On the ASP.NET tab, click the More Tags icon again to insert another control.

The Tag Chooser should open to the same list of validation controls we were just looking at in Step 3 (**Figure 6.13**). If not, navigate back to that list using the instructions in Step 3.

8. Double-click asp:ValidationSummary from that list.

Its Tag Editor opens.

9. In the Tag Editor, enter "vsSummary" in the ID text box and "The following errors occurred:" in the Header Text text box. In the Display Mode text drop-down menu, select "BulletList" and click OK to create the control (**Figure 6.14**).

The result will be a control that acts as a central location for all validation error messages so that they appear together in a bulleted list.

continues on next page

PREPROGRAMMED VALIDATORS

115

10. Verify that your code matches that in **Script 6.2**, and then preview your page by pressing F12.

You'll find that the new validation controls aren't visible until you try to submit the form with the field that represents the txtEmail control left empty. If you do that, an asterisk will appear next to the errant field, and below the Submit button will be a list containing the "Email is required" error message.

✔ Tip

- If you leave the text attribute blank instead of typing an asterisk, the error message will display wherever the validation control is placed in the document.

You're probably already thinking about instances where you could use these controls in your own projects. You've also probably thought of harder things to validate, such as making sure the data entered into txtEmail is actually formatted like an email address. In the next section, we'll work with controls that handle more complex validation scenarios.

Value-based validators

The Required Field Validator presented in the previous section doesn't inspect the value of the field it validates—it only makes sure that there's data in that field. However, it's often necessary to validate the actual data in the field as well. There are three controls specifically designed to validate the data within the form elements. The first validation control, called asp:RangeValidator, ensures that the data in the field falls within a given range.

The second control, asp:CompareValidator, can compare the data to a specific value. In this case, it checks to see if the data in the assigned control is greater than, less than, or equal to a predetermined value. This control can also operate more dynamically,

Script 6.2 Validation controls look a great deal like other controls in code, except that they have different attributes to set.

```
1  <%@ Page Language="C#" ContentType=
   "text/html" ResponseEncoding="iso-8859-1" %>
2  <html>
3  <head>
4  <title>Untitled Document</title>
5  <meta http-equiv="Content-Type" content=
   "text/html; charset=iso-8859-1">
6  </head>
7  <body>
8  <form runat="server">
9    <table border="0" cellspacing="5"
      cellpadding="5">
10     <tr>
11       <td>Email</td>
12       <td>
13         <asp:textbox ID="txtEmail" runat=
           "server" />
14         <asp:requiredfieldvalidator
15             ControlToValidate="txtEmail"
16             Display="Dynamic"
17             ErrorMessage="Email is required."
18             ID="rfvEmail"
19             runat="server"
20             Text="*" />
21       </td>
22     </tr>
23     <tr align="center">
24       <td colspan="2">
25         <asp:button ID="btnSubmit" runat=
           "server" Text="Submit Form" /></td>
26     </tr>
27   </table>
28   <asp:validationsummary
29       DisplayMode="BulletList"
30       HeaderText="The following errors
       occured:"
31       ID="vsSummary"
32       runat="server" />
33 </form>
34 </body>
35 </html>
```

by comparing the value against another control's data at run time.

The third validation control, asp:Regular ExpressionValidator, matches the data against a *regular expression,* which is a defined pattern, such as the pattern of an email address. Regular expressions constitute a powerful scripting language that allows you to create custom validation rules for practically any validation requirement. To create regular expressions, you use a special set of scripting codes to define a pattern of characters against which to validate. Form data is then matched against this pattern. When it matches the pattern, `true` is returned; otherwise, `false` is returned. (You'll find a more detailed explanation of regular expressions in the "Regular Expressions" sidebar.)

Now we'll extend the Web Form we've been working with to verify that the email address follows the correct pattern. Validating an email address is particularly difficult because of all of the combinations that are possible. To accomplish this, we'll create a regular expression pattern using the asp:RegularExpressionValidator. We'll also gather data about the user's age and when he or she wants to be removed from the email list. For each of these new values, we'll add the correct validator to make sure the user's entries are acceptable. If any of the data is unacceptable, the form will not submit to the server and error messages that instruct users on what they need to correct before trying to submit the form again.

To use value-based validators:

1. Open the validate.aspx Web Form we were working with in "To use the asp:RequiredFieldValidator control."

2. In Design view, click to the right of the txtEmail control, and then on the ASP.NET tab, click the More Tags icon ⬚.

continues on next page

The Tag Chooser opens. In the right pane of the Tag Chooser, you should see the same list of validation controls you saw earlier (**Figure 6.15**). If not, refer to Step 3 of "To use the asp:RequiredFieldValidator control" to navigate to that list.

3. In the list of validation controls, double-click on asp:RegularExpressionValidator.

4. In the Tag Editor, set the following values (**Figure 6.16**):
ID: **revEmail**
Text: *****
Control to Validate: **txtEmail**
Validation Expression: **\w+([-+.]\w+)*@\w+([-.]\w+)*\.\w+([-.]\w+)***
Display: **Dynamic**
Error Message: **Email must contain a valid email address.**

Most of the settings for this control are similar to those we set for the asp:Required FieldValidator earlier—except for some strange-looking stuff in the Validation Expression field. This is what the regular expression pattern looks like for an email address. When the form is submitted, the pattern will be compared to the data in the txtEmail control. The validator will check to see if that data matches the regular expression pattern we've defined here. If it doesn't, the validator will stop the form from submitting and will instruct the user to correct the mistake. For a more detailed look at the syntax of regular expressions, see the "Regular Expressions" sidebar at the end of this stepped list.

5. Click OK to create the control in your form, and click Close to exit the Tag Chooser.

6. Back in Design view, right-click in the cell labeled Email. Then from the context menu that appears, select Tables > Insert Rows or Columns.

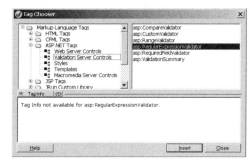

Figure 6.15 Select the asp:RegularExpressionValidator control from the Tag Chooser.

Figure 6.16 Use the Tag Editor to define the revEmail control.

PREPROGRAMMED VALIDATORS

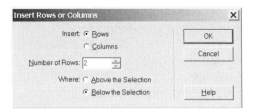

Figure 6. 17 You use the Insert Rows or Columns dialog box to insert two rows below the current row.

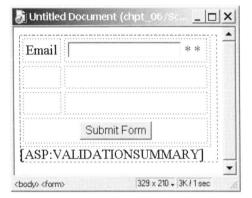

Figure 6.18 There will be two blank rows in the middle of the table when you're done inserting them.

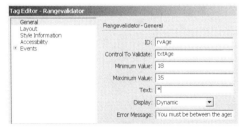

Figure 6.19 Use the Tag Editor to define the rvAge control.

The Insert Rows or Columns dialog box appears, allowing us to add two new rows to our table.

7. In the Number of Rows field, specify 2. Click the Below the Selection radio button, and then click OK (**Figure 6.17**).

This inserts the new rows below the first row (**Figure 6.18**).

8. In the first cell of the new second row, type "Age".

9. Move one cell to the right. From the Insert bar, click on the ASP.NET tab and then click on the asp:textbox icon ⬚ to start the Tag Editor. In the ID text box, enter "txtAge" and click OK.

10. Place your cursor to the right of the new txtAge control. On the ASP.NET tab, click the More Tags icon ⬚ and double-click asp:RangeValidator.

The asp:RangeValidator's Tag Editor opens.

11. In the Tag Editor, set the following values (**Figure 6.19**):

ID: **rvAge**
Control to Validate: **txtAge**
Minimum Value: **18**
Maximum Value: **35**
Text: *****
Display: **Dynamic**
Error Message: **You must be between the ages of 18 and 35.**

The new fields for this control are the Minimum and Maximum Value fields. They allow us to set a valid range for our txtAge control's data.

continues on next page

PREPROGRAMMED VALIDATORS

12. Click OK to save your settings.

You've probably noticed that we still have an asp:RequiredFieldValidator for the txtEmail control, but we don't have one for txtAge. Don't be misled. Even though this field has an asp:RangeValidator assigned to it, the user can still leave it blank because value-based validators don't fail when their assigned controls are left blank. You need both validation controls only if you want data to be both required and checked. Here we're allowing our users to leave txtAge blank.

13. In the first cell of the table's blank third row, enter "Remove On."

14. Click in the remaining blank cell to the right of "Remove On." On the ASP.NET tab, click the asp:textbox icon ![ab] to open the Tag Editor. In the ID text box, enter "txtRemoveOn" and click OK.

15. Click to the right of the new txtRemoveOn control in Design view. Once again, click the More Tags icon in the ASP.NET tab to open the Tag Chooser ![].

16. In the list of ASP.NET validation controls, double-click asp:CompareValidator. Its Tag Editor opens.

17. Set the following values in the Tag Editor (**Figure 6.20**):

ID: **cvRemoveOn**
Text: *****
Control to Validate: **txtRemoveOn**
Value to Compare: **1/1/2004**
Operator: **GreaterThanEqual**
Type: **Date**
Display: **Dynamic**
Error Message: **You must be on the list until at least January 1, 2004.**

Because we're comparing txtRemoveOn to a static value, we set the Value to Compare field instead of the Control

to Compare field (the latter attribute would be used to compare the control's value to the value of another field). This validator also allows you to specify the data type to expect, which we set to Date. And it asks how to make the comparison, such as GreaterThanEqual, like we chose here. The rest of the fields are much the same as the other validation controls we've used so far.

18. Click OK to save your settings.

19. Use **Script 6.3** to make sure there's nothing misspelled and press F12 to preview the page.

To test the page's validation functions, try submitting the page with different combinations of values for the input fields.

Can you believe we added all that functionality without typing one line of code? The best part is that you won't have to maintain the validation scripts.

However, while these controls solve most validation problems, they can't always handle unique ones. For custom validation scenarios, you still may have to write some code. For that purpose, we use the asp:CustomValidator. We'll be working with that control in the following section.

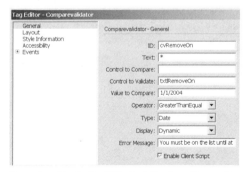

Figure 6.20 Use the Tag Editor to define the cvRemoveOn control.

Script 6.3 All the values and settings necessary to define the different types of validation controls are set using attributes.

```
1  <%@ Page Language="C#" ContentType=
   "text/html" ResponseEncoding="iso-8859-1" %>
2  <html>
3  <head>
4  <title>Untitled Document</title>
5  <meta http-equiv="Content-Type" content=
   "text/html; charset=iso-8859-1">
6  </head>
7  <body>
8  <form runat="server">
9    <table border="0" cellspacing="5"
     cellpadding="5">
10     <tr>
11       <td>Email</td>
12       <td>
13         <asp:textbox ID="txtEmail" runat=
           "server" />
14         <asp:requiredfieldvalidator
15           ControlToValidate="txtEmail"
16           Display="Dynamic"
17           ErrorMessage="Email is required."
18           ID="rfvEmail"
19           runat="server"
20           Text="*" />
21         <asp:regularexpressionvalidator
22           ControlToValidate="txtEmail"
23           Display="Dynamic"
24           ErrorMessage="Email must contain a
             valid email address."
25           ID="revEmail"
26           runat="server"
27           Text="*"
28           ValidationExpression="\w+([-+.]\w+)
             *@\w+([-.]\w+)*\.\w+([-.]\w+)*" /> </td>
29     </tr>
30     <tr>
31       <td>Age</td>
32       <td>
33         <asp:textbox ID="txtAge" runat=
           "server" />
34         <asp:rangevalidator
35           ControlToValidate="txtAge"
36           Display="Dynamic"
```

Script 6.3 *continued*

```
37           ErrorMessage="You must be between
             the ages of 18 and 35."
38           ID="rvAge"
39           MaximumValue="35"
40           MinimumValue="18"
41           runat="server"
42           Text="*" />
43       </td>
44     </tr>
45     <tr>
46       <td>Remove On</td>
47       <td>
48         <asp:textbox ID="txtRemoveOn"
           runat="server" />
49         <asp:comparevalidator
50           ControlToValidate="txtRemoveOn"
51           Display="Dynamic"
52           ErrorMessage="You must be on the
             list until at least January 1, 2004."
53           ID="cvRemoveOn"
54           Operator="GreaterThanEqual"
55           runat="server"
56           Text="*"
57           Type="Date"
58           ValueToCompare="1/1/2004" />
59       </td>
60     </tr>
61     <tr align="center">
62       <td colspan="2"> <asp:button
         ID="btnSubmit" runat="server"
         Text="Submit Form" /></td>
63     </tr>
64   </table>
65   <asp:validationsummary
66     DisplayMode="BulletList"
67     HeaderText="The following errors
       occured:"
68     ID="vsSummary"
69     runat="server" />
70 </form>
71 </body>
72 </html>
```

Regular Expressions

Regular expressions are used to describe patterns in strings. They are flexible, powerful tools that can represent almost any kind of pattern. For example, you can define an expression to locate an email address using the fifth character from the start of the string; or you can make sure the entire string is exactly five numbers long.

The syntax used to describe regular expressions is, in essence, a scripting language with it's own unique format. You can see an example of the syntax in Step 4 of "To use value-based validators." That example describes an email address.

Following is a brief sampling of some of the syntax used to describe regular expressions. This list is limited, but it will get you started—and help you understand the example in Step 4 that describes an email address.

A Matches the literal character *A*. You can specify any character this way.

[ ] Surrounds a set of characters. A match occurs if any one of the characters in the set is found. For example, in the range [a-z], any lowercase letter *a* through *z* will satisfy this pattern.

. Matches any single character except the new-line character.

**** Indicates that the following character is a specialized one, not a literal one. Or if it's usually specialized (such as *), it should be taken literally.

\d Indicates a specialized character that matches any digit. This is equivalent to [0-9].

\w A specialized character that matches any number, any letter, or the underscore symbol. Equal to [a-zA-Z0-9_].

* Matches zero or more occurrences of the preceding pattern. This symbol is used for defining a pattern consisting of repeating elements.

+ Matches one or more occurrences of the preceding pattern. This symbol is used for defining a pattern consisting of repeating elements.

? Matches the preceding pattern zero or one times.

( ) Groups a pattern into one unit. Often used in conjunction with the *, +, and ? syntax within complex patterns.

continues on next page

Regular Expressions, *continued*

Using this syntax, let's walk through the email address pattern:

`\w+([-+.]\w+)*@\w+([-.]\w+)*\.\w+ ([-.]\w+)*`

It starts by expecting one or more letters, numbers, or underscores:

`\w+`

Then within parentheses it looks for a dash, plus, or period, followed by one or more letters, numbers, or underscores zero or more times:

`([-+.]\w+)*`

Then the literal character @ should appear before one or more letters, numbers, or underscores:

`@\w+.`

After that should be a dash or dot, followed by one or more letters, numbers, or under-scores. The * indicates that this should occur zero or more times:

`([-.]\w+)*`

Then follows the literal period character and one or more letters, numbers, or underscores:

`\.\w+`

Finally, it expects zero or more occurrences of the pattern describing a dash or dot, followed by one or more letters, numbers, or underscores:

`([-.]\w+)*`

For a more in-depth understanding of regular expressions and their syntax, you'll find many books and Web sites dedicated to this topic. *Mastering Regular Expressions, 2nd Edition*, by Jeffrey E.F. Friedl is a popular reference book on this subject.

Custom Validators

So far in this chapter we've looked at some really useful controls that will satisfy our most common validation needs. However, there are times when those controls won't be able to handle complex or unique validation requirements for our forms. For the more complex scenarios, we have the asp:CustomValidator.

The asp:CustomValidator control allows us to define client-side and server-side functions for form validation. That way, we can validate our form in a unique way and still have the benefit of alerting the user of a validation error immediately, while maintaining the security of server-side validation.

One scenario in which a Custom Validator is needed is when a control requires validation only some of the time. In the following instructions, for example, only one selection from a drop-down text box needs more information.

To create an asp:CustomValidator control:

1. Open the Web Form we were working with in "To use value-based validators." Make sure the page shows both Code and Design views by clicking the Show Code View and Show Design View icon ▦ .

2. In Design view, click to the left of the txtRemoveOn control. From the Insert bar, click on the ASP.NET tab, and then click on the asp:dropdownlist icon to insert a Drop-down List control (**Figure 6.21**).
   The asp:dropdownlist control's Tag Editor opens.

3. In the ID text box, enter "ddlRemoveOn" and click OK.

Figure 6.21 Click the asp:dropdownlist icon on the ASP.NET tab to start the Tag Editor dialog box.

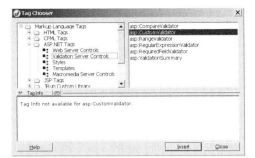

Figure 6.22 Select the asp:CustomValidator control from the Tag Chooser.

Figure 6.23 Use the Tag Editor to define the customvRemoveOn control.

4. In the page's code, between the opening and closing tags of the ddlRemoveOn control, type the following:

```
<asp:dropdownlist ID="ddlRemoveOn"
runat="server">
  <asp:listitem Value="none">
    Select One
  </asp:listitem>
  <asp:listitem Value="never">
    Never Remove
  </asp:listitem>
  <asp:listitem Value="remove">
    Set Date
  </asp:listitem>
</asp:dropdownlist>
```

We're hard-coding the list items here, but you could just as easily add them dynamically using the technique covered in the "To bind data to a control" in Chapter 4.

5. Back in Design view, position the cursor to the right of the cvRemoveOn Compare Validator control. On the ASP.NET tab, click the More Tags icon ⎒ .

The Tag Chooser dialog box's right pane displays the list of validation controls (**Figure 6.22**).

6. Double-click asp:CustomValidator.

Its Tag Editor opens (**Figure 6.23**).

If you need help listing the validation controls in the right pane of the box, refer to Step 3 of "To use the asp:RequiredFieldValidator control" earlier in this chapter.

continues on next page

CUSTOM VALIDATORS

7. In the asp:CustomValidator's Tag Editor, set the following values:

ID: **customvRemoveOn**
Text: *****
Client Validation Function: **validateRemoveOn**
Control to Validate: **ddlRemoveOn**
Display: **Dynamic**
Error Message: **Need to set a date.**

All of this should be familiar to you now, except for the Client Validation Function. This is the name of the JavaScript function that will do the validation on the client's computer when the form is submitted.

8. Click OK to create the control in your form. Then click Close to exit the Tag Chooser.

Now we have to define the client-side validation function using JavaScript specified for the customvRemoveOn control in the last step.

9. Click just in front of the </head> tag in the code of the page and typing the following:

```
<script language="JavaScript">
function validateRemoveOn(src, args)
{
    var ddlValue = document.all("ddlRem
oveOn").options[ document.all("ddlR
emoveOn").selectedIndex ].value;

    if( ( ddlValue == "none" ) ||
        ( ddlValue == "remove" &&
        document.all("txtRemoveOn")
        .value == "" ) )
    {
        args.IsValid = false;
    }
    else
    {
        args.IsValid = true;
    }
}
</script>
```

All custom validation functions, whether client-side or server-side, take two parameters: the source object and the arguments object. It is the arguments object that has the IsValid parameter, which needs to be set with the result of your validation check.

In this function we're checking the current selection of the ddlRemoveOn control. The function will result in an invalid status if the user either hasn't made a selection from the ddlRemove control or has chosen "Set Date" without actually setting the date in the txtRemoveOn control.

Remember that only the asp:RequiredField Validator control reacts to a blank value in the validated control. That means that if we had left the `Value` attribute blank on our "Select One" list item and that was the option that was selected by the form user, then our custom validation script would not be initiated.

10. Before we add the function for handling the server-side validation of our control, let's register it in the `Page_Load` function. Place your cursor placed above the JavaScript block we just added. On the ASP.NET tab, click the Page_Load icon 🗎 to insert Dreamweaver's default code into our page. Insert the highlighted code below in the `Page_Load` function:

```
protected void Page_Load(Object Src,
EventArgs E)
{
    this.customvRemoveOn.ServerValidate
    += new ServerValidateEventHandler(
    this.customvRemoveOn_ServerValidate
    );
}
```

Remember from Chapter 5 that this code is programmatically adding the `customvRemoveOn_ServerValidate` event-handling function to the control's ServerValidate delegate. If you need a refresher on what this function is doing, refer to Chapter 5 for a discussion of controls and their events.

11. We'll need to write that function now that the Web server is going to be looking for it. You'll find the following code is similar to the client-side version. Enter it just after the `Page_Load` function but still inside the same script block so it will run on the server.

```
void customvRemoveOn_ServerValidate(
Object src, ServerValidateEventArgs
args )
{
    String ddlValue = ddlRemoveOn.Selec
    tedItem.Value;

    if( ( ddlValue == "none" ) ||
        ( ddlValue == "remove" &&
        txtRemoveOn.Text == String
        .Empty
        )
      )
    {
      args.IsValid = false;
    }
    else
    {
      args.IsValid = true;
    }
}
```

As you can see, it does the same sort of check as the client-side version of the function. But it's important to have the server-side version in case hackers bypass your client-side code and because the JavaScript may not execute on the client machine.

If you wanted to use just the server-side function, you could do so by not specifying a function in the `ClientValidation Function` attribute of the customvRemove On control. However, the user would incur a round-trip to the server during validation, increasing network traffic.

12. With all the code we've added to this page, you'll definitely want to check your page against **Script 6.4** to catch any errors. Then press F12 to preview the page in your browser.

Now if you try to submit the form with bad data, you'll see that our custom validator catches it every time. You can test the server-side function by removing the `ClientValidationFunction` attribute of the customvRemoveOn control, as discussed in the previous step, and running the page again.

Custom validation controls are powerful, as you can see. You'll find yourself relying on them frequently in your Web development career. And, if you design them right, you may be able to reuse them, similar to the preprogrammed validation controls provided with ASP.NET that we discussed earlier in this chapter.

Now your Web Forms are able to gather data into databases. The next two chapters will prepare you for saving the validated data gathered by your Web Forms to a database. In Chapter 7 we'll discuss databases in general and how to create one. Then in Chapter 8 we'll work directly with databases using Web Forms.

Script 6.4 Custom validation controls may have server and client-side validation controls defined for them. This is a good habit to develop, and because the code is very similar for both functions, it's easy to do.

```
1  <%@ Page Language="C#" ContentType=
   "text/html" ResponseEncoding="iso-8859-1" %>
2  <html>
3  <head>
4  <title>Untitled Document</title>
5  <meta http-equiv="Content-Type"
   content="text/html; charset=iso-8859-1">
6  <script runat="server">
7  protected void Page_Load(Object Src,
   EventArgs E)
8  {
9    this.customvRemoveOn.ServerValidate += new
     ServerValidateEventHandler(this.customvRem
     oveOn_ServerValidate);
10 }

11 void customvRemoveOn_ServerValidate( Object
   src, ServerValidateEventArgs args )
12 {
13   String ddlValue = ddlRemoveOn.Selec
     tedItem.Value;
14   if( ( ddlValue == "none" ) ||
15     ( ddlValue == "remove" &&
16       txtRemoveOn.Text == String.Empty
17     )
18   )
19   {
20     args.IsValid = false;
21   }
22   else
23   {
24     args.IsValid = true;
25   }
26 }
27 </script>
28 <script language="JavaScript">
29 function validateRemoveOn( src, args )
30 {
31   var ddlValue = document.all("ddlRemoveOn")
     .options[ document.all("ddlRemoveOn").selec
     tedIndex ].value;
32   if( ( ddlValue == "none" ) ||
33     ( ddlValue == "remove" &&
34       document.all("txtRemoveOn").value == ""
35     )
36   )
37   {
38     args.IsValid = false;
39   }
```

(script continues)

Script 6.4 *continued*

```
40   else
41   {
42     args.IsValid = true;
43   }
44 }
45 </script>
46 </head>
47 <body>
48 <form runat="server">
49   <table border="0" cellspacing="5" cellpad
     ding="5">
50     <tr>
51       <td>Email</td>
52       <td>
53         <asp:textbox ID="txtEmail"
           runat="server" />
54         <asp:requiredfieldvalidator
55           ControlToValidate="txtEmail"
56           Display="Dynamic"
57           ErrorMessage="Email is required."
58           ID="rfvEmail"
59           runat="server"
60           Text="*" />
61         <asp:regularexpressionvalidator
62           ControlToValidate="txtEmail"
63           Display="Dynamic"
64           ErrorMessage="Email must contain a
             valid email address."
65           ID="revEmail"
66           runat="server"
67           Text="*"
68           ValidationExpression=
             "\w+([-+.]\w+)*@\w+([-.]\w+)
             *\.\w+([-.]\w+)*" /> </td>
69     </tr>
70     <tr>
71       <td>Age</td>
72       <td>
73         <asp:textbox ID="txtAge"runat=
           "server" />
74         <asp:rangevalidator
75           ControlToValidate="txtAge"
76           Display="Dynamic"
77           ErrorMessage="You must be between
             the ages of 18 and 35."
78           ID="rvAge"
79           MaximumValue="35"
80           MinimumValue="18"
81           runat="server"
82           Text="*" />
83       </td>
84     </tr>
```

(script continues)

Script 6.4 *continued*

```
                    script
85    <tr>
86      <td>Remove On</td>
87      <td>
88        <asp:dropdownlist ID="ddlRemoveOn"
          runat="server">
89          <asp:listitem Value="none">Sel
            ect One</asp:listitem>
90          <asp:listitem Value="never">Never
            Remove</asp:listitem>
91          <asp:listitem Value="remove">Set
            Date</asp:listitem>
92        </asp:dropdownlist>
93        <asp:textbox ID="txtRemoveOn"
          runat="server" />
94        <asp:comparevalidator
95          ControlToValidate="txtRemoveOn"
96          Display="Dynamic"
97          ErrorMessage="You must be on the list
            until at least January 1, 2004."
98          ID="cvRemoveOn"
99          Operator="GreaterThanEqual"
100           runat="server"
101         Text="*"
102         Type="Date"
103         ValueToCompare="1/1/2004" />
104       <asp:customvalidator
105         ClientValidationFunction=
            "validateRemoveOn"
106         ControlToValidate="ddlRemoveOn"
107         Display="Dynamic"
108         ErrorMessage="Need to set a date."
109         ID="customvRemoveOn"
110         runat="server"
111         Text="*"></asp:customvalidator>
112     </td>
113   </tr>
114   <tr align="center">
115     <td colspan="2"> <asp:button ID=
        "btnSubmit" runat="server" Text=
        "Submit Form" /></td>
116     </tr>
117 </table>
118 <asp:validationsummary
119     DisplayMode="BulletList"
120     HeaderText="The following errors occured:"
121     ID="vsSummary"
122     runat="server" />
123 </form>
124 </body>
125 </html>
```

USING
DATABASES IN
DREAMWEAVER

The database has become the data storage technology of choice for nearly every type of application that stores and retrieves large amounts of data. Early on, applications had to use what are called "flat files" to store data. To do this, programmers needed to write functions that would handle the insertion and deletion of data from the file, not to mention the functions required to search for and retrieve desired data.

Because it was difficult to write these functions every time a program needed to store data, a software-based solution called a Database Management System (DBMS) was born. This solution centralized data storage, retrieval, and manipulation functions in one product, and provided improved data storage, management, and retrieval technology.

The DBMS is primarily a stand-alone application that contains predefined functions that enable other applications to store, manage, and retrieve data. Programmers can reuse these predefined functions, so they don't have to write new ones each time. Two common types of DBMSs are object-oriented (ODBMS) and relational (RDBMS). Since RDBMS is the more widely used of the two, we'll focus on that type in this chapter.

Today's RDBMS has become robust, complex, and scalable. Fortunately, most RDBMSs use the Structured Query Language (SQL) for data definition, retrieval, and manipulation, so moving from one product to another doesn't usually require a big learning curve. However, even within the category of relational databases, each vendor's DBMS offering differs somewhat, so take into consideration the strengths and weaknesses of each vendor's DBMS when making your choice.

In this chapter, we'll learn about relational databases and the different options, and then we'll install our choice: the Microsoft Data Engine (MSDE). After building a database, we'll incorporate it into a Web Form using Dreamweaver MX, and then create a link between the database and the Web Form that will let us actually retrieve data.

Preparing the Database

Databases are where you store the data that you'll use to dynamically populate your Web pages. An e-commerce site is a common example of a site that uses a database to dynamically populate its Web pages with content. Using a database to store the product information rather than putting it directly in a Web page provides a leap forward in efficiency. One benefit is that product information need only be entered once in the database, even though it may appear on many different Web pages. So when, say, a product's price changes, you only have to make the change once—in the database; the change will then automatically update in every place the product price appears on the Web site. Another benefit of only having to enter the information once is that you minimize the chance of introducing typos—or even of missing a page during the update process.

To store the product information in a database, we must design and create a database that's designed to handle that type of data. First, however, we'll need to decide which RDBMS to use. There are many to choose from, each with different strengths and weaknesses.

Relational Database Management Systems

In choosing an RDBMS, some criteria to consider are capabilities, price, scalability, ease of use, and how standard it is. By *standard*, we mean that it adheres to SQL 92, the definition of SQL devised by the ANSI standards body. An RDBMS that sticks to this standard will make it much easier for you to migrate if you need to someday—which happens more often than you might think. As far as price is concerned, there are many free RDBMSs available. MySQL and Firebird are two popular open source databases. Both are powerful

and standard, although they do require some setup and administrative effort. And their lack of good graphical interfaces to ease those chores may make these databases not worth it to some users.

Microsoft Access's great graphical interface makes database creation and management easy. However, it's not free, and its Jet data engine doesn't scale very well—nor does it stick to the standards. In fact, the Jet data engine isn't a true relational database engine. It uses many of the same concepts but leaves out key elements, such as true relational integrity, views, and stored procedures. The "Access vs. SQL Server" sidebar discusses the differences in more detail.

To counter the Jet data engine's limitations, you can use Microsoft's SQL Server or the Oracle database as the back end to Access. This lets you still use Access's nice graphical interface, while using a more robust RDBMS as the back end. Unfortunately, both SQL Server and Oracle are pricey. A really good, essentially free alternative is the Microsoft Data Engine (MSDE), and it comes on the Access installation CD-ROM.

MSDE is sort of a baby SQL Server, in that it doesn't scale quite as well. But if you ever exceed its limitations, it'll map directly into SQL Server without your having to change any code. The best part is that you can use it as the database engine behind Access instead of the Jet data engine, so you can take advantage of Access's great interface and still have a powerful, relational system on the back end.

Because of all these advantages, we've chosen it as our database engine for this book. If you already have a favorite RDBMS, feel free to use it instead. Just make sure that any SQL code we use is correctly adjusted to work with your choice.

✔ Tips

- With Microsoft Access, you can deploy a database powered by the Jet data engine without having Access installed on the target of deployment. However, if you choose to use MSDE over Jet, the computer on which you install your database will need to have either MSDE or SQL Server installed.

- You can use the Upsizing wizard that comes with Access to ease your transition to SQL Server if you do choose Access's Jet data engine and need to migrate later. The tool translates Access's nonstandard SQL to SQL Server–compliant code.

Access vs. SQL Server

Access was originally created to store data in a local file. The data in that file was meant to be available to only one Access front end at a time. While Access has become more capable of handling many users at once, it still isn't meant for such work. Therefore, Microsoft refers to Access's Jet database engine as a file server, whereas it refers to SQL Server and its smaller sibling MSDE as client/server data engines. Microsoft's Knowledge Base article Q222135 available at http://support.microsoft.com/default.aspx?scid=KB;EN-US;Q222135, shows how strongly the company feels about this:

"While Microsoft Jet is consciously (and continually) updated with many quality, functional, and performance improvements, it was not intended (or architected) for the high-stress performance required by 24x7 scenarios, ACID transactions, or unlimited users, that is, scenarios where there has to be absolute data integrity or very high concurrency."

In the same article Microsoft recommends using SQL Server for Web applications, because it's been designed and tested for that type of use. You may instead use MSDE for smaller-scale needs, since it uses the same engine as SQL Server.

Access also has different objects than SQL Server. These are some of the differences:

- A *select query* in Access is called a *view* in SQL Server

- *Action* and *parameterized queries* are *stored procedures* in SQL Server

- *Relationships* in Access are *database diagrams* in SQL Server

In addition, Access has different syntax for delimiters and SQL. It even uses different data types.

With all these differences, it can sometimes be hard to start using a real relational database after getting used to Access. However, it's well worth the effort, as Access is really the nonstandard one in the bunch. All the other database systems are quite similar to SQL Server, so learning one makes it easier to migrate to and understand the syntax of the others.

PREPARING THE DATABASE

133

To install MSDE:

1. Double-click a file called setupsql.exe found in the \Sql\x86\Setup folder available on your Microsoft Office or Access installation CD-ROM.

   This starts the MSDE installation program, which prompts you to pick an installation preference (**Figure 7.1**).

2. Accept the default setting of Local Install and click Next.

   The Welcome screen appears.

3. The Welcome screen alerts you to exit all other Windows programs. Click Next after you've done so.

   The User Information dialog box appears (**Figure 7.2**).

4. Enter your name and company, and click Next.

   You'll see the Setup Type dialog box (**Figure 7.3**).

Figure 7.1 Select the Local Install as the installation method for MSDE.

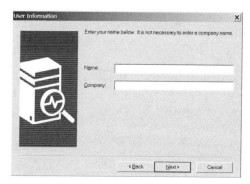

Figure 7.2 Enter your name and company's name into the MSDE installation program.

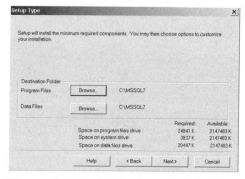

Figure 7.3 Set the installation directories for MSDE.

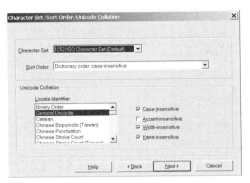

Figure 7.4 Choose the character set and sort order MSDE should use.

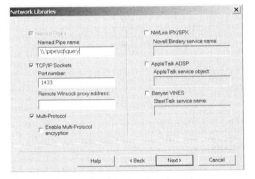

Figure 7.5 Accept the default network settings.

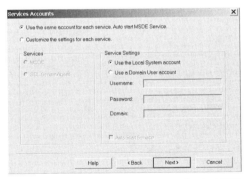

Figure 7.6 Use the Local System account for the MSDE Service.

5. Either accept the default locations for the program and data files, or customize those settings by clicking the Browse buttons. To accept the file destinations, click Next.

The Character Set/Sort Order/Unicode Collation dialog box appears (**Figure 7.4**). This screen lets you choose the character set and default sort order for your databases.

6. Review the defaults for this dialog box. If you deal with languages other than English, you may need to make changes. Then click Next to accept the settings.

The Network Libraries dialog box appears (**Figure 7.5**).

7. The default settings in the Network Libraries screen should be correct. The only reason you might need to change anything is if you're on a network that doesn't comply with these defaults. In that case, check with the network administrator for the appropriate settings. Click Next to continue.

The Services Accounts dialog box appears (**Figure 7.6**). We recommend changing the Domain User account from the default entry to an account specifically created for the database application to use. However, since this would require you to have the access and knowledge to create a Domain account, the next best setting is a Local System account. We'll set that next.

8. Select the "Use the Local System account" radio button found in the Service Settings panel. Click Next.

The Start Copying Files screen appears now that the installation program has the information it needs.

continues on next page

PREPARING THE DATABASE

9. Click Next to start copying files to your computer (**Figure 7.7**).

10. After the files have been copied, click Finish to close the installation program. And to make sure everything is running cleanly, restart your computer now.

In the next task, we'll begin defining our MSDE database using the front end tools in Access.

To use Microsoft Access 2000 or later as MSDE's front end:

1. Start Access 2000 or later (we used Access 2000 in the making of this book).

2. From the File menu, choose New.
The New dialog box opens (**Figure 7.8**).

3. From the General tab, select Project (New Database). Then click OK.
A File dialog box opens.

4. Name your Access project "PartsAreUs.adp," and click Create.
Now that you've created the Access Project, the Microsoft SQL Server Database wizard will start.

5. In the first text box, set the SQL Server you would like to use to (local) from the drop-down list, and name the database "PartsAreUs" in the bottom text box (**Figure 7.9**).

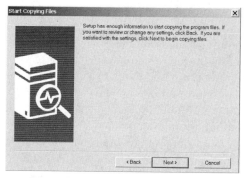

Figure 7.7 The MSDE installation program is now ready to copy files to your computer.

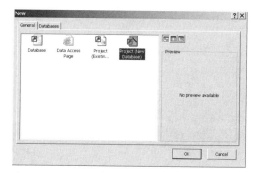

Figure 7.8 Create a Project with a new database in Microsoft Access.

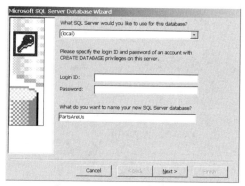

Figure 7.9 In the Microsoft SQL Server Database wizard, set the server to (local), provide a Login ID and password, and name the database "PartsAreUs."

6. You'll also need to provide a log-in ID and password so that the wizard can create the database. For the log-in ID, either you can make it a Windows account that's a member of the Administrators group and specify a password, or you can use the default MSDE "sa" account with no password. Click Next to continue.

Remember that MSDE is really just a baby SQL Server, so that's why Access doesn't distinguish between them.

7. In the final screen of the wizard, click Finish.

The wizard creates the database and returns you to Access.

That's all it takes to set up Access as MSDE's front end. Now that we've set up the database, we need to create the tables in which to store data.

Your first database

For the purposes of this book, we've decided to use an e-commerce example in creating our database. This example should be relatively easy to follow since most of you have had plenty of experience buying things online.

A Web site has a few prerequisites that allow it to handle online sales. First, it needs to have a list of products for sale. Second, it needs a way to store information about the items that a customer wants to order. And third, it needs a way for the customer to pay. We'll concern ourselves with the first two.

Right now, we'll create a simple database that has three tables. The first table, which we'll call Parts, will store information about the products we're selling. The second table, called Orders, will store each customer's information, such as name, address, and phone number. A third table will keep track of the individual items that make up a customer's order. We'll call that OrderItems. We won't be creating a table that stores payment information, however, since we won't be implementing a fully operational e-commerce Web site. And last, we'll establish the relationships between the three tables to make our database operational.

To create a Parts table in the database:

1. Open the PartsAreUs database in Microsoft Access.

   The PartsAreUs dialog box opens (**Figure 7.10**).

2. In the Objects list, select Tables. Then double-click the Create Table in Design View icon 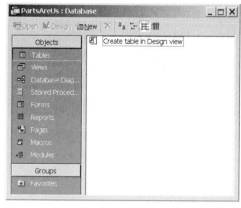 on the right.

   This opens the Choose Name dialog box for your new table (**Figure 7.11**).

3. Enter the name "Parts" in the name box, and click OK.

   This opens the new Parts table in Design view (**Figure 7.12**).

Figure 7.10 The tables list in the PartsAreUs dialog box.

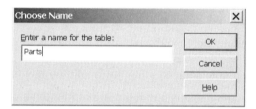

Figure 7.11 The Choose Name dialog box for the Parts table.

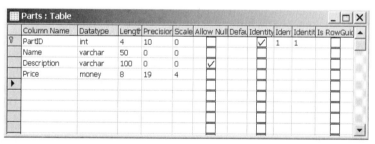

Figure 7.12 The Parts table in Design view. Its columns include the PartID primary key, Name, Description, and Price.

4. In Design view, create a column called "PartID" with a data type of "int." Uncheck the Allow Nulls check box. Then check the Identity check box found further to the right. Finally, make PartID a primary key by clicking the Primary Key icon found at the top of Access (**Figure 7.13**).

Let's quickly review what each of these actions accomplishes. The datatype int is short for Integer. This datatype will allow numbers without decimals into this column.

The Allow Nulls check box needs to be cleared for columns we never want the user to leave blank. Leaving it checked means we allow the field to be left blank and, as a result, we might accidentally create a part with no name. This would surely confuse customers and possibly our program.

Checking the Identity check box makes PartID automatically increment by one, starting at one, every time a part is added to the table. These values are inserted into the PartID field and used as unique keys to identify each row of part data. You can change the starting number and the increment by adjusting the values in the Identity Seed and Identity Increment fields, but the default values are fine for this example.

The Primary Key icon allows you to designate a column that will be used to uniquely identify a row of data. The Primary Key field will be useful later when you want to retrieve a specific row of data from the database. You'll normally want to assign at least one of your columns as the Primary Key.

If you look at Figure 7.12, you'll see a little key icon appear to the left of the PartID row.

Note that in Design view, each row that we define will actually become a column when we view the table in Datasheet view.

continues on next page

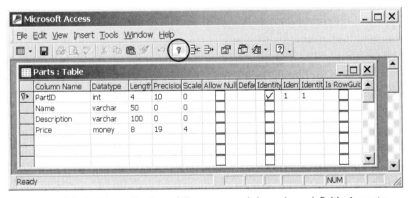

Figure 7.13 Click the Primary Key icon while your cursor is in a column definition's row to make that column a primary key.

PREPARING THE DATABASE

139

5. On the next row (still in Design view), add a column called "Name" and set its data type to "varchar." The default length of 50 is fine, but clear the Allow Nulls check box.

6. Add a "Description" column below Name, also of type "varchar." Change the length to 100, since we'll need a little more room for part descriptions; and clear the Allow Nulls check box.

7. Add one last row called "Price." Change its data type to "money" and clear its Allow Nulls check box. Now close the table's Design view, and save your changes when prompted to do so. You're now back in the PartsAreUs dialog box you opened in Step 1.

Our last step will be to add some sample data to the Parts table.

8. Double-click the Parts table found on the right side of the dialog box. In the window that opens, add the following Parts:

Name: Doohickey
Description: The part you will love forever.
Price: $25.00

Name: Whatchamacallit
Description: A one size fits all part that will solve more problems than we can count.
Price: $14.93

Name: Thingamabob
Description: If you have this part you will never need another. It is that wonderful!
Price: $9.26

Notice that the PartID column automatically populates with the values of 1, 2, and 3, respectively, as you move from one row to the next (**Figure 7.14**).

After entering those three parts, you can close the window.

Next, we'll create a table to store each customer's order information.

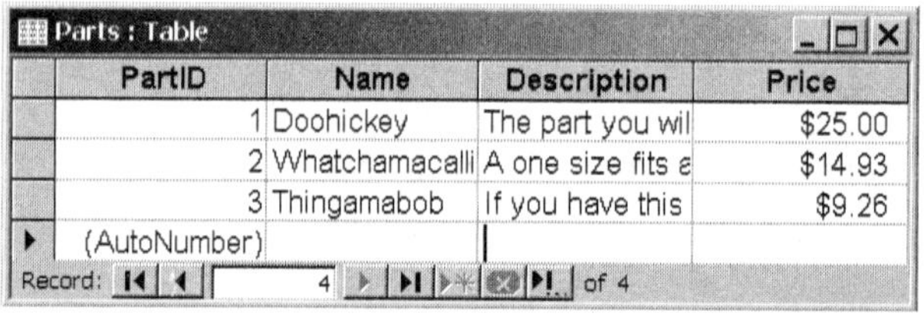

Figure 7.14 The data contents of the Parts table.

To create an Order table in the database:

1. On the right side of the PartsAreUs dialog box, double-click the Create Table in Design View icon 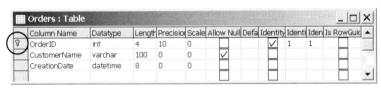 to open the Change Name dialog box. Name the table Orders, and click OK.

   This opens the Order table in Design view.

2. In the Design view of the Orders table, create a column called "OrderID." Set its data type to "int," and clear its Allow Nulls check box. Then select the Identity check box to make the column automatically increment. Also, make the row a primary key by clicking the Primary Key icon.

   A little key graphic will appear to the left of the row (**Figure 7.15**).

3. In the row below the OrderID definition, create a column called "CustomerName." Change its data type to "varchar," and set the length to 100. Keep Allow Nulls checked this time so we can wait to ask for the customer's name until checkout time.

4. The last column to add to the Orders table should be called "CreationDate." Change its data type to "datetime," and clear the Allow Nulls check box. Close the Order table and save your changes when prompted.

   Next, we'll add the last table—the OrderItems table.

Figure 7.15 The Orders table in Design view. It includes a primary key column called OrderID, and the CustomerName and CreationDate columns.

To create an OrderItems table in the database:

1. On the right side of the PartsAreUs dialog box, double-click the Create Table in Design View icon 🔳.

   The Change Name dialog box opens.

2. Set the name to "OrderItems" and click OK.

   The OrderItems table will open. It's a little different, in that it will contain columns you've seen before.

3. First add a column called "OrderID." Set the data type to "int" and clear its Allow Nulls check box.

   This column should match the primary key column of the Orders table, because it will store the same sort of data (**Figure 7.16**). However, this one won't automatically increment its value. It will store only what we insert into it.

4. In the next row, add a column called "PartID." Set its data type to "int" and clear its Allow Nulls check box.

5. Add one more column and call it "Quantity." Assign it a data type of "int," and clear its Allow Nulls check box.

   Next, we'll need to create a primary key, but this time it will consist of two columns, not just one.

6. Select both OrderID and PartID by clicking the gray area to the left of the column names while holding down the Shift key. Then click the Primary Key icon 🔑.

You'll see a little key graphic appear to the left of each row.

Primary keys must be unique in a table. When there is only one column in the primary key, each value in that column must be unique. However, when two columns are in the key, only the combined value of both columns needs to be unique. Therefore, the OrderID 1 can be in the OrderID column as many times as we want, as long as each PartID value is different from the others that share the OrderID of 1.

We have one more task to do before we're finished creating our database. We need to create relationships between the three tables so that MSDE will help enforce the relational integrity of our database that is inferred by the OrderID and PartID key columns. For example, when adding an order to the Orders table, we'd want to be sure the PartID value existed in the Parts table; conversely, we wouldn't want to remove a part from the Parts table that had orders placed on it. This kind of data consistency (also known as relational integrity) can be managed by the database when relationships are defined. To help us create these relationships, Access provides a graphical tool called a diagram.

	Column Name	Datatype	Length	Precision	Scale	Allow Null	Defa	Identity	Iden	Iden	Is RowGuid
🔑	OrderID	int	4	10	0						
🔑	PartID	int	4	10	0						
	Quantity	int	4	10	0						

Figure 7.16 The OrderItems table's Design view, containing the two-column primary key OrderID and PartID, plus the Quantity column.

To create the relationships among the tables:

1. On the left of the PartsAreUs dialog box, click Database Diagrams, and then double-click the Create Database Diagram in Designer icon 🗗.

   This opens a blank diagram.

2. To add tables to the blank diagram, click the Show Table icon found near the top of Access (**Figure 7.17**). Then in the Show Table dialog box that appears, click the + (plus) sign next to Tables.

   This displays a list of the available tables (**Figure 7.18**). To add the tables to the diagram, click and drag each of them

from the dialog box to the diagram window behind it. When you're done, you can close this dialog box.

3. Back in the diagram, add a relationship between the Parts table and the OrderItems table by dragging the PartID column from the Parts table to the OrderItems table.

   The Create Relationship dialog box will open, with everything preset for you. Just read over the settings to make sure they're correct, and click OK (**Figure 7.19**).

continues on next page

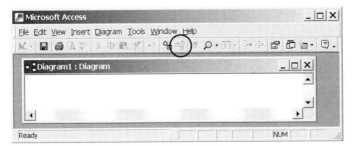

Figure 7.17 Click the Show Table icon to open a dialog box that contains a list of tables you can add to a diagram.

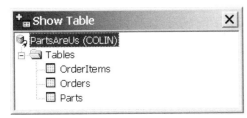

Figure 7.18 A list of tables in the Show Table dialog box.

Figure 7.19 Creating a relationship between the Parts and OrderItems tables.

Next, we'll create a relationship between the Orders table and the OrderItems table.

4. Drag the OrderID column from the Orders table to the OrderItems table.

   This opens the Create Relationship dialog box (**Figure 7.20**).

5. Again, make sure the settings are correct, and click OK.

   The resulting diagram has two lines, each with a key at one end and an infinity sign at the other. One line links the Parts and OrderItems tables, and the other links the OrderItems table with the Orders table (**Figure 7.21**). The infinity signs both point toward the OrderItems table, signifying that many Parts can be assigned to one Order and many Orders can contain the same part.

6. Close the diagram, and when prompted name it PartsAreUs Diagram.

   Notice that the prompt also verifies that you want to alter the three tables. This alteration is the addition of the relationships you just created among the tables (**Figure 7.22**).

We now have a database that can handle e-commerce data. A real database, of course, would have a Customers table and so on, but this one will get us started. In the next section, we'll put our database to use.

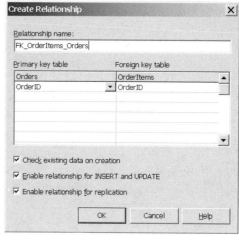

Figure 7.20 Creating a relationship between the Orders and OrderItems tables.

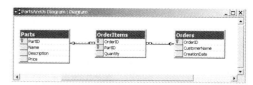

Figure 7.21 The final PartsAreUs Diagram.

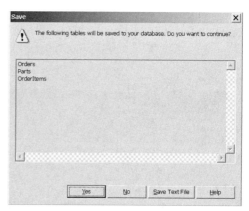

Figure 7.22 Saving the diagram will cause the tables to be altered to contain the relationships.

Working with a Database in Dreamweaver

In the previous section we looked at the different DBMS options available to us. We chose the MSDE data engine because it's more robust, reliable, and scalable—and it works well with Access, giving us a nice interface. Then, using Access, we created a basic e-commerce database called PartsAreUs.

Now, we'll start working with Dreamweaver again to incorporate the PartsAreUs database in a Web Form. We recommend creating a new site called PartsAreUs that we'll use for the next section, as well as the next chapter. If you need help creating a site, reread "To define a site for your local server" in Chapter 3.

Database connectivity

In the new Dreamweaver site you created for PartsAreUs, you'll find the Database tab on the Application panel group filled with several instructions.

Essentially these instructions inform you that in order to connect to a database, you'll need to create a Connection object. A *Connection object* is what lets Dreamweaver interact with your database, and it comes in two forms: OLE DB and SQL Server. An OLE DB Connection is a more generic object that lets Dreamweaver communicate with many different types of databases, ranging from Access to Oracle. The SQL Server Connection object is more specialized for communicating with SQL Server and MSDE. This specialization makes it more efficient than the generic OLE DB Connection object, improving performance.

Because we chose MSDE as our DBMS, we'll create a SQL Server Connection. However, if you chose a different DBMS, you'll need to create an OLE DB Connection. Here are a couple tips to get you started:

◆ The interfaces for creating the two types of connections are similar, though the OLE DB dialog box has a couple of extra buttons (**Figure 7.23**).

◆ The Build button provides a more complex interface (**Figure 7.24**) that provides greater flexibility in defining the settings for the data sources to which you can connect.

◆ To lessen the time it takes you to create the object, the Templates button provides some preformatted connection strings for common data sources, such as an Oracle database (**Figure 7.25**).

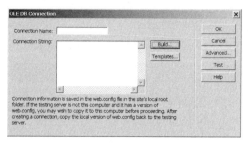

Figure 7.23 The OLE DB Connection dialog box.

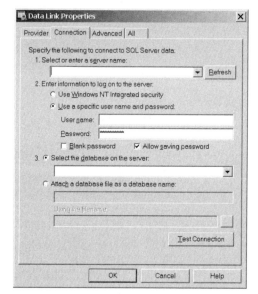

Figure 7.24 For greater flexibility, the Build button on the OLE DB Connection dialog box produces the DataLink Properties dialog box.

Figure 7.25 The Templates button on the OLE DB Connection dialog box opens a list of available connection string templates for commonly used data sources.

WORKING WITH A DATABASE IN DREAMWEAVER

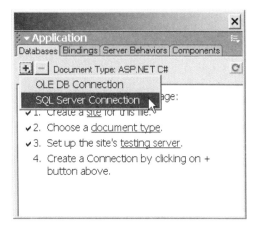

Figure 7.26 The list of available connection types in the Application panel group.

Figure 7.27 A correctly modified connection string in the SQL Server Connection dialog box.

To create a SQL Server Connection object:

1. From the Application panel group in Dreamweaver, click on the Databases tab, and then click the + (plus) sign icon.

   This opens a drop-down list of available connection types (**Figure 7.26**). If the Application panel group isn't visible, choose Databases from the Window drop-down list at the top of Dreamweaver.

2. Select SQL Server Connection.

   This opens the SQL Server Connection dialog box (**Figure 7.27**).

3. In the Connection Name text box, enter the name "PartsAreUs." Then change the Connection String box's default value as follows:

   Persist Security Info=False;
   Data Source=;
   Initial Catalog=PartsAreUs;
   User ID=sa;
   Password=;

   Because the server is your local computer in this instance, you can use a period instead of the actual computer's name in the DataSource= line. Otherwise, you would have had to put either the name of the computer or its IP address. We're also just using MSDE's default username (sa) and a blank password here. For greater security you would need to create a unique username and password with rights only to this database.

4. Click the Test button to make sure Dreamweaver can connect to the database with these settings, and then click OK.

   You should now be back at the Database tab with the PartsAreUs Connection object visible.

continues on next page

WORKING WITH A DATABASE IN DREAMWEAVER

5. Try expanding the PartsAreUs Connection object, as well as the Tables group that appears under, it by clicking their respective + (plus) signs. You can go one more level down by clicking the + sign next to dbo.OrderItems as well if you want to see the column details for that table (**Figure 7.28**).

6. Finally, review the web.config file found at the root of your site and shown in **Script 7.1**. In it you'll see the PartsAreUs connection string that we just defined in what is known as an application setting. *Application settings* are how ASP.NET defines variables that are to be used by a Web site's code. Dreamweaver stores the database connection information in these settings. This lets us make the connection string readily available to our code from page to page. You can also create your own application settings if you need to make a variable available throughout your site.

✔ Tip

■ The *dbo* in dbo.OrderItems is simply SQL syntax to denote the name of the user who created that table. The letters stand for *database owner*.

Now that we've created a connection to our database, lets start using it. The next section shows you how.

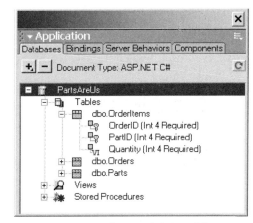

Figure 7.28 The partially expanded view of the PartAreUs database on the Databases tab.

Script 7.1 After creating a Connection object, the values that define how to connect to the database are stored as application settings in the web.config file.

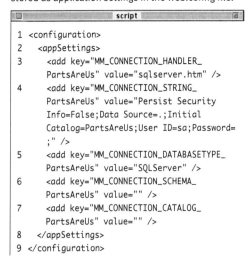

```
1  <configuration>
2    <appSettings>
3      <add key="MM_CONNECTION_HANDLER_
       PartsAreUs" value="sqlserver.htm" />
4      <add key="MM_CONNECTION_STRING_
       PartsAreUs" value="Persist Security
       Info=False;Data Source=.;Initial
       Catalog=PartsAreUs;User ID=sa;Password=
       ;" />
5      <add key="MM_CONNECTION_DATABASETYPE_
       PartsAreUs" value="SQLServer" />
6      <add key="MM_CONNECTION_SCHEMA_
       PartsAreUs" value="" />
7      <add key="MM_CONNECTION_CATALOG_
       PartsAreUs" value="" />
8    </appSettings>
9  </configuration>
```

Binding to database data

ASP.NET uses an object called a *DataSet* to collect data from a database. If you've dealt with other server-side scripting languages such as ASP, you'll know this type of object by the name of *Recordset*. However, a DataSet is based on XML and is more flexible than a Recordset, so the terms aren't interchangeable.

You have a lot of flexibility in creating DataSet objects, so you can retrieve exactly the data you want. Dreamweaver's DataSet tool enables you to retrieve data from a database without having to even know SQL. But for those times when you need that extra bit of control over the code, the Dataset tool offers an advanced interface that gives you direct access to the SQL itself.

To create a DataSet in Dreamweaver, you'll have to look under the Bindings tab of the Application panel group. Dreamweaver refers to the process of linking data from the database to a DataSet as *binding*. In the Bindings tab, you can bind to more than just a DataSet. The most likely candidate for binding to something other than a DataSet is a stored procedure.

A *stored procedure* is essentially a predefined function in a database written in an SQL-like programming language. In the case of SQL Server and MSDE, the programming language is called Transact SQL—or T-SQL for short. Stored procedures generally execute faster because they're precompiled. Therefore, they're a good place to store SQL code if it's going to be run often.

Since DataSets are used more often, we'll create one below in order to give our customers a list of products from which to order. We'll use the simple interface of the DataSet tool so that we won't need to type any SQL; however, the "SQL Select Statements" sidebar will help you understand any SQL you do see.

To create a DataSet object:

1. Open the PartsAreUs site in Dreamweaver. Then create a new Web Form, and name it "PartsList.aspx."

2. From the Application panel, click on the bindings tab, and then click on the + (plus) sign icon.

   This displays a list of possible bindings you can make (**Figure 7.29**).

3. Select DataSet.

   This opens the DataSet dialog box (**Figure 7.30**). Make sure the DataSet dialog box is in Simple mode by checking for a button on the right side labeled Advanced. If instead you find a button labeled Simple, you're in Advanced mode. Click the Simple button to switch interfaces.

4. Set the Name box to "dsPartsList." Then from the Connection drop-down list, select PartsAreUs.

   This is the same Connection object we created in the "To create a SQL Server Connection object" earlier.

5. From the Table drop-down list, select dbo.Parts. Switch the Columns radio button from All to Selected. Now, while holding down the Control key, click PartID, Name, and Price in the list of columns. Click OK when you're done.

   You'll see the results in two places. The first place is in the Bindings tab, where you'll see each column we specified when creating dsPartsList (**Figure 7.31**). The second place is in the code of the Web Form itself (**Script 7.2**). In fact, the Bindings tab merely displays a graphical representation of the code that's at the top of your Web Form.

   Save your page. We'll deal with displaying the data in Chapter 8.

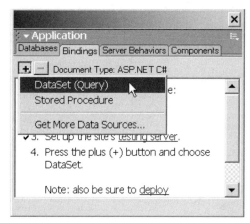

Figure 7.29 Selecting the DataSet binding option from the Bindings tab.

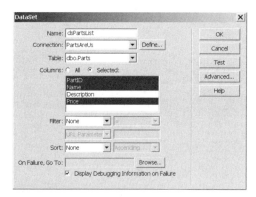

Figure 7.30 Creating the dsPartsList DataSet object using the DataSet dialog box's simple interface.

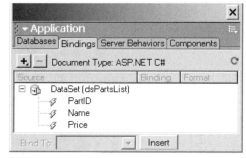

Figure 7.31 The graphical representation of the dsPartsList DataSet.

Script 7.2 The application settings defined in the web.config file are used to dynamically set the values of a DataSet's attributes.

```
                    script
 1 <%@ Page Language="C#" ContentType=
   "text/html" ResponseEncoding="iso-8859-1" %>
 2 <%@ Register TagPrefix="MM" Namespace=
   "DreamweaverCtrls"Assembly="DreamweaverCtrls,
   version=1.0.0.0,publicKeyToken=
   836f606ede05d46a,culture=neutral" %>
 3 <MM:DataSet
 4   id="dsPartsList"
 5   runat="Server"
 6   IsStoredProcedure="false"
 7   ConnectionString='<%# System.Configuration.
     ConfigurationSettings.AppSettings
     ["MM_CONNECTION_STRING_PartsAreUs"] %>'
 8   DatabaseType='<%# System.Configuration.
     ConfigurationSettings.AppSettings["MM_CONN
     ECTION_DATABASETYPE_PartsAreUs"] %>'
 9   CommandText='<%# "SELECT PartID, Name,
     Price FROM dbo.Parts" %>'
10   Debug="true" >
11 </MM:DataSet>
12 <MM:PageBind runat="server" PostBackBind=
   "true" />
13 <html>
14 <head>
15 <title>Untitled Document</title>
16 <meta http-equiv="Content-Type" content=
   "text/html; charset=iso-8859-1">
17 </head>
18 <body>
19 </body>
20 </html>
```

By looking at the code in your PartsList.aspx Web Form, you'll see how Dreamweaver uses the application settings created for the PartsAreUs Connection object. They dynamically populate the values of the ConnectionString and DatabaseType attributes of the MM:DataSet control.

Another important thing that you'll discover in the code is a page-level command that looks like the following:

```
<%@ Register TagPrefix="MM" Namespace=
"DreamweaverCtrls"Assembly="Dreamweaver
Ctrls,version=1.0.0.0,publicKeyToken=
836f606ede05d46a,culture=neutral" %>
```

This command registers with the Web server a Dynamic Link Library (DLL) file that's provided by Dreamweaver. A *DLL file* represents a grouping of callable functions. The actual Dreamweaver MX DLL can be found in the following directory:

C:\Program Files\Macromedia\Dreamweaver MX\Configuration\ServerBehaviors\Shared\ ASP.Net\Scripts

This DLL file must be copied into the bin directory of your Web site so that the Web server can find it. It contains the definition of the MM:DataSet control, as well as a host of other controls that Dreamweaver refers to as server behaviors. You'll see the DLL file in every page that uses a server control, so don't be surprised to have it at the top of most of your pages.

We'll display the Parts data in the PartsList.aspx Web Form in Chapter 8. In that chapter, we'll display the data using the DataSet we created here and manipulate the data in the database—all within Web Forms.

WORKING WITH A DATABASE IN DREAMWEAVER

SQL Select Statements

SQL is a language used in databases to define and manipulate data. The language contains many commands, but the most commonly used one is the select command. The reason is that this command retrieves the data.

To satisfy all the requirements of retrieving data from a database, the command is designed to be extremely flexible. In its simplest form, it can retrieve all data from a table such as the following:

```
SELECT * FROM dbo.Parts
```

But it can also incorporate limiting statements, and even sub–select statements. The actual syntax definition of a select statement is too long and complex to include here, but the following is a short version:

```
SELECT list-of-columns
[ INTO table ]
FROM table
[ JOIN table ON column=column ]
[ WHERE condition ]
[ GROUP BY column ]
[ HAVING condition ]
[ ORDER BY column [ ASC | DESC ] ]
```

Using this syntax we could create a select statement that joins the Parts table to the OrderItems table and then to the Orders table so that we can see all the parts in an order. We could even limit the search to include only OrderID 1 and OrderID 2, and sort the results in reverse alphabetical order. Such a command would look like the following:

```
SELECT o.OrderID, p.Name
FROM Parts p
JOIN OrderItems i
  ON i.PartID = p.PartID
JOIN Orders o
  ON o.OrderID = i.OrderID
WHERE o.OrderID = 1
  OR o.OrderID = 2
ORDER BY p.Name DESC
```

For a more complete look at the full complexity of SQL select statements we suggest looking for a book or Web site that best suits your needs. To view Microsoft's select statement documentation, go to http://msdn.microsoft.com/library/en-us/tsqlref/ts_sa-ses_9sfo.asp

DATA-DRIVEN WEB FORMS

In the last chapter, we covered database basics. We chose and installed Microsoft Data Engine (MSDE) as our Database Management System (DBMS). Then, using MSDE, we created a database to store parts and orders data. Finally, we created a Connection object and a DataSet object in Dreamweaver to retrieve that data.

In this chapter we'll learn how to display that data in a Web Form to make the form dynamic. Then we'll expand on the concept of displaying data by creating a Master-Detail page set in which we initially limit the display of data and provide links for viewing the detailed data at the discretion of the user. Finally, we'll create Web Forms that we'll use to manipulate the data stored in the database.

Visual Data Representation

Displaying data is the job of every developer of a dynamic Web site. Data display options range from tables filled with numbers to charts and graphs.

To make the page more readable, we sometimes purposely omit some of the available data from view so that we don't overwhelm the viewer. However, the data we leave out still might be important to the customer, so we still need to make it available. By creating a Master-Detail Web Form set, we can summarize data on a Master page and then provide links to a Details page for more data.

In the next section, we'll show you how to display the parts data for the DataSet object we created in Chapter 7. Then, in the Master-Detail Web Forms section, we'll build a Master-Detail set to display all available data to the customer.

Displaying data

On the Web, data is usually displayed in tabular format. This is because tables work well in Web browsers and because people have become accustomed to rows and columns from years of seeing them in printed format. We could use charts and graphs instead, but they're harder to program, they aren't always the best way to present the data, and they haven't been around as long as tables have.

The data we're going to display is from the PartsAreUs database that we created in Chapter 7 (see "Your First Database" for more information). Let's quickly review what other

things we did so that we'll easily pick up where we left off: We created a Connection object in Dreamweaver called PartsAreUs to enable Dreamweaver to communicate with the PartsAreUs database (see "To create a SQL Server Connection object" in Chapter 7). Then we created a PartsList.aspx Web Form in which we made a DataSet object called dsPartsList that would retrieve the PartID, Name, and Price columns from the Parts table in the PartsAreUs database.

Here we'll continue with the PartsList.aspx Web Form. In it we'll create an object called a *DataGrid* and assign to it the dsPartsList DataSet. A DataGrid is a flexible control that takes the data it's given, in this case the dsPartsList DataSet, and automatically displays the data in a preformatted HTML table. The DataGrid control is very flexible. It can automatically display all columns of data in a simple table, or you can define selected columns and specify how each should be displayed. The DataGrid dialog box Dreamweaver provides only scratches the surface of what a DataGrid is really able to do, so don't limit your imagination to just what you see there. To access the real potential of DataGrid controls, you have to dig into the code. "The DataGrid Control" sidebar on the next page reviews some of the DataGrid's capabilities.

The DataGrid Control

ASP.NET's DataGrid control is the easiest way to display data in a table. It has five types of columns, seven common region styles, and two properties for hiding either the header or the footer.

The column types let you specify the behavior you want the data to have. They are as follows:

◆ **BoundColumn.** This is the default column type and is used to display the data as text.

◆ **ButtonColumn.** This column produces a command button for each row of data. The button can be used for actions such as adding or deleting a row.

◆ **EditCommandColumn.** This produces a command button for each row. The button enables the data in that row to be edited.

◆ **HyperLinkColumn.** This creates a hyperlink for each row. The links range from static text linking to a set page, to data-driven text linking to different pages.

◆ **TemplateColumn.** This style enables customization of the output. It's most useful for having custom controls within the column.

By default, the `AutoGenerateColumns` property is set to `True`. That will cause all the columns of data to be mapped to one BoundColumn each. If you need more control over the DataGrid, you can set that property to `False` and state exactly which columns you want displayed in your DataGrid and in what order.

Then there are the styles. Styles are for customizing the look of the DataGrid's output. The styles are made of Cascading Style Sheet attributes, and there's one style for each region of a DataGrid:

◆ **ItemStyle.** This specifies how each item in the DataGrid should appear when rendered to a table row.

◆ **AlternatingItemStyle.** To increase readability you may specify a different look for every other item in the DataGrid (for example, you might add shading to alternate rows).

◆ **EditItemStyle.** This is the style to be used when an item is selected for editing.

◆ **SelectedItemStyle.** This is the style to be used when an item is selected by the user.

◆ **PagerStyle.** When the data consumes more than one page, this style defines how the region containing the paging links should appear.

◆ **HeaderStyle.** This defines the look that the header of the DataGrid should have.

◆ **FooterStyle.** This defines the look that the footer of the DataGrid should have.

It's possible to define even more styles than this for specific items, but this at least gives you a sense of the DataGrid's power and flexibility. We haven't even mentioned yet that you can manipulate a DataGrid programmatically at execution time, as well as during the design phase using the markup code that we'll create in the next set of instructions. For that information, however, you'll have to look at the documentation. One location for more information is http://msdn.microsoft.com.

VISUAL DATA REPRESENTATION

To display data in a Web Form:

1. In the PartsAreUs site we created in Chapter 7, open the page called PartsList.aspx (it looks like **Script 8.1**). In the Bindings tab, you'll see a DataSet called dsPartsList (**Figure 8.1**).

If any of this is unfamiliar, please review "Working with a Database in Dreamweaver" in Chapter 7.

2. Set the view of PartsList.aspx to show both code and design by clicking the Show Code and Design Views icon on the Document toolbar (**Figure 8.2**).

3. Click in the Design portion of the page. Then from the Insert bar, click on the Application tab, and then click the DataGrid icon (**Figure 8.3**).

This will open a dialog box for creating a DataGrid control.

Script 8.1 Here we see the markup for a DataSet that uses the settings from the web.config file to connect to the database and retrieve the data from the PartID, Name, and Price columns of the Parts table.

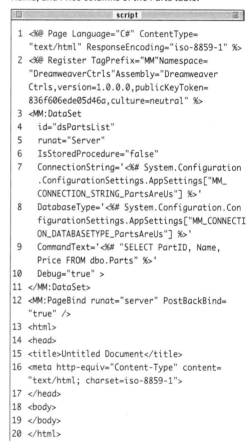

```
script

1 <%@ Page Language="C#" ContentType=
   "text/html" ResponseEncoding="iso-8859-1" %>
2 <%@ Register TagPrefix="MM"Namespace=
   "DreamweaverCtrls"Assembly="Dreamweaver
   Ctrls,version=1.0.0.0,publicKeyToken=
   836f606ede05d46a,culture=neutral" %>
3 <MM:DataSet
4   id="dsPartsList"
5   runat="Server"
6   IsStoredProcedure="false"
7   ConnectionString='<%# System.Configuration
    .ConfigurationSettings.AppSettings["MM_
    CONNECTION_STRING_PartsAreUs"] %>'
8   DatabaseType='<%# System.Configuration.Con
    figurationSettings.AppSettings["MM_CONNECTI
    ON_DATABASETYPE_PartsAreUs"] %>'
9   CommandText='<%# "SELECT PartID, Name,
    Price FROM dbo.Parts" %>'
10  Debug="true" >
11 </MM:DataSet>
12 <MM:PageBind runat="server" PostBackBind=
   "true" />
13 <html>
14 <head>
15 <title>Untitled Document</title>
16 <meta http-equiv="Content-Type" content=
   "text/html; charset=iso-8859-1">
17 </head>
18 <body>
19 </body>
20 </html>
```

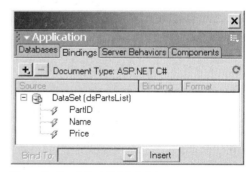

Figure 8.1 The dsPartsList DataSet.

Figure 8.2 Change the view so you can see both code and design simultaneously.

Figure 8.3 You'll find the DataGrid icon on Application tab of the Insert bar.

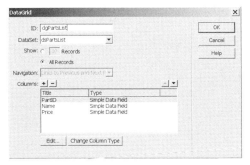

Figure 8.4 The DataGrid dialog box is where we'll create the dgPartsList DataGrid.

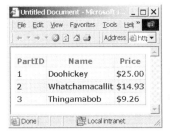

Figure 8.5 The PartsList.aspx file as rendered in Internet Explorer.

4. In the ID text box, enter "dgPartsList" and in the DataSet text box, enter "dsPartsList" (**Figure 8.4**).

This is the same DataSet we created for this Web Form in "To create a DataSet object" in Chapter 7.

5. For the Show option, click the radio button beside All Records, and click OK.

This closes the dialog box and creates the DataGrid object.

The last thing we have to do is alter the code a little so that our Price field gets formatted correctly as money.

6. In the page's Code view, click just before the /> in the control that looks like this:

```
<asp:BoundColumn DataField="Price"
      HeaderText="Price"
      ReadOnly="true"
      Visible="True" />
```

Then add the `DataFormatString` attribute with the value "{0:C}". This means that the column's data (that's the 0) should be formatted as currency (that's the C). The modified code will look like this:

```
<asp:BoundColumn DataField="Price"
      HeaderText="Price"
      ReadOnly="true"
      Visible="True"
      DataFormatString="{0:C}" />
```

"The DataFormatString Attribute" sidebar discusses additional formatting options.

7. Finally, review your page's code against **Script 8.2** on the next page to check for inconsistencies. Then press the F12 key to open the page in your default browser.

You'll see that our DataGrid automatically created a readable table listing the parts and their prices (**Figure 8.5**).

VISUAL DATA REPRESENTATION

Script 8.2 Starting with a DataSet, we add a DataGrid to the page so that we can have all the data automatically formatted into an HTML table when rendered in a browser.

```
                              script
1  <%@ Page Language="C#" ContentType="text/html" ResponseEncoding="iso-8859-1" %>
2  <%@ Register TagPrefix="MM" Namespace="DreamweaverCtrls"Assembly="DreamweaverCtrls,version=
   1.0.0.0,publicKeyToken=836f606ede05d46a,culture=neutral" %>
3  <MM:DataSet
4    id="dsPartsList"
5    runat="Server"
6    IsStoredProcedure="false"
7    ConnectionString='<%# System.Configuration.ConfigurationSettings.AppSettings["MM_CONNECTION_STRING
     _PartsAreUs"] %>'
8    DatabaseType='<%# System.Configuration.ConfigurationSettings.AppSettings["MM_CONNECTION_DATABASETY
     PE_PartsAreUs"] %>'
9    CommandText='<%# "SELECT PartID, Name, Price FROM dbo.Parts" %>'
10   Debug="true">
11 </MM:DataSet>
12 <MM:PageBind runat="server" PostBackBind="true" />
13 <html>
14 <head>
15 <title>Untitled Document</title>
16 <meta http-equiv="Content-Type" content="text/html; charset=iso-8859-1">
17 </head>
18 <body>
19 <form runat="server">
20 <asp:DataGrid AllowPaging="false"
21   AllowSorting="False"
22   AutoGenerateColumns="false"
23   CellPadding="3"
24   CellSpacing="0"
25   DataSource="<%# dsPartsList.DefaultView %>" id="dgPartsList"
26   runat="server"
27   ShowFooter="false"
28   ShowHeader="true" >
29 <HeaderStyle HorizontalAlign="center" BackColor="#E8EBFD" ForeColor="#3D3DB6" Font-Name="Verdana,
   Arial, Helvetica, sans-serif" Font-Bold="true" Font-Size="smaller" />
30 <ItemStyle BackColor="#F2F2F2" Font-Name="Verdana, Arial, Helvetica, sans-serif" Font-Size="smaller"
   />
31 <AlternatingItemStyle BackColor="#E5E5E5" Font-Name="Verdana, Arial, Helvetica, sans-serif" Font-
   Size="smaller" />
32 <FooterStyle HorizontalAlign="center" BackColor="#E8EBFD" ForeColor="#3D3DB6" Font-Name="Verdana,
   Arial, Helvetica, sans-serif" Font-Bold="true" Font-Size="smaller" />
33 <PagerStyle BackColor="white" Font-Name="Verdana, Arial, Helvetica, sans-serif" Font-Size="smaller" />
34   <Columns>
35     <asp:BoundColumn DataField="PartID"
36       HeaderText="PartID"
37       ReadOnly="true"
38       Visible="True"/>
39     <asp:BoundColumn DataField="Name"
40       HeaderText="Name"
41       ReadOnly="true"
42       Visible="True"/>
```

(script continues on next page)

Script 8.2 *continued*

```
                        script
43    <asp:BoundColumn DataField="Price"
44       HeaderText="Price"
45       ReadOnly="true"
46       Visible="True"
47       DataFormatString="{0:C}" />
48    </Columns>
49 </asp:DataGrid>
50 </form>
51 </body>
52 </html>
```

The DataFormatString Attribute

You can use the `DataFormatString` attribute of an asp:BoundColumn control to specify how you want the data formatted when it's rendered in the browser. We did this in Step 6 of the previous exercise. We used the currency format, but other common formats are available as well.

The formatting string consists of a 0 (zero), which represents the data to be formatted, followed by a colon, and then the code representing the format. All of this needs to be inside curly braces '{}' in order to be dynamic. Anything outside the curly braces will be taken literally.

Here are the common format codes:

C Currency format: the dollar sign, followed by a number with two decimal places.

D Decimal format: D should be followed by a number to specify how many decimal places to show (for instance, {0:D2} shows 2 decimal places).

E Exponential (scientific) format.

X Hexadecimal format.

These codes are case insensitive, with the exception of the X formatting code, whose case dictates the case of the hexadecimal characters when it's rendered in the browser.

✔ Tip

■ Instead of clicking the DataGrid icon from the Application Tab in the Insert Panel in Step 3, you can also go to the Application panel, click on the Server Behaviors tab, and select Data Grid from the menu.

The page we just created lists the parts in our database for the customers to see. However, the customers have no way to read the parts' descriptions, let alone buy the parts. We'll solve that problem in the next section, "Master-Detail Web Forms."

Master-Detail Web Forms

Master-Detail Web Forms are a very common approach to displaying data as they allow you to summarize data on a page and add links for users to view detailed data. The *Master page* shows summary information and includes links to a *Detail page,* which as the name suggests provides the detailed information. By creating Master-Detail pages, you can limit the information you display on the Master page to a manageable amount by linking to the less essential but still important information on the Detail pages. This empowers visitors to delve further into the data as their interest warrants.

After displaying data in our Web Form, our customers can now see a list of the parts of our database. But they won't know much about each part because we currently have no description available. To better serve our customers, we'll create a way for them to click on a part in the list to get more details about that part. We'll start by altering the PartsList.aspx Web Form a little.

To create a Master Web Form:

1. Open the PartsList.aspx Web Form once again.

   This will make its dgPartsList control available in the list on the Application panel group's Server Behaviors tab (**Figure 8.6**).

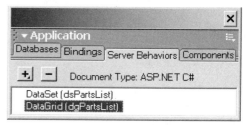

Figure 8.6 A list of Server Behaviors that are in the PartsList.aspx page.

2. Double-click dgPartsList in that tab.

   This opens the dgPartsList DataGrid's dialog box so we can edit the control (**Figure 8.7**).

3. In the Columns list, select PartID. Then click the Change Column Type button, and select Hyperlink from the list that appears.

   The Hyperlink Column dialog box opens (**Figure 8.8**).

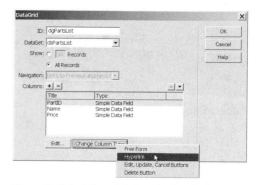

Figure 8.7 Select Hyperlink from the list of column types available in the DataGrid dialog box.

   The Hyperlink Column dialog box allows you to define settings for the hyperlink. The Hyperlink Text portion of the dialog box defines the text the user will click in order to go to the Detail page. You can either enter static text if you want the same text to appear for every link or reference a data field from a DataSet to use dynamic text for each link. Similarly, the linked (or Detail) page, which is the page the user will go to when the link is clicked, is defined in the Linked Page portion of the dialog box. The link can be a static URL, making the user always go to the same linked page; or it can be a dynamic URL by using a data field from a DataSet.

Figure 8.8 Use the Hyperlink Column dialog box to configure the linking to the PartDetail.aspx Web Form.

   The Hyperlink Column dialog box that's open is already set to use dynamic text for both the Hyperlink Text and Linked Page. We will need to enter a mix of static and dynamic text for the linked page's URL.

4. In the second Format String field of the Hyperlink Column dialog box, type the following:

`PartDetail.aspx?PartID={0}`

The second Format String field is the last field in the dialog box and relates to the linked page. What we're doing here is linking to a page called PartDetail.aspx, which we're about to create. The portion after the question mark is called the Querystring, and in it we're passing a variable called `PartID`. Then using syntax similar to that we used for the `DataFormatString` attribute in Step 6 of "To display data in a Web Form," we're dynamically setting the variable's value to the PartID on each row of the DataGrid.

Note: If the PartDetail.aspx page had already existed during this step, we could have used the dialog box's Browse button to find and select it. That would have populated this field automatically.

5. Click OK to return to the DataGrid dialog box, and then Click OK to close DataGrid dialog box and save your changes.

6. Save the PartsList.aspx Web Form.

Next, we'll create the PartDetail.aspx file that this page links to.

To create a Detail Web Form:

1. Start by creating a new Web Form, and name it "PartDetail.aspx."

If you need a reminder, the process for creating a new Web Form is outlined in "To create a new Web Form" in Chapter 4.

2. From the Insert bar, click on the Application tab, and then click the DataSet icon 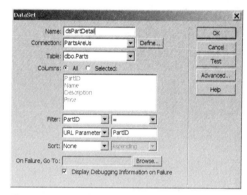, which is the first one on the left.

This opens the DataSet dialog box (**Figure 8.9**).

Figure 8.9 Create the dsPartDetail DataSet so it will retrieve only the part whose PartID matches the PartID value in the Querystring.

3. In the Name text box, enter "dsPartDetail." In the Connection drop-down menu, choose PartsAreUs. In the Table drop-down menu, choose dbo.Parts.

This time we want to retrieve all the columns, but we need a filter.

Figure 8.10 Use the testing dialog box for parameterized DataSets to make sure the dataset works correctly.

4. In the Filter drop-down menu, select PartID. In the drop-down field to the right, select the equal sign (=) as the operator. In the third drop-down menu, select URL Parameter as the data type, and in the fourth, enter "PartID" as the name of the URL Parameter.

5. Before closing the dialog box, click the Test button.

A testing dialog box opens (**Figure 8.10**).

6. Enter "1" into the Test Value field. Click OK.

This retrieves the part whose PartID is 1.

7. Now you can close the testing window and click OK in the DataSet dialog box to close it as well.

Because we're retrieving only one part from the database, we'll create a table that displays the data ourselves, rather than having Dreaweaver build one automatically.

Figure 8.11 Click the Insert Tables icon to open its dialog box.

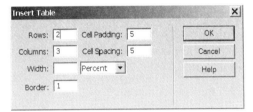

Figure 8.12 Use the Insert Table dialog box to create a table to display the part data.

Figure 8.13 Merge the two table cells by using the Merge Selected Cells Using Spans icon on the Property inspector.

8. From the Insert bar, click on the Tables tab, and then click the Insert Table icon (**Figure 8.11**).

This opens the Insert Table dialog box (**Figure 8.12**).

9. In the dialog box, set Rows to 2, Columns to 3, and Border to 1. Then set both the Cell Padding and the Cell Spacing fields to 5. Click OK.

This creates the table and closes the dialog box.

10. In the Design view of the page, select all three cells in the bottom row of the table we just created. Then on the Property inspector, click the Merge Selected Cells Using Spans icon (**Figure 8.13**).

continues on next page

VISUAL DATA REPRESENTATION

11. Now that we have a table, drag the PartID field from the Bindings tab into the first field.

The following will appear in the first cell of the table in Design view (**Figure 8.14**):

`{dsPartDetail.PartID}`

And if you look in the page's code you'll find this:

```
<%# dsPartDetail.FieldValue(
"PartID", Container ) %>
```

These both mean that the value of the PartID field will be inserted into this cell of the table.

12. Drag the Name field on the Bindings tab down into the table's second cell. To format the Name field, we'll use the formatting menu that appears for the Name field in the Bindings tab. You can locate it by looking to the right of the Name field and clicking on the down arrow in the format column.

The formatting menu drops down (**Figure 8.15**).

13. From the formatting menu, select Trim > Both.

Trimming both sides (left and right) of a data field removes any extra spaces or tabs before and after the field's value.

```
    Untitled Document (chpt_08/Script_8-04.aspx)                        _ □ X
23  <table border="1" cellspacing="5" cellpadding="5">
24    <tr>
25      <td>
26        <%# dsPartDetail.FieldValue("PartID", Container) %>
27      </td>
28      <td>
29        <%# dsPartDetail.FieldValue("Name", Container).Trim() %>
30      </td>
31      <td>
32        <%# Double.Parse(dsPartDetail.FieldValue("Price", Container)).ToString("C") %>
33      </td>
34    </tr>
35    <tr>
36      <td colspan="3">
37        <%# dsPartDetail.FieldValue("Description", Container).Trim() %>
38      </td>
39    </tr>
40  </table>
```

```
{dsPartDetail.PartID}   {dsPartDetail.Name}   {dsPartDetail.Price}
{dsPartDetail.Description}
```

`<body> <table> <tr> <td>`   `822 x 111 ▾ 3K / 1 sec`

Figure 8.14 This is the resulting Code and Design view of the finished table.

Figure 8.15 The Trim submenu is located under the formatting menu for the Name field.

Figure 8.16 Select Default from the Currency submenu.

14. Again from the Bindings tab, drag the Price field down to the third cell of the table. From the Price field's formatting menu, select Currency > Default (**Figure 8.16**).

If you look in the page's code at what was entered for the Price field, you'll see the following:

```
<%# Double.Parse(dsPartDetail.Field
Value( "Price", Container ) ).ToStr
ing("C") %>
```

This code is similar to that seen in Step 11 in the way it still puts the Price data into the table cell but before doing so converts it to a numeric data type called Double. Then it converts that to a string formatted as currency using the C parameter.

15. Drag the Description field down to the big cell that makes up the bottom row of the table. Again, from the formatting menu, select Trim > Both to trim both sides of its value.

16. Save the file. To test, open PartsList.aspx and browse it in your default browser. Click on one of the PartIDs in the PartsList.aspx file to be transferred to the Detail page. The Detail page will be populated with the data matching the PartID you chose.

✔ Tip

■ If you have trouble executing the PartDetail.aspx file, try opening it from Dreamweaver by pressing F12 first. This, too, will fail, because it is not being passed the data it requires; however, it *will* force Dreamweaver to copy the file to your testing server so that it is available. Once you do this, the file should execute.

VISUAL DATA REPRESENTATION

Altering Database Content

So far in this chapter, we've built on our work in Chapter 7 to provide a way for our customers to view parts in our database with varying levels of detail. But what about the times when we want to add a new part, change a price, or remove a part that's been discontinued? We need a way to alter the data.

We could use Microsoft Access to edit the data in the tables, just as we used it to create the database in Chapter 7. However, what if we wanted to manipulate the data from anywhere in the world via the Internet? What if we wanted to create a custom interface to ease the management process? To solve those problems, we can create Web Forms that let us manipulate the data in the database by means of a Web interface. By designing our own Web Forms, we can control what data is available for editing and how the interface looks and behaves.

Updating data

The most common task performed on data is updating it. And with our database, we'll most commonly be updating prices, because parts go on sale and production costs fluctuate.

Fortunately, through the use of a DataGrid control we can easily edit the contents of our database. If you read "The DataGrid Control" sidebar earlier in the chapter, you know that this control has a predefined column type called the EditCommandColumn designed specifically for this sort of work. To use it, let's create a Web Form for editing our parts data.

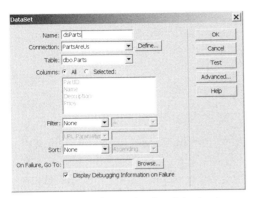

Figure 8.17 Use the dsParts DataSet dialog box to configure the DataSet.

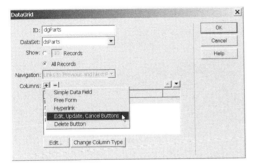

Figure 8.18 Select Edit, Update, Cancel Buttons from the list of available column types.

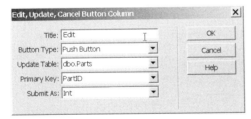

Figure 8.19 Create a new EditCommandColumn called Edit for the dgParts DataGrid.

To update database data using a Web Form:

1. Create a new Web Form and name it "PartEditor.aspx."

2. From the Application tab of the Insert bar, click the DataSet icon 📄 .

   The DataSet dialog box opens (**Figure 8.17**).

3. In the Name field, enter "dsParts." In the connection drop-down menu, select PartsAreUs. In the table drop-down menu, select dbo.Parts as the table to use. Click OK to create the DataSet.

4. On the Application tab, click the DataGrid icon 📄 .

   This opens the DataGrid dialog box (**Figure 8.18**).

5. In the the ID text box, enter "dgParts." In the DataSet drop-down menu, select dsParts. Change the Show setting from 10 Records to All Records. Then click the + (plus) sign to add a column to the list of columns. Select Edit, Update, Cancel Buttons from the list that appears.

   This opens the Edit, Update, Cancel Button Column dialog box (**Figure 8.19**).

6. In the Title field, enter "Edit." Then from the Button Type drop-down menu, select Push Button; and from the Update Table menu, select dbo.Parts. Click OK.

   This adds the new column to the Data-Grid dialog box's Columns list and closes the Edit, Update, Cancel Button Column dialog box.

continues on next page

7. In the DataGrid's list of columns, select the new column called Edit at the bottom of the list and click the up-arrow button until the column moves to the top of the list (**Figure 8.20**).

8. Select the Name column and click the Edit button found underneath the list.

This opens the Simple Data Field Column dialog box.

9. Uncheck the box labeled Read Only (**Figure 8.21**). Then click OK to close the dialog box.

This will enable us to edit the parts data.

10. Repeat Steps 8 and 9 for the Description and Price columns.

11. Finally, click the DataGrid dialog box's OK button to create the DataGrid and close the dialog box.

12. We're now ready to start editing the parts data. Press the F12 key to open the page in your browser. Try clicking the Edit button on the left side of the table.

It should refresh the page to make that row editable (**Figure 8.22**).

Deleting data from the database is equally easy. We could have added a Delete Button column to our list of DataGrid columns. It would require no more work than that. But rather than delete data, let's learn how to add it.

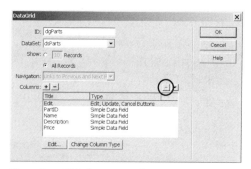

Figure 8.20 Click the up arrow button to move the new Edit column to the top of the list of columns.

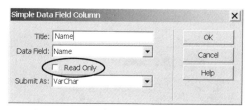

Figure 8.21 Clear the Read Only check box for the Name, Description, and Price columns so that they can be edited.

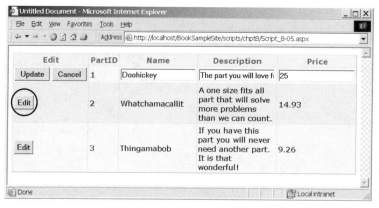

Figure 8.22 Use the Edit button to make a row of the PartsEditor.aspx file editable when rendered in Internet Explorer or another suitable Web browser.

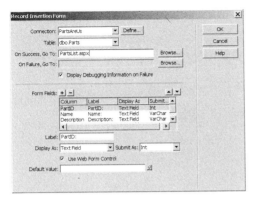

Figure 8.23 The Record Insertion Form dialog box lets you insert a new part into the database's Parts table.

Inserting data

Dreamweaver has one of the best tools ever created for inserting data into a database via a Web page. It's simple to use and easy to understand. You'll find the Record Insertion Form dialog box either on the Application tab of the Insert bar or on the Server Behaviors menu.

The Record Insertion Form works by inspecting the table you're planning to insert data into and then creating a list of fields that match up to the columns in the table. If you don't want to insert data into all the table columns, you can remove those fields from list. You can even set default values, data types, and form field types. This dialog box also has fields for setting where you want the user to be taken upon success or failure of the insertion procedure.

Let's create a new Web Form so that we can add some new parts for our customers to browse.

To insert data into a database using a Web Form:

1. Create a new Web Form and call it "AddPart.aspx."

2. From the Insert bar, click on the Application tab, and then click the Record Insertion Form icon ▦ .

   The Record Insertion Form dialog box opens (**Figure 8.23**).

   continues on next page

3. In the Connection text box, enter "PartsAreUs." In the Table drop-down menu, select dbo.Parts as the table to insert into, and in the On Success, Go To field, enter "PartsList.aspx."

   This is the same PartsList.aspx we created in "To display data in a Web Form" earlier in this chapter.

   We will keep the default of showing the debugging information upon failure to help us diagnose any problem that may occur.

4. Still in the Record Insertion Form dialog box, find the Form Fields list near the middle of the dialog box. Click the PartID column to select it, and then click the – (minus sign) button to remove the PartID column from the list.

   We don't want to insert data into this column, because the database is set to autogenerate this field value.

5. Lower in the Form Fields list you'll find Description. Select it, and then in the Display As drop-down list, change the selection from Text Field to Text Area.

   This will give the users more space to type in a part description (**Figure 8.24**).

6. Click OK.

   This will close the dialog box and create all the code necessary to insert data into the database's Parts table.

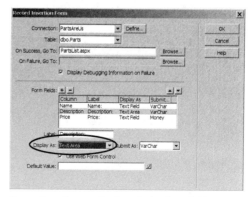

Figure 8.24 Change the Description form field's display type to Text Area to give the user more room to type a description.

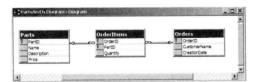

Figure 8.25 The PartsAreUs database Diagram illustrates the relataionships between the database tables. Here we see that the OrderItems table is dependant on the Orders table.

7. Press F12 to open the page in your browser, and start adding parts to the database.

   You'll find that when you click the Insert Record button, you'll be brought to the PartsList.aspx page, where you'll see the part you just added.

   If you try adding things like text into the price field, you'll get an error. This page is a prime candidate for adding validation controls to avoid such problems. If you're interested, go back to Chapter 6 and read all about validation controls and how they can help you.

Now that we've created pages that allow the site manager to edit the parts data, we'll now make it possible for customers to add these parts to their orders.

Inserting data (advanced)

So far we've seen ways to very simply update and insert data into the PartsAreUs database, but we still haven't seen a way for our customers to add parts to their orders. To accomplish this task, we'll need a way to insert data into the OrderItems table. But our database structure requires that there be an order in the Orders table before any items can be added to the OrderItems table (**Figure 8.25**). So if there isn't an order, we need to create it. If there is one, we need to reuse it.

Before we insert data into multiple database tables, we need to let our customers select a part to add to their order. We did something similar to this in the PartsList.aspx file that we worked on in the Master-Detail Web Forms section of this chapter, so the following instructions should sound familiar.

To make a list of parts to buy:

1. Create a new Web Form and call it "PartsToBuy.aspx." This Web Form will end up being almost identical to the PartsList.aspx file we finished in "To create a Master Web Form" earlier in this chapter.

2. On the Application tab, click the DataSet icon 🖳 .

    The DataSet dialog box opens (**Figure 8.26**).

3. In the Name field, enter "dsPartsToBuy." In the Connection drop-down menu, select PartsAreUs. Then in the Table drop-down menu, select dbo.Parts, and click OK.

    This creates the DataSet and closes the dialog box.

4. On the Application tab, click the Data-Grid icon 🖳 .

    This opens its dialog box.

5. In the ID text box, enter "dgPartsToBuy" and in the DataSet text box, enter "dsPartsToBuy." Also, select All Records to make sure that all data will be returned. Below, in the list of columns, select PartID and then click the Change Column Type button. Change the column to a Hyperlink column.

    The PartID's Hyperlink Column dialog box opens.

6. In the dialog box, type the following into the second Format String field (**Figure 8.27**):

    BuyPart.aspx?PartID={0}

    This format string is making the PartID column into hyperlinks that link to a BuyPart.aspx file that we'll soon create. For that page to recognize which part the customer is trying to buy, the PartID must be included in the Querystring.

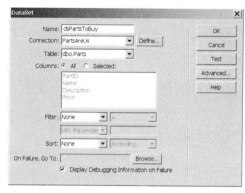

Figure 8.26 The DataSet dialog box is where we'll create the dsPartToBuy DataSet.

Figure 8.27 We use the Hyperlink Column dialog box to configure the PartID column as an HyperLinkColumn.

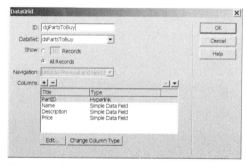

Figure 8.28 This is the resulting configuration for the dgPartsToBuy DataGrid.

7. Click OK.

This closes this dialog box and returns us to the DataGrid dialog box (**Figure 8.28**). All the work of defining our dgPartsToBuy control is done.

8. Click OK.

This closes the DataGrid dialog box.

9. Press F12 to view the new page in your default browser.

Next, we'll create the BuyPart.aspx file so we can actually add the parts to orders.

Now that we have a list of parts to add to our order, we need to be able to add them to the OrderItems table. Dreamweaver MX doesn't provide any tools that will help us do this sort of work easily. Instead, we'll need to program it ourselves. But before we do that, there are some things we need to review.

In the code we'll be writing, we'll be accessing some predefined classes provided by .NET. One of them, the DataSet, you're already familiar with, but the other three are new: SqlConnection, SqlCommand, and SqlDataAdapter. The SqlConnection class provides a way to connect to a database. The SqlCommand class lets us run SQL commands like `insert` statements on our target database. The SqlDataAdapter class retrieves data from the database results we generate.

You will also see a new command at the top of the page that looks like this:

```
<%@ Import Namespace="System.Data" %>
```

This statement makes a reference to a namespace. *Namespaces* are really just a hierarchical grouping for classes. ASP.NET uses namespaces to group similar classes together and to avoid naming conflicts. The namespace shown above is where the DataSet class is defined. The `System.Data.SqlClient` namespace is where the SqlConnection, SqlCommand, and SqlDataAdapter classes are defined.

The hierarchical structure of provided classes is probably starting to make more sense by now. These classes are organized in a tree-like fashion, beginning at the root level with the fundamental building-block-type classes, and then progressing upward, where each successive branched class is built from classes in the lower-level branches. Each tree level consists of similarly grouped classes and is assigned its own namespace. For example, the data-related classes will be found within the `System.Data` branch of the class hierarchy.

We're ready to create the page that will insert the item into the database. We'll split the process of creating the BuyPart.aspx Web Form into two sets of instructions. In the first set, we'll make the form in which the customer will type his or her name and the desired quantity of parts. In the second, we'll write the code to process the form.

To make the advanced data insertion form:

1. Create a Web Form called "BuyPart.aspx." We created a link to this file from PartsToBuy.aspx in Step 6 of "To make a list of parts to buy." Make both the code and the design visible by clicking the Show Code and Design Views icon 🖳 on the Document toolbar.

2. In the code, just after the \<body> tag, create a form in which we'll work. Make sure to set the runat attribute to "server" as follows:

```
<form runat="server">
</form>
```

3. Then in between the opening and closing \<form> tags, type the code shown below to add a hidden input field called hdnPartID. This field will hold the PartID specified on the Querystring for later use without the user seeing it.

   The body code of your page will end up looking like this:

```
<form runat="server">

<input type="hidden" id="hdnPartID"
name="hdnPartID" runat="server" />

</form>
```

4. On the Property inspector, click the Refresh button (**Figure 8.29**).

   This produces a red box with a little yellow icon inside it in the page's Design view. The red box represents the form created in Step 2. The yellow icon represents the hidden input field.

5. Click the page's Design view beside the yellow icon inside the red box. Then in the Insert bar's Common tab, click the Insert Table icon 🖼 .

   The Insert Table dialog box opens (**Figure 8.30**).

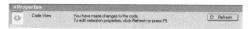

Figure 8.29 This is what the Property inspector looks like after altering the page's code. You must click the Refresh button to see the changes to the code reflected in the design.

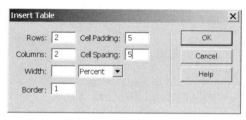

Figure 8.30 Use the Insert Table dialog box to create your HTML table.

Figure 8.31 The asp:textbox icon found on the ASP.NET tab.

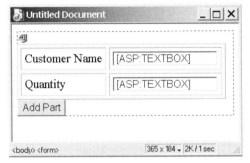

Figure 8.32 This is the Design view of the BuyPart.aspx page.

6. In the dialog box, set both Rows and Columns to 2. Then set both Cell Spacing and Cell Padding to 5. Set the Border to 1, and click OK.

   You've now inserted a table into the form.

7. Back in Design view, click in the left cell on the top row of the table. Enter "Customer Name."

8. Move to the left cell of the table's bottom row, and enter "Quantity."

9. Click in the right cell of the table's top row. Then from the Insert bar, click on the ASP.NET tab, and then click the asp:textbox icon (**Figure 8.31**).

   This opens the Tag Editor dialog box.

10. In the Tag Editor, set the ID to "txtCustomerName" and click OK.

    The dialog box closes.

11. Click into the *right* cell of the table's *bottom* row. This is the last blank cell of the table. On the ASP.NET tab, click the asp:textbox icon.

    This opens the Tag Editor dialog box.

12. In the Tag Editor, set the ID to "txtQuantity" and click OK.

13. Click in the white space to the right of the table in Design view to set the location for your next control. Then from the ASP.NET tab, click the asp:button icon.

    This opens the Tag Editor dialog box.

14. In the Tag Editor, set the ID to "btnAddPart" and Text to "Add Part." Click OK.

    The dialog box closes and the design of the page is now done (**Figure 8.32**)

Now we'll write the code to process the form. The following instructions comprise lots of code, so we'll write only a little at a time. Use **Script 8.3** on the next page as a reference to help you along.

Script 8.3 Once a customer has selected a part to buy, we need to insert an order into the Orders table and insert an item into the OrderItems table.

```
1  <%@ Page Language="C#" ContentType=
   "text/html" ResponseEncoding="iso-8859-1" %>
2  <%@ Import Namespace="System.Data" %>
3  <%@ Import Namespace="System.Data.SqlClient" %>
4  <html>
5  <head>
6  <title>Untitled Document</title>
7  <meta http-equiv="Content-Type" content=
   "text/html; charset=iso-8859-1">
8  <script runat="server">
9  protected void Page_Load(Object Src,
   EventArgs E)
10 {
11   SqlConnection conn = new SqlConnection(
     System.Configuration.ConfigurationSettings
     .AppSettings[ "MM_CONNECTION_STRING_Par
     tsAreUs" ] );
12   SqlCommand cmd;
13   SqlDataAdapter da;
14
15   if( ! IsPostBack )
16   {
17     hdnPartID.Value = Request.QueryString
       ["PartID"].ToString();
18   }
19   else
20   {
21     Int32 OrderID = 0;
22     if( Session["OrderID"] != null )
23     {
24       OrderID = Int32.Parse(
         Session["OrderID"].ToString() );
25     }
26     else
27     {
28       string today = System.DateTime.To
         day.ToString();
29       cmd = new SqlCommand("INSERT INTO
         Orders ( CustomerName, CreationDate )
         VALUES ( '" + txtCustomerName.Text +
         "', '" + today +"' )", conn);
30       cmd.Connection.Open();
31       cmd.ExecuteNonQuery();
32
33       da = new SqlDataAdapter("SELECT
         OrderID FROM Orders WHERE CustomerName
         = '" + txtCustomerName.Text + "' AND
         CreationDate = '" + today + "'", conn);
```

Script 8.3 *continued*

```
34       DataSet ds = new DataSet();
35       da.Fill(ds, "Orders");
36       cmd.Connection.Close();
37
38       OrderID = Int32.Parse( ds.Tables[ "Or
         ders" ].Rows[0][ "OrderID" ]
         .ToString() );
39       Session["OrderID"] = OrderID;
40     }
41
42     if( OrderID > 0 )
43     {
44       cmd = new SqlCommand("INSERT INTO
         OrderItems ( OrderID, PartID, Quantity
         ) VALUES ( " + OrderID + ", " +
         hdnPartID.Value +", " +
         txtQuantity.Text + ")", conn);
45       cmd.Connection.Open();
46       cmd.ExecuteNonQuery();
47       cmd.Connection.Close();
48       // transfer to another page here
49     }
50   }
51 }
52 </script>
53 </head>
54 <body>
55 <form runat="server">
56 <input type="hidden" id="hdnPartID" name=
   "hdnPartID" runat="server" />
57 <table border="1" cellspacing="5" cell
   padding="5">
58   <tr>
59     <td>Customer Name</td>
60     <td><asp:textbox ID="txtCustomerName"
       runat="server" /></td>
61   </tr>
62   <tr>
63     <td>Quantity</td>
64     <td><asp:textbox ID="txtQuantity"
       runat="server" /></td>
65   </tr>
66 </table>
67 <asp:button ID="btnAddPart" runat="server"
   Text="Add Part" />
68 </form>
69 </body>
70 </html>
```

To write advanced data insertion code:

1. Open the BuyPart.aspx file we were just working with. Change it to Code view by clicking the Show Code View icon on the Document toolbar (**Figure 8.33**).

2. Click just before the <html> tag to set your code insertion point. Then on the Insert bar's ASP.NET tab, click the Import Namespace icon .

   This sets the insertion point for the following code:

   ```
   <%@ Import Namespace="" %>
   ```

   Your cursor will be moved automatically to the point between the two quotes following Namespace.

3. Type "System.Data" so the code looks like this:

   ```
   <%@ Import Namespace="System.Data" %>
   ```

4. Again, place your cursor just in front of the <html> tag, and on the ASP.NET tab, click the Import Namespace icon. This time set the namespace to "System.Data.SqlClient"

   With these two namespaces imported, you'll have programmatic access to the DataSet, SqlConnection, SqlCommand, and SqlDataAdapter classes.

5. Move your cursor down in the file a little so it's just in front of the </head> tag. Then on the ASP.NET tab of the Insert bar, click the Page_Load icon.

   This inserts the default Page_Load function code.

6. Inside the Page_Load function but before the default if statement, add the following:

   ```
   SqlConnection conn = new SqlConnec
   tion( System.Configuration.Configura
   tionSettings.AppSettings[ "MM_CONNEC
   TION_STRING_PartsAreUs" ] );
   ```

   ```
   SqlCommand cmd;
   ```

   ```
   SqlDataAdapter da;
   ```

   This code defines three variables that we'll use in the rest of the function. The first one, conn, is a SqlConnection object that represents the connection to the database. It's assigned a new instance of the SqlConnection class using the application setting that was automatically set as a parameter in "To create a SQL Server Connection object" in Chapter 7.

   The second variable is a SqlCommand called cmd that represents the operations we can perform against the database using the connection.

   The third variable is a SqlDataAdapter called da that represents operations to access the results from the database operation.

   We'll create new objects for conn and cmd in the coming steps.

   continues on next page

Figure 8.33 Switch to see only code using the Show Code View icon.

7. Change the default `if` statement in the `Page_Load` function to the following:

```
if( ! IsPostBack )
{
  hdnPartID.Value = Request.QueryStr
ing["PartID"].ToString();
}
```

This `if` statement only allows the code it contains to run when the page is first visited (in other words, it's not a post back). When it does run, it sets the `hdnPartID` hidden form field's value to the PartID passed on the Querystring from the PartsToBuy.aspx page we created in "To make a list of parts to buy."

8. Immediately following the `if` statement, add an `else` clause. This `else` clause will execute during post back—in other words, when the form is being submitted for processing. In it we need to create a new variable call `OrderID` and check to see if an Order already exists for the current customer.

```
else
{
  Int32 OrderID = 0;
  if( Session["OrderID"] != null )
  {
    OrderID = Int32.Parse( Session["
    OrderID"].ToString() );
  }
}
```

Here we set a variable, OrderID of type Integer32 (this type of variable allows whole numbers only, using 32-bit precision), to zero and then checked to see if a session variable that's also called OrderID has already been defined. Session variables are unique per customer, per visit. We use a session variable here to indicate that an order already exists for this customer. If the OrderID is already defined, we extract it from the Session object and convert it from a String type to an Integer32.

If you want more information on session variables, refer to the "Moving Between Pages" section of Chapter 4.

9. We need to add an `else` clause to the `if( Session["OrderID"] != null )` clause. It will handle the instances where the session variable hasn't been set before by inserting an order into the Orders table for that customer. The code should look like this:

```
else
{
  string today = System.DateTime.Tod
ay.ToString();

  cmd = new SqlCommand( "INSERT INTO
Orders ( CustomerName, CreationDa
te ) VALUES ( '" + txtCustomerNam
e.Text + "', '" + today +"' )",
conn);

  cmd.Connection.Open();
  cmd.ExecuteNonQuery();
}
```

When the OrderID doesn't already exist, this code will insert an Order record with the customer's name and today's date into the Orders table using the objects stored in the `cmd` and `conn` variables.

The next step will deal with retrieving the OrderID that the database automatically creates when the `insert` statement is run. Having the database automatically create OrderIDs is great because it makes the database keep track of which one should be next. But it does force the developer to first insert the data and then retrieve the newly created OrderID.

10. To get the right OrderID, we'll retrieve the OrderID where the data matches the data we inserted in Step 9. Make sure the following code is placed within the **else** clause started in Step 8.

```
da = new SqlDataAdapter( "SELECT
OrderID FROM Orders WHERE CustomerNa
me = '" + txtCustomerName.Text + "'
AND CreationDate = '" + today + "'",
conn);
DataSet ds = new DataSet();
da.Fill(ds, "Orders");
cmd.Connection.Close();
```

The **ds** DataSet object is used here to hold the data retrieved by the **da** SqlDataAdapter object. You can see that the SqlDataAdapter fills the DataSet with data and names it **Orders**. Then the connection to the database is closed.

11. Finally, still within the **else** clause created in Step 8, we'll set the value of the OrderID and store OrderID as a session variable. Type in the following code to do so:

```
OrderID = Int32.Parse( ds.Tables["Or
ders"].Rows[0]["OrderID"].ToString()
);

Session["OrderID"] = OrderID;
```

12. Using the OrderID that we got from either the database or the session variable by now, we need to insert the item we're ordering into the OrderItems table. Insert the following code just after the } (closing curly brace) of the **else** clause we were just working inside of, but still inside the **else** clause created in Step 8:

```
if( OrderID > 0 )
{
  cmd = new SqlCommand( "INSERT INTO
  OrderItems ( OrderID, PartID,
  Quantity ) VALUES ( " + OrderID +
  ", " + hdnPartID.Value +", " +
  txtQuantity.Text + ")", conn );

  cmd.Connection.Open();
  cmd.ExecuteNonQuery();
  cmd.Connection.Close();
}
```

The check for having OrderID greater than zero is simply to make sure that we have a valid OrderID. The rest of the code is similar to that in Step 9. It opens the connection to the database, executes the **insert** statement, and then closes the database connection.

13. Compare what you've typed to Script 8.3 to make sure you didn't mistype something. Then press F12 to force Dreamweaver to copy your page to the testing server.

Doing so will cause an error, because you're not passing a PartID field in the Querystring, but it ensures the page won't fail by not being on the testing server.

14. Open the PartsToBuy.aspx Web Form in Dreamweaver and press F12. Click one of the PartID hyperlinks to go to the BuyPart.aspx page. Enter your name and your desired quantity. Click the Add Part button.

The page will look like all it did was refresh, because we aren't transferring to another page or displaying a "successfully completed" message.

continues on next page

15. Use Microsoft Access to view the contents of the Orders and OrderItems tables. You should find your order data in those two tables.

Of course, this is a very simplified Web Form, because it doesn't give you any feedback about your success and it doesn't do any data validation. But you now should have a good idea of what it takes to deal with more advanced data insertion scenarios. Though this task involved a lot of code, by now you should be getting the hang of programming ASP.NET Web Forms.

In the coming chapters we'll explore more advanced ASP.NET topics such as security, custom controls, Web services, and extending Dreamweaver with ASP.NET functionality.

ALTERING DATABASE CONTENT

CREATING A LOGIN SYSTEM

Once a site's dynamic content is created, it's frequently manipulated by adding, editing and displaying it in varying levels of detail in our Web pages. In the last chapter, we explored some of the various ways you can manipulate data, which leads us to the next topic: access security.

We clearly want customers to be able to add parts to their orders, for example, but we don't want them to be able to alter the parts prices, which are stored in the Parts table of our PartsAreUs database. So we need to create a login system for our PartsAreUs site that limits access to the Web Forms we created in Chapter 8 to manipulate our parts data.

A login system requires a list of users with access rights to the site. The obvious and most appropriate place to store a list of PartsAreUs users would be in a table that we could create in the PartsAreUs database. However, so that we can expose you to even more of what's possible in ASP.NET, we've decided to store the list of users in an XML file instead. Then by using your Web site's configuration file, web.config, we'll instruct the Web server to automatically limit access to a section of the PartsAreUs site. We'll create a Web Form that will accept the user's login information and compare it to the data stored in our list of users. As a result, only users who have credentials stored in our XML file will be granted access to the restricted area.

Limiting Web Form Access

Since anyone with a computer and an Internet connection can access the Internet, Web sites need a way to know who's accessing secure information on a site. If you plan to put secure information on your Web site without a security system to limit access, expect that information to be read by anyone in the world who wants to read it.

Often a Web site will contain both public and private information. On our PartsAreUs site, we want to limit access to the Web Forms, which allow users to add or edit the data contained in the Parts table of the PartsAreUs database. But we also want to make sure the Web Forms that let customers add parts to their orders are kept publicly available (or at least available to the extent that each customer can access his or her own records).

There's an easy way to limit access to Web Forms in ASP.NET Web sites. You use the web.config file to define settings for granting and limiting access to your Web pages.

The web.config file

The web.config file is a special XML file that's immensely useful for configuring settings that pertain to your Web site. Chapter 2 discussed how you can use the web.config file to define application settings that store things like database connection strings. You can also use it to configure how your site should handle debugging and tracing, both of which are useful for determining the causes of errors you or your users encounter. And you can also use the web.config file to configure access to your site's Web Forms.

We looked at the PartsAreUs site's web.config file in "To create a SQL Server Connection object" in Chapter 7. In the file, you could see the database connection information being stored as application settings. Here it is again shown in **Script 9.1**.

Notice how the web.config file is hierarchical in nature, as all XML files are. First there's a `configuration` element. In XML parlance this is called the document root, of which there can be only one. Within that is an element called `appSettings`. It contains several elements called `add`. Each `add` element is instructing the Web server to add an application setting using the name specified in the element's `key` attribute, with the value stated in the `value` attribute.

To configure Web site access security in the web.config file, we need to add some new elements. The following instructions detail how the file must change and what each new element means.

Script 9.1 The web.config file from Chapter 7 holds the settings necessary to connect to the PartAreUs database.

```
1  <configuration>
2    <appSettings>
3      <add key="MM_CONNECTION_HANDLER_PartsAreUs" value="sqlserver.htm" />
4      <add key="MM_CONNECTION_STRING_PartsAreUs" value="Persist Security Info=False;Data Source=
       .;Initial Catalog=PartsAreUs;User ID=sa;Password=;" />
5      <add key="MM_CONNECTION_DATABASETYPE_PartsAreUs" value="SQLServer" />
6      <add key="MM_CONNECTION_SCHEMA_PartsAreUs" value="" />
7      <add key="MM_CONNECTION_CATALOG_PartsAreUs" value="" />
8    </appSettings>
9  </configuration>
```

To configure user access in the web.config file:

1. Open the PartsAreUs site's web.config file in Dreamweaver MX.

   It will look like Script 9.1.

2. Start a new line after the `</appSettings>` tag, but before the `</configuration>` tag.

3. In the new line, type the following:

   ```
   </appSettings>
   <system.web>
       <authentication mode="Forms">
   </configuration>
   ```

   This code opens, but doesn't yet close, a new element called `system.web`. The `system.web` element is used in web.config files to encapsulate many Web site settings such as how the Web server should handle debugging for the site and, as seen here, the Web site's security settings.

   Immediately following the `system.web` element is the opening tag for the `authentication` element. In this context, *authentication* is the process of determining if a user is who they say they are. We can choose from four authentication modes. You'll find a complete discussion of these modes in the "Authentication Modes" sidebar later in this chapter. Here we chose Forms, which is short for Web Forms. That means we'll use Web Forms to authenticate the users.

4. On the line below the code we just added, add the following highlighted code to define how our site should handle forms-based authentication and then to close the `authentication` element that we opened in Step 3.

   ```
   <authentication mode="Forms">
     <forms name=".PARTSAREUSAUTH"
           loginUrl="Login.aspx"
           protection="All" />
   </authentication>
   ```

The `forms` element seen here defines three settings for the Web server. The `name` attribute declares the name of the *cookie* (a file placed on the visiting user's computer for the duration of their visit) that will store authentication information. The `loginURL` attribute identifies the Web page to which the user should be redirected if they haven't been authenticated yet.

5. Add the following highlighted code below the closing `</authentication>` tag to define who should be granted access to the site.

   ```
   </authentication>
   <authorization>
     <allow users="?" />
   </authorization>
   ```

   The `authorization` element can contain two elements: `allow` and `deny`. Here we're only defining the `allow` element. Our use of the question mark (?) as the value of the `users` attribute tells the Web server that all anonymous, or unauthenticated, users may enter the site. By not defining the `deny` element, we're saying that we're not denying anyone access to the site.

   You might be wondering why we just gave everyone free access to the site when this chapter is about limiting access. We'll get to that in a moment.

6. Last, we need to close out the `system.web` element by typing the following highlighted code:

   ```
       </authorization>
     </system.web>
   </configuration>
   ```

   continues on next page

7. Having finished altering the PartsAreUs site's `web.config` file, compare it to **Script 9.2** to check for errors. Then save it.

✔ Tip

■ You may sometimes need to synchronize your local Dreamweaver site with your site's defined testing server in order to copy manually edited web.config files to the testing server. The process is covered in "To synchronize your site" in Chapter 3.

So why did we open the site to all unauthenticated users? Many of the pages on our site are ones in which we want everyone to see—only a few pages are ones in which we want to limit access. The reason we're explicitly stating that all users may access our Web Forms, even though the site is fully open by default, is that there can be multiple web.config files.

Web sites may have more than one web.config file because the Web server reads the web.config file at the root of the site (or more accurately, the root of the application, as discussed in Chapter 2) when the user first visits the Web site. If the user then visits a Web Form in a subdirectory of the site, the Web server will check for a web.config file in that subdirectory, too. If a web.config file exists in that subdirectory and redefines a setting defined in the root's web.config file, the redefinition will override the root configuration file's setting, but only for the files in that subdirectory.

The following two sets of instructions will make this more clear. First we'll organize the PartsAreUs site into a directory structure. Then we'll create a new web.config file in a subdirectory. In that new web.config file, we'll limit access to some of our Web Forms by redefining the `authorization` element.

Script 9.2 The system.web element of the web.config file contains the security settings for the site.

```
script

1  <configuration>
2    <appSettings>
3      <add key="MM_CONNECTION_HANDLER_PartsAreUs" value="sqlserver.htm" />
4      <add key="MM_CONNECTION_STRING_PartsAreUs" value="Persist Security Info=False;Data Source=.;
         Initial Catalog=PartsAreUs;User ID=sa;Password=;" />
5      <add key="MM_CONNECTION_DATABASETYPE_PartsAreUs" value="SQLServer" />
6      <add key="MM_CONNECTION_SCHEMA_PartsAreUs" value="" />
7      <add key="MM_CONNECTION_CATALOG_PartsAreUs" value="" />
8    </appSettings>
9    <system.web>
10     <authentication mode="Forms">
11       <forms name=".PARTSAREUSAUTH" loginUrl="Login.aspx" protection="All" />
12     </authentication>
13     <authorization>
14       <allow users="?" />
15     </authorization>
16   </system.web>
17 </configuration>
```

Authentication Modes

When setting the authentication mode in the web.config file of a Web site, you can choose from four types of authentication:

- **Windows.** This form of authentication will check the user's credentials against Windows user accounts. For this to work, the user must have an account already set up in Windows. This form of authentication is great for a site that will be accessed only by company employees, because employees must have an account anyway. However, this isn't such a good option when the list of users is constantly changing.

- **Forms.** This form of authentication requires a Web Form–based mechanism to be created in order to authenticate the users trying to log in. The forms element must be defined so that the Web server will know which Web Form to redirect unauthenticated users to. This option requires the most work to set up, but it's the most flexible form of authentication because the Web Form can be created to suit your needs, and the list of users may be stored in any way you wish. The Web Form we create in this chapter will have to check the user trying to log in against a list of users that we maintain ourselves.

- **Passport.** Microsoft Passport is a technology that accommodates the use of one username and password for all sites that utilize Passport authentication. This option requires the passport element to be defined so that the Web server knows where to redirect unauthenticated users. Sites that use this as their authentication mechanism let Microsoft store the list of users. So although users only need to create one username and password for all the sites they access that use Passport, many people don't trust Microsoft for storing security information. For that reason, you need to consider carefully whether Passport is the best option for your site's authentication mechanism.

- **None.** Opt for no authentication only when anonymous users are expected to visit the site.

To organize the PartsAreUs site:

1. In Dreamweaver, go to the Files panel group and open the Site panel for the PartsAreUs site. If you don't see it, press the F8 key to open it

   You'll see the root of the PartsAreUs site (**Figure 9.1**).

2. Select the root of the site.

3. From the Site panel, select File > New Folder.

   This will create a new "untitled" folder at the root of the PartsAreUs site.

4. Rename the folder Secured.

5. Click the AddPart.aspx file that we created in "To insert data into a database using a Web Form" in Chapter 8, and drag it into the Secured folder.

   The Update Files dialog box opens (**Figure 9.2**). It verifies that you really want to move the file and automatically update its hyperlinks.

6. Click the Update button.

   This moves the page and updates its links, and then closes the dialog box.

7. Click the PartEditor.aspx file that we created in "To update database data using a Web Form" in Chapter 8 and drag it into the Secured folder.

   The Update Files dialog box opens again.

8. Click the Update button.

   This moves the file and updates the links, and then closes the dialog box.

Now we have a site with one subdirectory called Secured. In that subdirectory will be the two Web Forms capable of altering the Parts table's data (**Figure 9.3**). Now we'll create the new web.config file in the Secured folder to limit access to those two Web Forms.

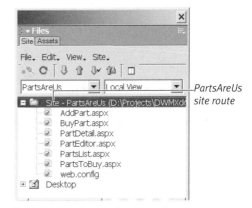

PartsAreUs site route

Figure 9.1 The PartsAreUs site on the Site panel shows all files within the site.

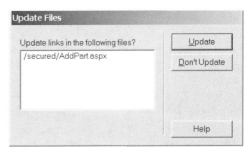

Figure 9.2 The AddPart.aspx file's Update Files dialog box verifies that you really want to move the file to the Secured folder.

Figure 9.3 This is the PartsAreUs site after moving the files into the Secured folder.

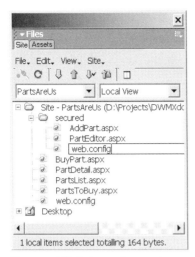

Figure 9.4 This is the newly named web.config file within the Secured folder.

To create a new web.config file:

1. Select the Secured folder. From the Site panel, select File > New File.

   A new file named "untitled.aspx" will appear under the Secured folder.

2. Rename untitled.aspx to "web.config."

   The web.config file appears in the Secured folder (**Figure 9.4**).

3. In the Site panel, double-click the web.config file that resides in the Secured folder.

   The file opens and is ready to be edited.

4. Select all of the default content in the file and delete it.

5. Then with the document blank, type the following:

   ```
   <configuration>
     <system.web>
       <authorization>
         <deny users="?" />
         <allow users="*" />
       </authorization>
     </system.web>
   </configuration>
   ```

   This code is similar to what we entered in the web.config file at the root of the PartsAreUs site in Step 5 of "To configure user access in the web.config file" earlier in this chapter. Here we're redefining the authorization setting for this subdirectory.

   The `deny users="?"` setting specifies that only users who have been authenticated will be allowed access. The `allow users="*"` setting permits access to all users.

   continues on next page

6. Save the web.config file. Then open the AddPart.aspx file in Dreamweaver, and press F12 to open it in your default browser.

Because you haven't been authenticated yet, you will be redirected by the Web server to the `Login.aspx` file as stated in the web.config file at the root of the site. However, because the file doesn't yet exist (we'll create it later in the chapter), you'll see an error in the browser (**Figure 9.5**).

The setting defined in Step 5 above denies access to unauthenticated users by setting the `deny` element's `users` attribute to a question mark (?). Also, users that have been authenticated are allowed access to the files in the Secured subdirectory because the `allow` element's `users` attribute was set to the asterisk (*).

Now that we've used multiple web.config files in setting up security, we need to provide a way for our users to log in.

In the next section, "Using XML files in Web Forms," we'll create the XML file that stores the list of users who are allowed to add and edit parts records. Then we'll create a Web Form to authenticate users listed in the file.

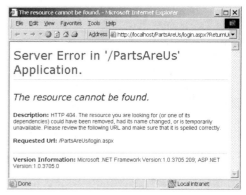

Figure 9.5 Here is the error message in Internet Explorer stating that the Login.aspx file could not be found.

LIMITING WEB FORM ACCESS

Using XML Files in Web Forms

We've decided to use XML to store data you can use in your Web Forms. Let's start by going over exactly what XML is.

XML is a file format that's been around for several years now and it's useful for storing textual data in a hierarchy. XML files consist of HTML-like tags that describe data. XML files must be written in a specific way: All data element tags must be closed; they must be correctly nested so they are closed in the opposite order that they were opened; and all data element attributes must be placed in quotes. When a file meets these requirements, it's called *well-formed*.

Well-formed XML documents are easy for both people and computers to read. This is different than file formats of the past, because files that are easily read by humans are rarely easily read by computers and vice versa.

However, the real power of XML is that as long as the file is well formed, it can contain any data you wish. You can make up the names of the elements yourself, or you can use predefined ones. In the case of the web.config file, there are specific elements and a set hierarchy that we must use: For example, the `appSettings` and `system.web` elements have to be within the `configuration` element.

To create our list of users identifying who may access the Web Forms we placed inside the Secured folder, we'll define our own XML elements. We'll adhere to the following format:

```
<secured_users>
  <user>
    <username />
    <password />
  </user>
</secured_users>
```

We're going to allow any number of user elements to exist inside the `secured_users` document root element, though each user element will contain only one `username` and one `password` element.

In the following instructions, we'll create the XML file that will list our secured users.

To create a list of users:

1. With the PartsAreUs site open in Dreamweaver, select File > New.

   The New Document dialog box opens (**Figure 9.6**).

2. In the Category list on the left, select Basic Page. Then in the list that appears on the right, select XML. Finally, click the Create button.

   The dialog box closes and a new XML document opens. The first line of the document contains the standard statement that appears at the top of most XML documents:

   ```
   <?xml version="1.0" encoding=
   "iso-8859-1"?>
   ```

   It simply states that this file is an XML file.

3. In the line immediately following this statement (Line 2), open the document root element by entering `<secured_users>`.

   Now with our document root defined, we can start adding users.

4. Add a user whose username is "ted" and password is "parts" by entering the following highlighted XML code:

   ```
   <secured_users>
     <user>
       <username>ted</username>
       <password>parts</password>
     </user>
   ```

Figure 9.6 Create a new XML document using the New Document dialog box.

Script 9.3 All users allowed to access the Secured folder will need to have a user element defined in the users.xml file.

```
1  <?xml version="1.0" encoding="iso-8859-1"?>
2    <secured_users>
3      <user>
4        <Username>ted</username>
5        <password>parts</password>
6      </user>
7      <user>
8        <username>tracey</username>
9        <password>areus</password>
10     </user>
11 </secured_users>
```

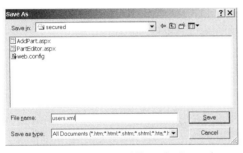

Figure 9.7 Save the users.xml file to the Secured folder.

5. Now let's add another user to the list: This time the username should be "tracey" and the password "areus."

```
    </user>
    <user>
      <username>tracey</username>
      <password>areus</password>
    </user>
```

6. To ensure the document is well formed, we have to close the `secured_users` element opened in Step 3.

```
    </user>
  </secured_users>
```

7. Now compare your file to **Script 9.3** to make sure there are no mistakes. Then save it in the Secured folder with the name "users.xml" (**Figure 9.7**).

In order to authenticate these two users, we'll need a Web Form that takes a user-name and a password and compares them to the values stored in the users.xml file. We'll cover that in the following section.

USING XML FILES IN WEB FORMS

Searching XML documents

For users to gain access to the two Web Forms in the secured subdirectory, they need to log in to the site. To log in, users must enter their usernames and passwords in a Web Form that we'll create. Then that Web Form will compare that username and password to the data in the users.xml file we created in "To create a list of users." If data in the file matches the values supplied by the user trying to log in, then the user will be granted access to the files located in the Secured subdirectory.

Before we discuss the code that will compare the information entered by the user to the data stored in the XML file, let's create the Web Form that will act as the login page. Then, because we already know we have valid user data stored in the users.xml file, we'll compare the user's login information against the data store in users.xml to authenticate the user. We'll now look at the code to authenticate the user.

To design the login page:

1. Create a new Web Form and call it Login.aspx. (If you need a refresher, the process of creating a new Web Form is outlined in "To create a new Web Form" in Chapter 4.)

2. From the Insert bar, click the Common tab, and then click the Show Code and Design Views icon to display both Code and Design views of the page (**Figure 9.8**).

3. In the page's code, just after the <body> tag, type the following to create a form in which to work:

   ```
   <form runat="server">
   </form>
   ```

   When you click in the Design view of the page, a red box will appear. It represents the form you just created.

Figure 9.8 See both code and design simultaneously by clicking the Show Code and Design Views icon in the Document toolbar.

4. With your cursor blinking inside the red box, go to the Common tab and click the Insert Table icon ▦ .

This opens the Insert Table dialog box (**Figure 9.9**).

5. Set Rows and Columns to 2. Set the Border to 1. Then set both the Cell Padding and Cell Spacing fields to 5. Click OK.

This creates the table and closes the dialog box.

6. Back in Design view, click into the left cell on the top row of the table. Type "Username" (**Figure 9.10**).

7. Move to the left cell of the table's bottom row and type "Password."

8. Click in the right cell of the table's top row. Then from the Insert bar, click on the ASP.NET tab, and click the asp:textbox icon (**Figure 9.11**).

The Tag Editor dialog box opens.

continues on next page

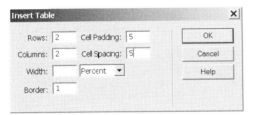

Figure 9.9 Use the Insert Table dialog box to easily create an HTML table.

Click here to insert the button login control

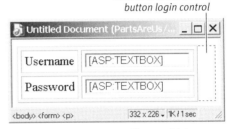

Figure 9.10 The login form will start with just a table that has labeled text fields.

asp.button icon　*asp.label icon*　*asp.textbox icon*

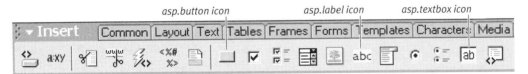

Figure 9.11 The ASP.NET tab has icons to insert the necessary controls for this form.

USING XML FILES IN WEB FORMS

9. In the ID text box, enter "txtUsername" and click OK (**Figure 9.12**).

The Tag Editor closes.

10. Back in Design view, click in the right cell of the table's bottom row. This is the last blank cell of the table. On the ASP.NET tab, click the asp:textbox icon [ab].

The Tag Editor dialog box opens (**Figure 9.13**).

11. In the ID text box, type "txtPassword." Then in the Text Mode drop-down menu, choose Password. Click OK to continue.

The Tag Editor closes.

12. In Design view, click in the white space to the right of the table to set the location for your next control. Then from the ASP.NET tab, click the asp:button icon [⌐].

Its Tag Editor opens.

13. In the ID text box, enter "btnLogin" and in the Text text box, type "Login." Click OK to continue.

The Tag Editor closes.

14. Back in Design view, click in the white space next to the btnLogin control and press Enter to move to the next line. Then from the ASP.NET tab, click the asp:label icon [abc].

The Tag Editor opens.

15. In the ID text box, type "lblErrorMsg" and in the Text text box, enter "Invalid username and password. Please try again." Then in the list on the left of the Tag Editor, select Style Information.

The screen will change to display the control's style setting fields (**Figure 9.14**).

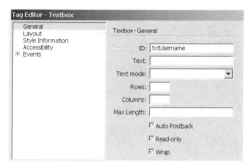

Figure 9.12 Use the Tag Editor to quickly create a text field.

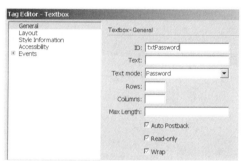

Figure 9.13 Change the password's Text mode to make the field a password field.

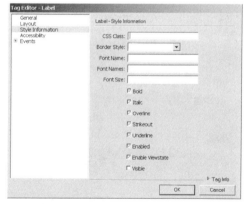

Figure 9.14 Make the lblErrorMsg control invisible by default using the Tag Editor.

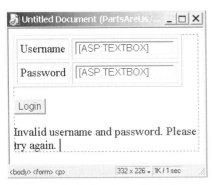

Figure 9.15 The Design view of the login.aspx page displays an error message here.

16. Back on the right side of the newly updated Tag Editor, clear the Visible check box. Click OK.

The Tag Editor closes.

You will see the error message in the design even though its Visibility is set to false (**Figure 9.15**).

17. Save the file.

Now that we know where all the data we'll need for our authentication check comes from, we can start investigating the login process.

XPath Syntax

XPath uses the hierarchical relationship of elements as the basis for its syntax. The most basic notation in XPath is a forward slash (/).

The forward slash by itself represents the root of the document, but it can be placed between the names of two elements to show that one will be found within the other. Using the users.xml document created in "To create a list of users," we can create the expression /secured_users/user to address all the user elements contained within the secured_users element that will be found at the root of the document.

However, if the forward slash is repeated (//), then we mean any element anywhere in the document that matches what we're looking for. An example would be //user, where we want all elements named user found anywhere in the document, whether they're under the secured_users element or not. But this syntax is slower, because the search isn't limited to the secured_users element's contents.

Limitations are placed on search statements by using the square brackets ([]). The XPath expression //user [username = 'ted'] would find user elements anywhere in the documents that contained a username element whose value was ted.

If our sample XML document instead had username as an attribute of the user element, we would need to alter the syntax slightly. The '@' symbol is used in XPath to identify attributes, so the new XPath expression would be //user [@username = 'ted'].

XPath is a complex syntax and is used in many ways we're not able to fully describe here. If you need more information, there are many books and Web sites dedicated to it. One good book on the subject is *XPath and XPointer*, by John E. Simpson, from O'Reilly Press.

We already know that we need to search the users.xml file for a user element containing username and password elements that match the username and password values entered in the login page. We just need to know how to search an XML document.

We can search an XML document by first loading it into the computer's memory. After it's in memory, we'll use a function called SelectSingleNode to search the document for a single user element. The function name includes the word *node,* because when working with an XML element in code, that element is referred to as a node. There's also a function called SelectNodes if you're looking for a collection of elements, but we won't need that for our login process.

The syntax used to define what you're looking for in an XML document is called XPath (it stands for XML Path Language). We'll create an XPath expression as a parameter to the SelectSingleNode function. That expression will define the search for a user element. Then we'll limit the search in the XPath expression to make a match only when the username and password elements' values match those entered in the Web Form. The "XPath Syntax" sidebar describes XPath in more detail.

In the following instructions, we'll finish coding the Login.aspx page we created in "To design the login page." When we're done, we'll have a fully functioning login page.

To write code to authenticate a user:

1. In the code of the Login.aspx file we created in "To design the login page," place your cursor just in front of the <html> tag at the top of the file. Then from the Insert bar's ASP.NET tab, click the Import Namespace icon to automatically insert the following code into the page (**Figure 9.16**):

   ```
   <%@ Import Namespace="" %>
   ```

2. Alter the code that has been automatically inserted into the page so that the System.Xml namespace is imported. The result will look like this:

   ```
   <%@ Import Namespace="System.Xml" %>
   ```

   System.Xml is the namespace that includes all XML classes.

3. Create a new line after the code you just entered, and then on the ASP.NET tab, again click the Import Namespace icon to automatically insert code.

4. Alter the Namespace attribute to Namespace="System.Xml.Xpath" The result will look like this:

   ```
   <%@ Import Namespace="System.Xml" %>
   <%@ Import Namespace="System.Xml.XPa
   th" %>
   ```

   This namespace will give us access to classes that we'll need in order to search the XML file for the user's information during a login attempt.

Import Namespace icon   Page_Load icon

Figure 9.16 The ASP.NET tab has icons to insert default code for you.

5. Repeat this process two more times to import the `System.Web.Security` and `System.IO` namespaces so that the code importing namespaces includes four separate statements, as follows:

```
<%@ Import Namespace="System.Xml" %>
<%@ Import Namespace="System.Xml.XPa
th" %>
<%@ Import Namespace="System.Web.Sec
urity"%>
<%@ Import Namespace="System.IO" %>
```

The `System.Web.Security` namespace is the location in which the classes relating to security are defined, and the `System.IO` namespace is the location in which the classes needed to open and read the users.xml file are defined. (We created that file in "To create a list of users," earlier in this chapter.)

6. Now that you've imported the necessary namespaces, move your cursor down the page to just in front of the `</head>` tag. Then on the ASP.NET tab, click the Page_Load icon 🖺.

This inserts the default `Page_Load` function that looks like the following :

```
<script runat="server">
protected void Page_Load(Object Src,
EventArgs E)
{
   if (!IsPostBack) DataBind();
}
</script>
```

7. Alter the default `Page_Load` function to look like the following:

```
protected void Page_Load( Object Src,
EventArgs E)
{
   if( IsPostBack )
   {
     lblErrorMsg.Visible = false;
   }
}
```

This code verifies that when the page is in post-back mode (after the btnLogin control is clicked by the user, causing the page to post back to the server), the lblErrorMsg control is not visible.

8. On the line following the statement setting the lblErrorMsg's `Visible` property to `false`, create a new XMLDocument object like so:

```
lblErrorMsg.Visible = false;
XmlDocument xmlDoc = new XmlDocu
ment();
```

The `xmlDoc` variable created here will be a reference to an object that holds the contents of the users.xml document in memory so that we can search it.

9. Now we need to load the users.xml document into the xmlDoc object. Insert the following lines of code:

```
XmlDocument xmlDoc = new
XmlDocument();
xmlDoc.Load( new FileStream(
Server.MapPath( "users.xml" ),
FileMode.Open, FileAccess.Read ) );
```

In order to load the users.xml document, we needed to enlist the help of the FileStream class. The FileStream class allows us to read data from users.xml. To create a new FileStream object, the FileStream class constructor needs the path to the document we're loading. The `Server.MapPath` function provides that. The FileStream class also needs to know what we're doing with the file. You see from the `FileMode.Open` statement that we're opening it. And it needs the access type it should use when trying to open the file. We only want to read the users.xml file right now, so we put `FileAccess.Read` as the desired access style.

We have the users.xml file loaded into our `xmlDoc` variable, so now we can search it.

continues on next page

USING XML FILES IN WEB FORMS

10. Enter the following code on the next line of the code you just entered:

```
XmlNode xmlNode =
xmlDoc.SelectSingleNode(
"/secured_users/user [ username = '"
+ txtUsername.Text + "' and password
= '" + txtPassword.Text + "' ]" );
```

As we said before, searching an XML document is done with an XPath expression. XPath searches XML by describing the relationships between elements and putting limitations on those relationships in the expression to reduce the data returned by the search. Here we're searching for a user element within the secured_users root element. That's the "/secured_users/user" part. Then we're limiting that search to just the user that contains username and password elements that match the "txtUsername" and "txtPassword" controls' values from the Web Form.

If there's a match for the search, the user element will be returned as a reference in the xmlNode variable. If there isn't a match, the xmlNode variable will be set to null.

11. Having stored the result of the search in the xmlNode variable. Let's use that variable's value to see if we should grant access to the secured Web pages.

```
if ( xmlNode != null )
{
  FormsAuthentication.RedirectFro
  mLoginPage( "*" , false );
}
else
{
  lblErrorMsg.Visible = true;
}
```

This code checks if xmlNode is not equal to null, meaning that a user element was found in the search. If that's the case, then the user is granted access to the secured page they tried to open and are redirected back to it. This is accomplished using the following command:

```
FormsAuthentication.RedirectFr
omLoginPage
```

This command performs all the actions required once a user has been authenticated, including redirecting the user to the page they originally requested.

The code in the else statement is run if xmlNode is equal to null. In that case the error message in the lblErrorMsg control is shown to the user.

12. Compare your code to **Script 9.4** to make sure you didn't miss anything, and save the file.

That's it! You can check that your login page works by pressing F12 to open one of the files in the Secured folder in the browser. You should be automatically redirected the way you were when you tested the results of "To create a new web.config file," but this time the Login.aspx page exists. Use the credentials of one of the users defined in the users.xml file to be redirected back to the secured file you tried to access.

✔ Tip

■ If you browse directly to the Login.aspx file and successfully log in, you'll be redirected to the default.aspx file whether you have a file by that name or not.

In this chapter we've implemented a custom security framework for our Web site by using the security features of ASP.NET. In the next chapter we'll start learning how to write our own ASP.NET controls.

Script 9.4 Opening and searching an XML file only requires a few lines of code, though they are complex. However, authorizing a user to access secured areas of a site is extremely easy.

```
1 <%@ Page Language="C#" ContentType="text/html" ResponseEncoding="iso-8859-1" %>
2 <%@ Import Namespace="System.Xml" %>
3 <%@ Import Namespace="System.Xml.XPath" %>
4 <%@ Import Namespace="System.Web.Security" %>
5 <%@ Import Namespace="System.IO" %>
6 <html>
7 <head>
8 <title>Untitled Document</title>
9 <meta http-equiv="Content-Type" content="text/html; charset=iso-8859-1">
10 <script runat="server">
11 protected void Page_Load(Object Src, EventArgs E)
12 {
13   if( IsPostBack )
14   {
15     lblErrorMsg.Visible = false;
16
17     XmlDocument xmlDoc = new XmlDocument();
18     xmlDoc.Load( new FileStream( Server.MapPath("users.xml" ), FileMode.Open, FileAccess.Read) );
19     XmlNode xmlNode = xmlDoc.SelectSingleNode( "/secured_users/user [ username = '" + txtUsern
       ame.Text + "' and password = '" + txtPassword.Text + "' ]" );
20
21     if ( xmlNode != null)
22     {
23       FormsAuthentication.RedirectFromLoginPage("*", false);
24     }
25     else
26     {
27       lblErrorMsg.Visible = true;
28     }
29   }
30 }
31 </script></head>
32 <body>
33 <form runat="server">
34   <table border="1" cellspacing="5" cellpadding="5">
35     <tr>
36       <td>Username</td>
37       <td><asp:textbox ID="txtUsername" runat="server" /></td>
38     </tr>
39     <tr>
40       <td>Password</td>
41       <td><asp:textbox ID="txtPassword" runat="server" TextMode="Password" /></td>
42     </tr>
43   </table>
44   <p>
45     <asp:button ID="btnLogin" runat="server" Text="Login" />
46   </p>
47   <p>
48     <asp:label ID="lblErrorMsg" runat="server" Text="Invalid username and password. Please try
       again." Visible="false"></asp:label>
49   </p>
50 </form>
51 </body>
52 </html>
```

AUTHORING CUSTOM USER CONTROLS

Keeping a consistent look and feel throughout a Web site requires more than just using the same color scheme and fonts on all the pages. It requires that recurring elements, such as the header and the navigation bar, appear the same on all the site's pages. Because these elements need to be identical for every page, it's most efficient to write their HTML definitions only once.

The common technique of separating recurring elements of a Web site's pages into their own files is, in fact, one of the first ways Web pages were made dynamic. After separating them, developers reincorporate them into their Web pages dynamically by referencing these element-definition files using an Include command. When the Web server sends the page to a visiting user, it replaces each Include command with the contents of the file to which the command refers. The dynamic assembly of the page appears seamless to the site visitor, and the developer is spared having to write and maintain the same code for every page.

In ASP.NET, however, there's yet another alternative. Developers can use custom user controls to define recurring page elements instead of include files. Custom controls are much more powerful than include files because they share the same characteristics as Web Forms, such as ASP.NET controls, event processing, and dynamic programmability. However, user controls can't be viewed directly in a browser; for security reasons they are accessible only from within Web Forms.

In this chapter we'll create our own custom user controls, ranging from simple ones that show only HTML to fully dynamic controls that handle their own events. After creating each one, we'll reference it from a Web Form just as easily as we reference other controls, such as asp:textbox.

Creating and Using Custom Controls

In addition, to using include files for HTML that needs to be repeated, developers have also used include files as function libraries when working in ASP to avoid having to replicate commonly used functions. Function libraries provide developers with a technique for organizing and grouping code modules. So by using include files for common functions, developers can more easily reuse and maintain the code, since coding changes only have to be made one time.

However, there's another technique for replicating functions that obviates the need for include files. Using class libraries from Microsoft and Macromedia, we now can use namespaces to achieve the same results that include files provide. You may remember that in Chapter 8 we showed you how to reference namespaces for gaining access to predefined classes. In "To write advanced data insertion code" in that chapter, we demonstrated how namespaces are used to organize libraries of predefined code. In addition, we can create our own unique namespaces to organize our own class files, which we discuss in Chapter 11.

While include files remain a viable technique for storing reusable definitions of commonly used page elements, ASP.NET user controls have their own advantages, which you'll discover in this section. We're also going to take a look at a handy bit of functionality available to us in ASP.NET called *caching*, which makes our pages execute faster by reducing the amount of work the Web server must do to serve our pages.

Creating a user control

User controls can contain many of the same elements as Web Forms and are considered almost like mini- Web Forms. Because they're meant to be plugged into the body of full Web Forms, user controls don't contain `<html>` and `<body>` tags. But they can contain other HTML and standard ASP.NET server controls such as asp:textbox and asp:button.

Most often, user controls are used to define things like page headers and navigation bars that will appear in many of a site's Web Forms. In the next exercise we'll create a user control—a page header that displays a title and the current system time formatted in a table. Then we'll insert the user control into a page. To use the control, we'll reference it inside of a Web form.

To create a user control:

1. Create a Web Form. (If you need a refresher, see "To create a new Web Form" in Chapter 4.)

2. Make both the code and design visible by clicking the Document toolbar's Show Code and Design Views icon (**Figure 10.1**). Then save the new page as "Header.ascx."

    Notice that the extension is .ascx, not .aspx. Using a *c* instead of a *p* indicates that the file is a control, not a page. Not only does this help us identify controls when looking at a list of files, but it also keeps users from being able to browse directly to our user controls. The Web server won't be able to serve up a user control directly.

Figure 10.1 The Show Code and Design Views icon on the Document toolbar.

Figure 10.2 Click the Insert Table icon on the Common tab to open the Insert Table dialog box.

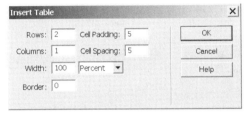

Figure 10.3 The Insert Table dialog box lets you create the Header control's table.

3. Go into the code, where you'll find the standard ASP.NET page declaration, which looks like the following:

`<%@ Page Language="C#" ContentType= "text/html" ResponseEncoding= "iso-8859-1" %>`

The standard declaration tells the Web server that this file is a page. We need to change this declaration to inform the Web server that this file is a control.

4. Alter the code by changing Page to Control and deleting the `ContentType` and `ResponseEncoding` attributes. It will end up looking like this:

`<%@ Control Language="C#" %>`

We deleted the `ContentType` and `Response-Encoding` attributes, because those declarations will be made by the Web Form in which we'll place this control.

5. Still in the code, delete everything below the declaration statement that we just altered in Step 4.

We won't need any of it because this is a user control, not a Web Form.

6. Now click in the design area. Go to the Insert bar, click on the Common tab, and then click the Insert Table icon (**Figure 10.2**).

This opens the Insert Table dialog box.

7. In the Insert Table dialog box, set Rows to 2 and Columns to 1 (**Figure 10.3**). Also change Width to 100, and in its related drop-down list select Percent. Then change Border to 0, and set both Cell Padding and Cell Spacing to 5. Click OK.

This creates the table and closes the dialog box.

8. Click in the table's top cell in Design view and enter "Page Header."

continues on next page

CREATING AND USING CUSTOM CONTROLS

9. Highlight the text you just typed, and then right-click it to open a context menu. In the menu's Paragraph Format submenu, select Heading 1 (**Figure 10.4**).

10. With the cursor still positioned in the cell, go to the Property inspector and from the Horizontal Alignment drop-down list, select Center (**Figure 10.5**).

11. Place your cursor in the second row of the table. Then on the Property inspector, select Horizontal Alignment > Right.

12. Enter "The time is: " in that row.

13. Go into the table control's code and find the HTML that defines the cell we were just working on. It should look like the following:

`<td align="right">The time is: </td>`

Place your cursor just in front of the `</td>` tag and type:

`<%= System.DateTime.Now.ToString() %>`

This will cause the Web server to place the current date and time formatted as a String into the control at this location. The resulting cell definition should look like this:

`<td align="right">The time is: <%= System.DateTime.Now.ToString() %></td>`

14. Compare your completed file against **Script 10.1** to check for inconsistencies, and then save it.

To avoid the error of the page not being on the testing server later on, browse to the control by pressing F12. This will cause an error message, "This type of page is not served," to appear in the browser, but it will force Dreamweaver to upload to file to the testing server.

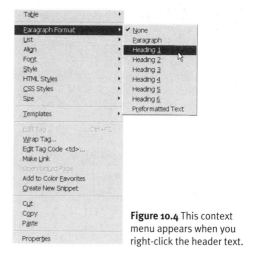

Figure 10.4 This context menu appears when you right-click the header text.

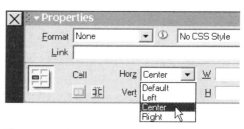

Figure 10.5 Selecting Center from the Property inspector's Horizontal Alignment drop-down list lets you position the text.

Script 10.1 This simple user control will display a table showing the current time.

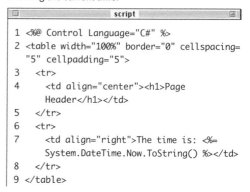

```
1  <%@ Control Language="C#" %>
2  <table width="100%" border="0" cellspacing=
   "5" cellpadding="5">
3    <tr>
4      <td align="center"><h1>Page
       Header</h1></td>
5    </tr>
6    <tr>
7      <td align="right">The time is: <%=
       System.DateTime.Now.ToString() %></td>
8    </tr>
9  </table>
```

Figure 10.6 View just the page's code by clicking the Show Code View icon on the Document toolbar.

To incorporate a user control:

1. Create a new Web Form and call it "Container.aspx."

    This Web Form will contain the user control we just created in the previous steps.

2. Make the code visible by clicking the Document toolbar's Show Code View icon (**Figure 10.6**).

    In the code at the top of the file, you'll find the standard ASP.NET page declaration:

    ```
    <%@ Page Language="C#" ContentType=
    "text/html" ResponseEncoding=
    "iso-8859-1" %>
    ```

    Since this declaration defines the ContentType and ResponseEncoding attributes, we don't need to define them in our control (.ascx) files.

3. Create a blank line below the page declaration, and type the following code:

    ```
    <%@ Register TagPrefix="VQP"
    TagName="Header" Src="Header.ascx" %>
    ```

    This command registers the Header.ascx control we created earlier and assigns it a Tag Name of Header. The TagPrefix attribute states the namespace we'll use to ensure that our control's name is unique. Here we set it to "VQP". The TagName is the name we'll use when we need to reference our control in this Web Form. It can be anything, as long as it's unique within the TagPrefix namespace. For obvious reasons, we set it to "Header". Then the Src attribute identifies the file that contains our control's definition.

continues on next page

CREATING AND USING CUSTOM CONTROLS

4. Now move your cursor down to just after the <body> tag. Type the following to locate the control at the top of the page:

```
<VQP:Header id="ctrlHeader" runat=
"server" />
```

See how we used the values from the TagPrefix and TagName attributes set in Step 3? We also had to give the control a unique ID for this page and set the runat attribute to "server".

5. That's it! Compare your page to **Script 10.2** and then save it. Browse to the file by pressing F12. You should see in your Container.aspx file the contents of your Header.ascx control.

Caching

In computer terms, a *cache* is a storage location in memory with a fast access time. It's used for storing frequently used files or data in order to speed up the server's response time. ASP.NET allows developers to cache the results from the execution of whole Web Forms or just individual user controls. When the same Web Form or control is subsequently requested, the results are retrieved from the cached location without having to be rerun. This enables users to get their Web pages faster. It also eases the load on the Web server, because the cached page or user control doesn't have to be rendered into HTML every time it's accessed.

To demonstrate caching, we're going to alter our Header.ascx user control and Container.aspx Web Form.

Script 10.2 To use a custom user control, register its definition file with a namespace and name. Then simply use it in the page as if it were any other control.

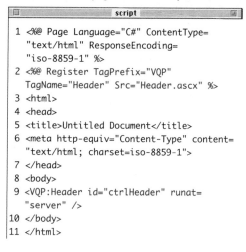

```
1  <%@ Page Language="C#" ContentType=
   "text/html" ResponseEncoding=
   "iso-8859-1" %>
2  <%@ Register TagPrefix="VQP"
   TagName="Header" Src="Header.ascx" %>
3  <html>
4  <head>
5  <title>Untitled Document</title>
6  <meta http-equiv="Content-Type" content=
   "text/html; charset=iso-8859-1">
7  </head>
8  <body>
9  <VQP:Header id="ctrlHeader" runat=
   "server" />
10 </body>
11 </html>
```

To cache a user control:

1. Open the Header.ascx control we created in the first stepped list in this chapter. Make sure the code is visible by clicking the Document toolbar's Show Code View icon .

2. Move your cursor to the end of the first line in the file and press Enter.

   This creates a new blank line on the second line of the file.

3. In the second line, type the following:

   ```
   <%@ OutputCache Duration="10"
   VaryByParam="none" %>
   ```

   This directive states that the control should be cached by the Web server for 10 seconds. It also sets the `VaryByParam` attribute to `"none"`, which indicates that the page won't have multiple versions cached. We can store multiple versions of a control in cache if the user control's content is dependent on `get` or `post` parameters, but we'd need to list those parameters here for that to occur. The `get` or `post` parameters are those that come into the page on the Querystring (attached to the end of a URL) or via form submission, respectively. The "OutputCache Page Directive" sidebar discusses other available caching options.

4. Save the Header.ascx user control, and press F12 to force Dreamweaver to upload the changed file to the testing server.

   Remember you'll get an error here because you aren't allowed to browse the user control directly.

To test a cached user control:

1. Open the Container.aspx Web Form in Dreamweaver, and make sure the code is visible by clicking the Document toolbar's Show Code View icon .

2. In the page's code, place your cursor just in front of the `</body>` tag, and type the following:

   ```
   Really the time is:
   <%= System.DateTime.Now.ToString() %>
   ```

   You should recognize this from the Header.ascx file. This code has the Web server place the current time into the page when you browse to it.

3. Save the Container.aspx file and press F12.

   This will open the page in your default browser; you should see that the time in the header is the same as the time in the body of the page. However, if you press F5 to refresh the page, the two times will be different because the header has been cached by the Web server and thus not reprocessed. Press F5 again after the 10 seconds has passed, and the two times will match once again.

Caching can be set for longer periods of time simply by increasing the number of seconds stated in the `Duration` attribute of the OuputCache page directive. If our content had been dependent on `get` or `post` parameter values, we could have stated which parameters should cause the server to re-render the control for those values. This would have caused multiple copies of the control to be stored in cache memory, each for the specified duration. There are more attributes available that we could have set, but we didn't need them here.

The OutputCache Page Directive

Caching is available both for full Web Forms and for user controls alone. When caching is enabled, the page or control is rendered into HTML upon its first use and then stored in the Web server's cache memory for fast access for the rest of the defined storage duration. This relieves the Web server of having to process and render the page or control every time a user requests it within the defined caching duration. When the duration runs out, the process starts over.

To provide for dynamic content in pages and controls, multiple versions of the page or control can be stored in the cache. These versions are differentiated by values of the get or post parameters, by browser type, by custom strings stated in the global.asax file, by HTTP headers, or by user control properties, which are covered in the Dynamic User Controls section of this chapter.

Here is a list of the available attributes for the OutputCache page directive:

- **Duration.** A required attribute that sets the amount of time in seconds the Web Form or user control is to be stored in the cache memory before being refreshed upon the next request.

- **VaryByParam.** An attribute that lists the get or post parameters, separated by semicolons. The parameters in this list should affect the contents of the Web Form or user control. For each value of each stated parameter, the cache will store a new copy of the Web Form or user control for the specified duration. This will allow all versions of the dynamic Web Form or user control to be cacheable. If only one version will exist for the Web Form or user control, this attribute's value may be set to "none". This attribute is required for Web Forms. It's also required for user controls unless the VaryByControl attribute is defined.

- **VaryByControl.** This attribute lists the user control properties, separated by semicolons. For each value a listed property is set to, the user control will be re-rendered and stored in the cache for the defined duration.

- **VaryByCustom.** This attribute's value may be set to browser in order for a different version of the Web Form or user control to be cached for each browser type. Alternatively, a custom value may be used, but that requires that the HttpApplication.GetVaryByCustomString method be overridden in the global.asax file.

- **VaryByHeader.** HTTP/1.1 cache-control headers define the types of data a browser can send and receive. This attribute lets a developer cache different versions of a Web Form or user control depending on those headers.

Dynamic User Controls

Being able to cache multiple versions of user controls is just one of the ways that ASP.NET user controls go beyond the capabilities of include files. Another advantage ASP.NET user controls have is that they can contain dynamic content. In this section, we show you how.

So far in this book, we've only used properties on controls such the asp:label control, and mostly we've used the Text property, a shared property common to various controls including asp:label and asp:textbox. Changing the value of the Text property in code lets us dynamically change the text displayed to visitors.

You may also remember that properties such as the Text property of the asp:label control map directly to the `Text` attribute of the asp:label control in the markup. To see an example of what we mean, the following is the markup of an asp:label control with its `Text` attribute set to `"Sample Text"`:

```
<asp:label id="lbl" text="Sample Text" />
```

Then in the code we have access to the Text property, which allows us to change the text from "Sample Text" to "Changed Text":

```
lbl.Text = "Changed Text";
```

We can create custom user controls that expose properties in just the same way. Doing so allows us to customize the user control either in code through the defined property or in markup through an attribute associated with the property. The following instructions show you how.

To create a dynamic user control:

1. Open the Header.ascx file in Dreamweaver, and make sure the code is visible by clicking the Document toolbar's Show Code View icon ◆ .

   (We created the Header.ascx user control in "To create a user control" earlier in this chapter.)

2. Delete the line at the top of the file that looks like this:

   ```
   <%@ OutputCache Duration="10"
   VaryByParam="none" %>
   ```

   This is the OutputCache page directive that we just added in "To cache a user control." We're removing it because we no longer want to cache this control.

3. Now with your cursor in the second line, just before the `<table>` tag, enter the following to create a script section for your control:

   ```
   <script language="C#" runat="server">
   </script>
   ```

4. In the script section, between the opening `<script>` and closing `</script>` tags, type the following lines of code to define two private variables:

   ```
   private String HeaderText = "Page
   Header";
   private String BGColor = "lightgrey";
   ```

   These two variables are defined as `private`, which means no code outside of this user control can change their values. We will be using them to store values used for setting the text and the background color of our header table. We set default values in case the developer who incorporates this control into a Web Form doesn't set them.

continues on next page

5. In the next line, below the code we just added, enter the following code to expose our private variables through property definitions:

```
public String Text
{
  get { return HeaderText; }
  set { HeaderText = value; }
}
public String Color
{
  get { return BGColor; }
  set { BGColor = value; }
}
```

These properties define specialized functions used to store (**set**) and retrieve (**get**) values assigned to our private variables. Defining properties is preferred over defining variables, because properties are more secure and provide a standardized interface, even though extra data manipulation may be needed to validate the values before they're set. We didn't need to manipulate the data here, but we could have added logic to verify that the value being stored for our member variable was acceptable. This is done by adding the verification code directly inside the set method of the property definition.

Script 10.3 Make a user control dynamic via properties by defining the code for those properties to be set and writing the property values out as HTML.

```
 1 <%@ Control Language="C#" %>
 2 <script language="C#" runat="server">
 3 private String HeaderText = "Page Header";
 4 private String BGColor = "lightgrey";
 5 public String Text
 6 {
 7   get { return HeaderText; }
 8   set { HeaderText = value; }
 9 }
10 public String Color
11 {
12   get { return BGColor; }
13   set { BGColor = value; }
14 }
15 </script>
16 <table width="100%" border="0"
    cellspacing="5" cellpadding="5"
    bgcolor="<%= BGColor %>" >
17   <tr>
18     <td align="center">
19         <h1><%= HeaderText %></h1>
20     </td>
21   </tr>
22   <tr>
23     <td align="right">
24         The time is:
25         <%= System.DateTime.Now.ToSt
           ring() %>
26     </td>
27   </tr>
28 </table>
```

6. We need to change the control's content a little to make use of our new properties. Add the `bgcolor` attribute to the `<table>` tag, and set it equal to "`<%= BGColor %>`" in order to dynamically set the background color of the table. The resulting change will look like this:

```
<table width="100%" border="0"
cellspacing="5" cellpadding="5"
bgcolor="<%= BGColor %>" >
```

7. Then find where the text of the first row's cell is set to "`Page Header`". Highlight that text and replace it with `<%= HeaderText %>`. The result will cause the definition of the first row's cell to look like this:

```
<td align="center">
  <h1><%= HeaderText %></h1>
</td>
```

8. You can check your file against **Script 10.3** and then save the file. Make sure to press F12 to force Dreamweaver to copy the file to the testing server, even though doing so will cause an error in the browser.

To incorporate a dynamic user control:

1. Open the Container.aspx file in Dreamweaver, and make sure the code is visible by clicking the Document toolbar's Show Code View icon .

(We created the Container.aspx user control in "To incorporate a user control" earlier in this chapter.)

2. In the code of the page, place your cursor just after the `<body>` tag and type the following:

```
<form runat="server">
```

3. Then move your cursor to just before the `</body>` tag. Close the form you just opened by typing `</form>`.

4. Place your cursor just before the `</form>` tag you just added. From the Insert bar, click on the ASP.NET tab, and then click the asp:button icon (**Figure 10.7**).

The Tag Editor opens.

continues on next page

Figure 10.7 Insert an asp:button control by clicking its icon on the Insert bar's ASP.NET tab.

5. In the Tag Editor, set the ID to "btnChangeProperties" and the Text to "Change Properties." Then in the list on the left of the Tag Editor, click Events. This will open up a large text box on the right in which you should type "btnChangeProperties_OnClick" (**Figure 10.8**).

6. Move up to just before the </head> tag, and type the following code:

```
<script language="C#" runat="server">
void btnChangeProperties_OnClick(
Object sender, EventArgs E )
{
    ctrlHeader.Text = "Changed Text";
    ctrlHeader.Color = "White";
}
</script>
```

This code is the definition of the OnClick event handler for the btnChangeProperties control. It will change our header control's Text and Color properties when activated by a click of the button.

7. Now go to the code defining the ctrlHeader control and add the Text attribute. Set it to "Original Text" so the resulting tag will look like this:

```
<VQP:Header id="ctrlHeader" Text=
"Original Text" runat="server" />
```

We did this to set the user control's text for when the page is loaded. We're not using the default value of the user control's text since we'll be modifying this value programmatically. But we are accepting the default color.

8. After comparing your file to **Script 10.4**, save it and press F12 open the page in your default browser (**Figure 10.9**).

When you click the Change Properties button, you'll see different text and color settings for the user control (**Figure 10.10**).

Figure 10.8 Set the button's click event handler in the Tag Editor. OnClick is the default event for an asp:button control.

Script 10.4 Web Forms can manipulate the properties of a user control via markup as well as code.

```
1  <%@ Page Language="C#" ContentType=
   "text/html" ResponseEncoding=
   "iso-8859-1" %>
2  <%@ Register TagPrefix="VQP" TagName=
   "Header" Src="Header.ascx" %>
3  <html>
4  <head>
5  <title>Untitled Document</title>
6  <meta http-equiv="Content-Type" content=
   "text/html; charset=iso-8859-1">
7  <script language="C#" runat="server">
8  void btnChangeProperties_OnClick(Object
   sender, EventArgs E)
9  {
10   ctrlHeader.Text = "Changed Text";
11   ctrlHeader.Color = "White";
12 }
13 </script>
14 </head>
15 <body>
16 <form runat="server">
17 <VQP:Header id="ctrlHeader"
   Text="Original Text" runat="server" />
18 Really the time is: <%=
   System.DateTime.Now.ToString() %>
19 <asp:button ID="btnChangeProperties"
   runat="server" Text="Change Properties"
   OnClick="btnChangeProperties_OnClick" />
20 </form>
21 </body>
22 </html>
```

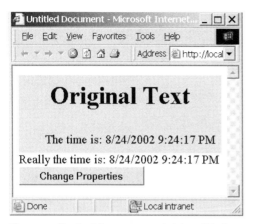

Figure 10.9 The Container.aspx page in Internet Explorer before the Change Properties button is clicked.

Figure 10.10 The Container.aspx page in Internet Explorer after the Change Properties button is clicked.

Event-handling user controls

User controls also can be configured to handle events. If you need a refresher—events are messages initiated by objects such as asp:button controls. Those messages are then intercepted by the Web server, which is configured to detect the event message and invoke a handler for that event. An *event handler* is a function created specifically to run when that event occurs.

Web Forms are able to handle events like button clicks. We saw an example of this in Steps 5 and 6 of the last exercise. That's because user controls share many of the same characteristics and elements as Web Forms, including the ability to handle events.

This capability makes user controls truly stand-alone elements of a page. In other words, they can be easily reused because they carry their functionality with them. They don't require each page they're referenced by to implement their code for them.

In the following list, we show you how to create a user control that handles its own events. First, it will have the visitor enter a name. Then the user control will save that name into a *cookie,* a small data file that a Web site places on the visitor's computer for the duration of the visit. Then the user control will use the data in the cookie to welcome the visitor into the site by name for the rest of that person's visit. This is an example of personalization.

We should point out, however, that this form of personalization doesn't work with all visitors, since individuals can set their computers to prevent a Web server from placing cookies onto their systems. Nevertheless, the use of cookies is so prevalent that most people leave the ability to write cookies enabled.

To handle events in a user control:

1. Create a Web Form so that you can change it into a user control and save it as "Personalizer.ascx." (If you need to refresh your memory, see "To create a user control" earlier in this chapter.)

   Make both the code and design visible by clicking the Document toolbar's Show Code and Design Views icon ⎄.

2. In the page's code, change the page declaration so that it reads like the following:

   `<%@ Control Language="C#" %>`

   Delete the rest of the page so that this code is the only thing left.

3. Click in the design of the page. From the Insert bar, click on the Common tab, and then click on the Insert Table icon ▦.

   This opens the Insert Table dialog box (**Figure 10.11**).

4. Set Rows to 2 and Columns to 3, and clear the Width field. Then set the Border to 1 and both Cell Spacing and Cell Padding to 5. Click OK.

   This creates the table and closes the dialog box.

5. In the page's Design view, select all three columns in the table's bottom row. Then in the Property inspector, click the Merge Selected Cells Using Spans icon (**Figure 10.12**).

   This will merge all the cells of the bottom row into one cell.

6. Now click in the left cell of the table's top row, and enter "What's your name?"

7. Move over one cell so that your cursor is blinking in the top row's middle cell. From the Insert bar, click on the ASP.NET tab, and then click on the asp:textbox icon (**Figure 10.13**) to start the Tag Editor.

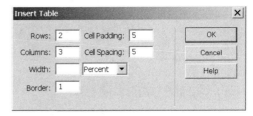

Figure 10.11 The Insert Table dialog box for the Personalizer.ascx user control.

Figure 10.12 Merge table cells using the Property inspector.

Figure 10.13 You can insert ASP.NET controls and code by using icons such as the asp:textbox on the ASP.NET tab.

Figure 10.14 Use the btnSetName control's Tag Editor to set the OnClick event handler.

8. In the Tag Editor, set the ID to "txtName" and click OK.

9. Move over one more cell so that your cursor is blinking in the right cell of the top row. From the ASP.NET tab, click on the asp:button icon ⊒ to start the Tag Editor.

10. In the Tag Editor, set the ID to "btnSetName" and Text to "Save." Then in the list on the left of the Tag Editor, click Events. This will open up a large text box on the right in which you should type "btnSetName_OnClick" (**Figure 10.14**).

11. Move your cursor to the bottom row's cell. From the ASP.NET tab, click the asp:label icon to start the Tag Editor.

12. In the Tag Editor, set the ID to "lblName" and click OK. We'll be setting this control's text dynamically later.

13. Go into the code and add the `ID` and `runat` attributes to the `<table>` tag as follows:

```
<table border="1" cellspacing="5"
cellpadding="5"
id="tbl" runat="server">
```

This will give us access to the table in code.

14. Add the `ID` attribute to the first of the table's `<tr>` tags. Set its value to `"row1"`. It should look like this:

```
<tr id="row1">
```

15. Do the same for the table's second `<tr>` tag. Set that `ID` attribute's value to `"row2"`.

16. Now place your cursor just before the `<table>` tag. Then from the ASP.NET tab, click the Page_Load icon to insert the code for the default `Page_Load` function.

17. Change the `Page_Load` function to read as follows:

```
protected void Page_Load( Object
Src, EventArgs E )
{
  HttpCookie cookie =
  Request.Cookies[ "Personalizer" ];
  if ( cookie != null )
  {
    ShowName(cookie.Values["Name"]);
  }
  else
  {
    row1.Visible = true;
    row2.Visible = false;
  }
}
```

This code creates a variable called `cookie` and sets it to hold the `Personalizer` cookie that may be sitting on the visitor's computer. The `if` statement verifies that `cookie` holds a value. If it does, a function called `ShowName` is called with the value associated with the cookie called `Name` passed as a parameter. We'll write the `ShowName` function in a moment.

If `cookie` doesn't hold a value (because it doesn't exist yet), then the top row of the table called "row1" is shown to the visitor and the bottom row, "row2," is not. This is because row1 collects the visitor's name, while row2 will display the name after it's been collected and stored in the cookie.

continues on next page

DYNAMIC USER CONTROLS

215

18. Now that the `Page_Load` function is set
to display the table's top row when
there's no cookie, we need to write the
function that will take the value of
`txtName` and save it to a cookie called
`Personalizer`. Just after the `Page_Load`
function, write the following code that
will handle the click event for the
btnSetName button:

```
void btnSetName_OnClick( Object
sender, EventArgs E )
{
  HttpCookie cookie =
    new HttpCookie( "Personalizer"
);
  cookie.Values.Add( "Name",
                    txtName.Text );
  Response.AppendCookie(cookie);
  ShowName( txtName.Text );
}
```

Here we're creating a new cookie called
`Personalizer`. It's the one we were
accessing in code in Step 17. Then we're
adding the text entered into `txtName` to
the cookie called `Name`. Next, we're sending the cookie to the visitor's computer
with the `Response.AppendCookie` function. Finally, we're calling the `ShowName`
function with the text that the visitor
entered into the txtName control.

19. The last bit of code we have to write
will display the visitor's name. We're
putting this code in its own function
so that we don't have to write it twice.
Enter the following code after the
btnSetName_OnClick function:

```
private void ShowName( String name )
{
  lblName.Text = "Welcome " + name;
  row1.Visible = false;
  row2.Visible = true;
}
```

Script 10.5 User controls can encapsulate their own event handlers, just as Web Forms can.

```
         ▤            script            ▣
 1 <%@ Control Language="C#" %>
 2 <script language="C#" runat="server">
 3 protected void Page_Load(Object Src,
   EventArgs E)
 4 {
 5   HttpCookie cookie =
     Request.Cookies[ "Personalizer" ];
 6   if ( cookie != null )
 7   {
 8     ShowName( cookie.Values[ "Name" ] );
 9   }
10   else
11   {
12     row1.Visible = true;
13     row2.Visible = false;
14   }
15 }
16 void btnSetName_OnClick(Object sender,
   EventArgs E)
17 {
18   HttpCookie cookie =
     new HttpCookie( "Personalizer" );
19   cookie.Values.Add( "Name", txtName.Text );
20
21   Response.AppendCookie(cookie);
22
23   howName( txtName.Text );
24 }
25 private void ShowName( String name )
26 {
27   lblName.Text = "Welcome " + name;
28   row1.Visible = false;
29   row2.Visible = true;
30 }
31 </script>
32 <table border="1" cellspacing="5"
   cellpadding="5" id="tbl" runat="server">
33   <tr id="row1">
34     <td>What's your name?</td>
35     <td><asp:textbox ID="txtName" runat=
       "server" /></td>
36     <td><asp:button ID="btnSetName"
       runat="server" Text="Save" OnClick=
       "btnSetName_OnClick" /></td>
37   </tr>
38   <tr id="row2">
39     <td colspan="3"><asp:label ID=
       "lblName" runat="server" /></td>
40   </tr>
41 </table>
```

You can see that this function takes the visitor's name as a parameter and then sets the text of the lblName control to a welcome message that incorporates the name. This effectively customizes the visitor's page. The function also hides the fields that the visitor used to enter a name by making row1 invisible, and it shows the user's personalized welcome message in row2.

20. Compare your code to **Script 10.5** to check for errors and then save it. Then press F12 to have Dreamweaver copy the file to the testing server, even though this will cause an error in the browser.

To incorporate an event-handling user control:

1. Open the Container.aspx file in Dreamweaver, and make sure the code is visible by clicking the Document toolbar's Show Code View icon ⟨⟩ .

2. In the code, just before the <html> tag, add the following code to register the user control we just created in the previous list:

```
<%@ Register TagPrefix="VQP" TagName=
"Personalizer" Src="Personalizer.ascx" %>
```

3. Now move your cursor down to just after the markup describing the Header control. It looks like this:

```
<VQP:Header id="ctrlHeader" Text=
"Original Text" runat="server" />
```

4. Just after this code, add the following:

```
<VQP:Personalizer id=
"ctrlPersonalizer" runat="server" />
```

continues on next page

DYNAMIC USER CONTROLS

217

5. Because our Personalizer control handles all its own events, we don't need to do any more! Compare your code to **Script 10.6** and then save it. To test the page, press F12 to open it in your default browser. Then enter your name in the text box, and click the Save button.

This will refresh the page. The text box and Save button will be gone, and in their place will be a message welcoming you by name. Your Container page will be personalized for as long as you have the browser open. As soon as you close the browser, though, the cookie will be removed from your computer, and the page will no longer be personalized.

If you think storing data in cookies in your own projects will be beneficial and that the risk of your visitors disabling cookies in their Web browser settings is manageable, then by all means consider using them. You can define how long they should remain after the browser is closed. For example, you could set the expiration using a date. All you'd need to do is set the cookie's Expires property to a specific date, such as 12/31/2004. Or, to keep the cookie on your visitor's computer indefinitely, you can set that property to `DateTime.MaxValue` like this:

`cookie.Expires = DateTime.MaxValue;`

This concludes our introduction to user controls. In the next chapter, we'll be working with custom server controls, which require more coding, but are even more powerful.

Script 10.6 By having the Personalizer user control define its own event handlers, the Web Form that contain it doesn't need to define that code.

```
1 <%@ Page Language="C#" ContentType=
   "text/html" ResponseEncoding=
   "iso-8859-1" %>
2 <%@ Register TagPrefix="VQP" TagName=
   "Header" Src="Header.ascx" %>
3 <%@ Register TagPrefix="VQP" TagName=
   "Personalizer" Src="Personalizer.ascx" %>
4 <html>
5 <head>
6 <title>Untitled Document</title>
7 <meta http-equiv="Content-Type" content=
   "text/html; charset=iso-8859-1">
8 <script language="C#" runat="server">
9 void btnChangeProperties_OnClick(Object
   sender, EventArgs E)
10 {
11   ctrlHeader.Text = "Changed Text";
12   ctrlHeader.Color = "White";
13 }
14 </script>
15 </head>
16 <body>
17 <form runat="server">
18 <VQP:Header id="ctrlHeader" Text=
   "Original Text" runat="server" />
19 <VQP:Personalizer id="ctrlPersonalizer"
   runat="server" />
20 Really the time is: <%=
   System.DateTime.Now.ToString() %>
21 <asp:button ID="btnChangeProperties" runat=
   "server" Text="Change Properties" OnClick=
   "btnChangeProperties_OnClick" />
22 </form>
23 </body>
24 </html>
```

Authoring Custom Server Controls

Have you been using some of the standard ASP.NET controls like asp:textbox and asp:DataGrid and found yourself wishing you could create your own? As developers, we're often limited to the functionality of the tools we choose and their available programming components because we can't customize them. Fortunately, ASP.NET custom server controls let you do just that.

Custom server controls are controls that we build ourselves to satisfy our unique needs. To create a custom control, we begin by inheriting the traits of an existing control that we'll use as base to add the functionality we need. When we inherit from an existing standard control, we have the opportunity not only to add functionality, but also to customize the built-in functionality of the control we're inheriting from. We can group several controls together and treat them like one control, or we can define one from scratch if necessary.

Custom server controls are incorporated into Web Forms using techniques (like the @Register directive) similar to those for the custom user controls we explored in Chapter 10. One important distinction, however, is that custom server controls are written entirely in code. You can't design the way they look in Dreamweaver the way you can a user control. However, while the fact that custom server controls are written exclusively in code makes them harder to create, they're much more flexible than user controls. For example, if the functionality you've built into a custom server control is needed in multiple Web sites, you can incorporate the control into all the sites simultaneously from a central location. You can even package them for sale and distribution.

In this chapter we'll build a custom server control and use it in a Web Form. Then we'll create a *composite control*—one that contains other controls—that can be bound to a data source. There's a lot of code writing in this chapter because custom server controls are built using program code, but the extra work will be worth it.

Using Custom Server Controls

In Chapter 10 we learned that custom user controls are essentially mini-Web Forms, because they're able to define HTML, they're dynamic in nature, and they're capable of handling their own events. One of the controls we created in Chapter 10 was a page header. It was meant to be used on any number of pages in a Web site. By turning the page header into a user control, we were able to define it only once, yet see the contents of that control at the top of any page that incorporated it.

User controls are great for grouping controls like asp:label, HTML, and code into components that can be reused in any page in a site, but they're not usually meant to be referenced more than once within the same Web page. Doing so can produce duplicate names and code blocks, especially when JavaScript code blocks are embedded in the user control.

You can follow certain steps if you want to use custom user controls more than once in the same page, but even that won't completely eliminate the problems. Take, for example, **Script 11.1**: It contains the HTML produced by executing the contents of the Personalizer custom user control we created in "To handle events in a user control" in Chapter 10. You can see that the value of each of the element's Name and ID attributes has "ctrlPersonalizer" appended it. The name, ctrlPersonalizer, comes from the user control's ID attribute that was set when we incorporated it into our page. That markup looked like this:

```
<VQP:Personalizer id="ctrlPersonalizer"
runat="server" />
```

Script 11.1 When user controls are rendered into HTML, the controls they contain are renamed to ensure the names are unique within the page.

```
1  <table id="ctrlPersonalizer_tbl" border="1"
     cellspacing="5" cellpadding="5">
2    <tr id="ctrlPersonalizer_row1">
3      <td>What's your name?</td>
4      <td>
5        <input
6          name="ctrlPersonalizer:txtName"
7          type="text"
8          id="ctrlPersonalizer_txtName" />
9      </td>
10     <td>
11       <input
12         type="submit"
13         name="ctrlPersonalizer:btnSetName"
14         value="Save"
15         id="ctrlPersonalizer_btnSetName" />
16     </td>
17   </tr>
18 </table>
```

The server automatically appends the value of the ID attribute to each element's ID and name attributes in order to guarantee that the values will be unique within the page. However, any JavaScript code blocks in our control would be inserted "as is" every time we used the control, resulting in its duplication. This doesn't always cause errors in the page, but it does make the pages messy and confusing.

Another limitation of user controls is that they can't contain other controls, text, or HTML between their opening and closing tags. In creating a dynamic user control in Chapter 10 (see "To create a dynamic user control"), we showed you how to make user controls dynamic. However, if we did something like the following, we would get an error:

```
<VQP:WillFail id="ctrlWillFail" runat=
"server"> Controls, Text, or HTML
</VQP:WillFail>
```

Custom server controls solve these problems. To illustrate how, we'll create one using the following stepped list. The control we'll create will display an image, with an optional caption placed below the image. It will also take a second image filename as input so that we can
create an image rollover effect.

We'll define properties to set the source attributes for the image tag, use JavaScript to perform the image source file swap and create the rollover effect, and accept text in between the opening and closing tags of our control to use as a caption. Because these next instructions include a bit of code, you might want to use **Script 11.2** on the next page as a guide.

Script 11.2 A server control can write HTML and Java-Script out to the browser by overriding the Render function. To ensure that the JavaScript appears only once, the OnPreRender function checks for the Java-Script function first, and then writes it to the browser if it doesn't exist.

```
1  using System;
2  using System.Web.UI;
3
4  namespace VQP
5  {
6    public class PictureBox : Control
7    {
8      private string ImgSrcOff;
9      private string ImgSrcOn;
10
11     public string ImageSourceOff
12     {
13       get { return ImgSrcOff; }
14       set { ImgSrcOff = value; }
15     }
16
17     public string ImageSourceOn
18     {
19       get { return ImgSrcOn; }
20       set { ImgSrcOn = value; }
21     }
22
23     protected override void OnPreRender(
         EventArgs e )
24     {
25       string SwitchImageScript = @"
26 <script language=""javascript"">
27 function switchImage(imgName, imgSrc)
28 {
29   if (document.images)
30   {
31     if (imgSrc != ""none"")
32     {
33       document.images[imgName].src = imgSrc;
34     }
35   }
36 }
```

(script continues)

Script 11.2 *continued*

```
37 </script>
38 ";
39     if ( ! Page.IsClientScriptBlockReg
         istered( "SwitchImageScript" ) )
40     {
41       Page.RegisterClientScriptBlock(
         "SwitchImageScript",
         SwitchImageScript );
42     }
43   }
44
45   protected override void Render(HtmlTex
       tWriter output)
46   {
47     string PictureBoxHTML = "<table style=
       'border: medium solid #000000;'>";
48     PictureBoxHTML += "<tr><td
       align='center'>";
49     PictureBoxHTML += "<img id='" + this
       .UniqueID + "' src='" + ImgSrcOff + "' ";
50     PictureBoxHTML += "onMouseOver=
       'switchImage(\"" + this.UniqueID +
       "\", \"" + ImgSrcOn + "\")' ";
51     PictureBoxHTML += "onMouseOut='switchI
       mage(\"" + this.UniqueID + "\", \"" +
       ImgSrcOff + "\")' />";
52     PictureBoxHTML += "</td></tr>";
53
54     if ( (HasControls()) && (Controls[0] is
       LiteralControl) )
55     {
56       PictureBoxHTML += "<tr><td align=
         'center'>";
57       PictureBoxHTML += ((LiteralControl)
         Controls[0]).Text;
58       PictureBoxHTML += "</td></tr>";
59     }
60
61     PictureBoxHTML += "</table>";
62
63     output.Write(PictureBoxHTML);
64   }
65  }
66 }
```

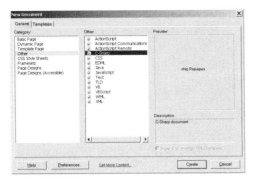

Figure 11.1 You can create a new C# file via the New Document dialog box.

To create a custom server control:

1. From the File menu at the top of Dreamweaver, choose New.

   The New Document dialog box opens.

2. In the New Document dialog box, click Other from the list of categories on the left (**Figure 11.1**). Then on the right, click C-Sharp. Click the Create button to close the dialog box and open the file. Save your file as PictureBox.cs.

3. Now in the file, type the following:

   ```
   using System;
   using System.Web.UI;
   ```

   You might recognize these two statements from Chapter 8 as namespace import commands. They make references to the System and System.Web.UI namespaces so that the compiler knows where to look for class definitions when it encounters a class that isn't defined in this file.

4. Now we need to create our own namespace to make sure that the class we're about to create has a unique name. Type the keyword namespace followed by a unique name, then encapsulate the block of code for the namespace in curly braces.

   ```
   namespace VQP
   {
   }
   ```

   Now that we have a namespace called VQP, we can create a class knowing it's uniquely named.

5. Within the VQP namespace's opening and closing curly braces, type the following highlighted code:

   ```
   namespace VQP
   {
     public class PictureBox : Control
     {
     }
   }
   ```

   continues on next page

This creates a publicly available class called PictureBox. Having a colon and then adding `Control` following the class name makes our new class inherit the functionality of the Control class. The Control class is the generic definition for all controls like asp:textbox and now PictureBox. Inheriting from Control allows us to reuse generic control functionality, while giving us the freedom to customize only the things we need to, like how our control should look.

6. Create two private member variables to hold the image filenames by adding the following highlighted code just inside of the class:

```
public class PictureBox : Control
{
  private string ImgSrcOff;
  private string ImgSrcOn;
}
```

Now we need to define the property methods for these two variables so that the control's user may access them safely.

7. Immediately after the code you entered in Step 6, type the following:

```
public string ImageSourceOff
{
  get { return ImgSrcOff; }
  set { ImgSrcOff = value; }
}
public string ImageSourceOn
{
  get { return ImgSrcOn; }
  set { ImgSrcOn = value; }
}
```

So far the code we've written hasn't been too different from what we wrote when we created a dynamic user control in Chapter 10 (see "To create a dynamic

user control" for more information). Now is where things start to diverge. We need to *override*, or create a new definition for, the Control class's Render method to customize how our control will look when it's rendered to the browser.

8. Type the following code, which uses the `override` keyword to accomplish the Render method's override. Then any code within the function will be unique to our class:

```
protected override void
Render(HtmlTextWriter output)
{
  output.Write(PictureBoxHTML);
}
```

When the server creates our control, this method is called automatically. The output parameter is set to an `HtmlTextWriter` capable of writing HTML to the visiting browser. Our `PictureBoxHTML` variable is written to the browser; but we haven't yet defined that variable. We'll do that next.

9. Just before the call to the output parameter's Write method in the last step, insert the following:

```
string PictureBoxHTML = "<table style=
'border: medium solid #000000;'>";
PictureBoxHTML += "<tr><td align=
'center'>";
PictureBoxHTML += "<img id='" +
this.UniqueID + "' src='" + ImgSrcOff
+ "' ";
PictureBoxHTML += "onMouseOver=
'switchImage(\"" + this.UniqueID +
"\", \"" + ImgSrcOn + "\")' ";
PictureBoxHTML += "onMouseOut=
'switchImage(\"" + this.UniqueID +
"\", \"" + ImgSrcOff + "\")' />";
PictureBoxHTML += "</td></tr>";
```

This code defines a literal string containing HTML text that defines a table with an image in the first row and stores it in the `PictureBoxHTML` variable. Notice that the image's `ID` attribute is set to `this.UniqueID`. The `this` is a reference to the object that represents our server control. The `UniqueID` property contains the value of our control's `ID` attribute, and this value is placed into the string at run time. The effect is that our rendered image will have the same ID as the one our control has.

We're not quite done yet. Before we add the closing table tag to the `PictureBoxHTML` variable, let's check for text between the server control's opening and closing tags.

Any time text or some other control is added between the opening and closing tags of a custom server control, it's added to a list called Controls. What we'll do is check to see if the first thing added to the Controls collection was text (including plain HTML), which is referred to as a LiteralControl. If it *is* text, we'll treat it as a caption to our image and place it in the second row of our table.

10. Type the following to check for the existence of a LiteralControl object between the opening and closing tags of our custom control:

```
if ( (HasControls()) && (Controls[0]
is LiteralControl) )
{
  PictureBoxHTML +=
    "<tr><td align='center'>";
  PictureBoxHTML += (
(LiteralControl) Controls[0] ).Text;
  PictureBoxHTML += "</td></tr>";
}
```

Here we're verifying that the Controls list contains controls that have the `HasControls()` function. Then we're making sure that the first control is text. A LiteralControl isn't limited to normal text but rather can include HTML that should be rendered into markup literally. Then we're adding another row and cell to our `PictureBoxHTML` variable. Inside the cell tag `<td>` we're adding the text of the first control in the Controls list (collection index numbers start at zero). And finally we close out the row cell and row.

11. Now we just have to close out the table by adding the following code just after the `if` statement we entered in Step 10:

```
PictureBoxHTML += "</table>";
```

If we left our control like this, we'd experience an error when we tried to use it in a page because we never defined the `switchImage` JavaScript function referenced in the `OnMouseOver` and `OnMouseOut` events of our images from Step 9.

12. To add the `switchImage` function to the page, we need to override another method inherited from the Control class. This one is called OnPreRender. It's called by the server just before the Render method we used in Step 8. Like the Render method, we'll override the OnPreRender method as follows:

```
protected override void
OnPreRender(EventArgs e)
{
}
```

continues on next page

13. Then within the overridden OnPreRender method, create the following variable to contain the text defining the JavaScript function:

```
string SwitchImageScript = @"
<script language=""javascript"">
function switchImage(imgName,
imgSrc)
{
  if (document.images)
  {
    if (imgSrc != ""none"")
    {
      document.images[imgName].src =
imgSrc;
    }
  }
}
</script>
";
```

This string probably looks a little funny to you because it's a special kind of string that starts with the @ symbol and is called a *verbatim literal* string. That means that everything in the string is taken verbatim, from new lines to escape characters. The only exception is the double–double quotes, as in `""javascript""`; that will end up reading as `"javascript"`. Verbatim literals are handy for storing JavaScript code that will look the same in the browser as we write it here. By the way, this `switchImage` function is found on Dreamweaver's Snippets panel in the Code panel group.

14. Now to ensure that the `switchImage` JavaScript function appears only once no matter how many times our control is used on the page, we need to use the `Page.IsClientScriptBlockRegistered` function. Given a keyname of our choosing, this function checks to see if any code has been registered with the page using that keyname. If it hasn't, we should register our JavaScript function under that keyname. (If we have already registered our function, we don't need to again.) Here's the code to do that:

```
if ( !
Page.IsClientScriptBlockRegistered(
"SwitchImageScript" ) )
{
  Page.RegisterClientScriptBlock(
    "SwitchImageScript",
    SwitchImageScript );
}
```

You see here that if the `"SwitchImageScript"` keyname hasn't been registered with the page yet, we register the `switchImage` function defined within the `SwitchImageScript` variable using that key. If another of our controls is used on the same page, it will find that the `"SwitchImageScript"` key has already been registered so it won't reregister the JavaScript function used for the image rollover.

15. After all that coding, we're finally done. You'll want to check your code against **Script 11.2** to make sure you didn't miss anything. Then save your file.

We aren't quite ready to use our custom server control. Custom server controls need to be compiled into Dynamic Link Library (DLL) files and copied to the bin directory of our Web site (or more correctly, our application, as explained in Chapter 2).

To compile a custom server control written in C# into a DLL file, we need to use the C# compiler. By default, it's located in the following directory: C:\ProgramFiles\ Microsoft.NET\FrameworkSDK\bin. However, you should be able to access it automatically from any directory using the command prompt. The following instructions explain how to compile your custom server control.

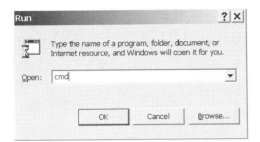

Figure 11.2 Open a command prompt from the Run dialog box.

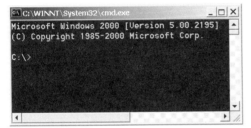

Figure 11.3 Type commands at the default command prompt.

To prepare a custom server control for use:

1. Click the Windows taskbar's Start button. Then click Run.

   This opens the Run dialog box.

2. In the Run dialog box, type "cmd" and press Enter (**Figure 11.2**).

   This will open a new command prompt window.

3. In the command prompt window (**Figure 11.3**), change to the directory that contains your PictureBox.cs file using the `cd` command, followed by the directory's full path. Make sure to put quotes around the path if it contains spaces. And if the directory is on a different drive than the one you're currently on, you'll have to change drives, too. For example, we'll change to drive D by typing "D:" at the prompt:

   `C:\>D:`

   Pressing Enter will change the prompt as follows:

   `D:\>`

   Then we'll change to the directory that contains our PictureBox.cs file:

   `D:\>cd "D:\Program Files\chpt11\"`

   Pressing Enter here will cause the prompt to change again, like so:

   `D:\Program Files\chpt11>`

   So now that we're in the directory that contains the PictureBox.cs file, we're ready to compile it.

4. To compile the PictureBox.cs file into a DLL file, we'll run the C# compiler called csc.exe on it. We'll also use a parameter (`/t:library`) to let the compiler know to make it into a DLL file and not a standard executable (.exe) file. Type the following and then press Enter:

   `csc.exe /t:library PictureBox.cs`

continues on next page

Note: Executable files don't need the .exe extension to run. You could have typed "csc" instead of csc.exe.

5. Assuming there were no errors reported during the compilation process, you now have a file in this directory called PictureBox.dll. Copy this file into the bin directory of your site using your favorite file copying method.

We're finally ready to use our PictureBox server control in a Web Form. Doing so is very much like adding a custom user control to a Web Form. The following instructions describe the process.

To incorporate a custom server control:

1. Create a Web Form. (See "To create a new Web Form" in Chapter 4 for more information.)

2. Make the code visible by clicking the Document toolbar's Show Code View icon (**Figure 11.4**).

3. Create a new blank second line in the code of the page, just after the page declaration command that looks like this:

```
<%@ Page Language="C#" ContentType=
"text/html" ResponseEncoding=
"iso-8859-1" %>
```

4. In the new blank second line, register the PictureBox.dll file with your page (this will require that the file exists within your site's bin directory):

```
<%@ Register TagPrefix="VQP"
Namespace="VQP" assembly=
"PictureBox" %>
```

Remember that files like DLL files and .exe files are called *assemblies* in .NET. Knowing this makes the page-level command more understandable. This command called Register assigns the PictureBox assembly, our DLL file, to the VQP namespace. It sets the tag prefix to VQP as well.

Figure 11.4 To see just the code, click the Show Code View icon on the Document toolbar.

5. Move down to just after the \<body> tag. We need to add a form element to our page so that the client JavaScript registration from Step 14 of "To create a custom server control" will work. Type the following:

```
<form runat="server">
</form>
```

6. Now just before the \</form> tag, add the following to use our PictureBox control:

```
<VQP:PictureBox
   id="pb1"
   ImageSourceOff="btnHome.jpg"
   ImageSourceOn="btnLocations.jpg"
   runat="server" >Caption Text
</VQP:PictureBox>
```

We're using the btnHome.jpg and btnLocation.jpg image files we first used in Chapter 5, so they should be handy. If not, you can get them out of their default location in Dreamweaver at C:\Program Files\Macromedia\Dreamweaver MX\ Samples\GettingStarted\Code\Assets\ images.

You may also use your own images instead if you wish.

7. To see the effects of our JavaScript registration, we'll add another PictureBox control to the page, just after the one we added in Step 6.

```
<VQP:PictureBox
   id="pb2"
   ImageSourceOff="btnLocations.jpg"
   ImageSourceOn="btnHome.jpg"
   runat="server" >Different Caption
   </VQP:PictureBox>
```

Notice that we flip-flopped the values of the ImageSourceOff and ImageSourceOn attributes. This is to help us see the difference between the two instances of the control when we test it.

That's all we need to do to use our custom PictureBox server control.

continues on next page

USING CUSTOM SERVER CONTROLS

8. Compare your file against **Script 11.3**, then save it. Press F12 to open your page in the default browser.

The page will have two images with captions enclosed within black boxes (**Figure 11.5**). When you move your mouse over the images, they should roll over to new images.

Also take a look at the source code of the rendered page. You'll find that there's only one copy of the `switchImage` JavaScript function, even though we used two controls.

An example of where you can apply controls similar to the one we've just built is when you want to create and reuse customized validation logic. We learned about the standard validation controls in Chapter 6 and found that there were situations that warranted the creation of a custom validation control containing your own validation logic. Often, you'll want to use custom validation control logic in many pages across several Web sites, but to accomplish this without some new technique, you'd have a fair amount of duplication cut out for you.

With custom server controls, you can create a customized validation server control, for instance, to validate the length of the text entered into an asp:textbox control. Once you've created the control, you can register that custom validation server control in a single location called the Global Assembly Cache (which we first discussed in Chapter 2). That way, you can use it in every one of your Web sites from that one location. Using the Global Assembly Cache, you can access a custom server control across multiple pages and sites, yet maintain just one, shareable copy of the control. The "Global Assembly Cache" sidebar discusses this option in more detail.

Script 11.3 A custom server control can be used any number of times within a Web Form.

```
1  <%@ Page Language="C#" ContentType=
   "text/html" ResponseEncoding="iso-8859-1" %>
2  <%@ Register TagPrefix="VQP" Namespace="VQP"
   assembly="PictureBox" %>
3  <html>
4  <head>
5  <title>Untitled Document</title>
6  <meta http-equiv="Content-Type" content=
   "text/html; charset=iso-8859-1">
7  </head>
8  <body>
9  <form runat="server">
10 <VQP:PictureBox
11   id="pb1"
12   ImageSourceOff="btnHome.jpg"
13   ImageSourceOn="btnLocations.jpg"
14   runat="server" >Caption Text</VQP:PictureBox>
15 <VQP:PictureBox
16   id="pb2"
17   ImageSourceOff="btnLocations.jpg"
18   ImageSourceOn="btnHome.jpg"
19   runat="server" >Different
     Caption</VQP:PictureBox>
20 </form>
21 </body>
22 </html>
```

Figure 11.5 This is the PictureBox control rendered in Internet Explorer.

The Global Assembly Cache

For a user control to be incorporated into pages in several Web sites, that control would need to be copied to each site. If the user control's developer needed to make changes to that control, the developer would have to change every Web site's copy of it—effectively reintroducing the very code-duplication problem that user controls were originally designed to solve.

The solution? You can store custom server controls in a central location, called the Global Assembly Cache (GAC), and then access them from any number of Web sites on the server. The GAC can even store multiple versions of the same control if required.

To store a control in the GAC, we need to do a few things first. We need to give our control what's called a *strong name*, which is a name that ensures that the control is unique and tamper-proof. This is important when storing your control in a central location on your server.

In order to give a control a strong name, you have to set its version number and assign it a public/private cryptographic key pair. You can set the version number to version 1.0.0.0 by adding the following code just after the namespace import statements:

```
[assembly:AssemblyVersionAttribute("1.0.0.0")]
```

Then you use the sn.exe tool to generate the key pair. The key pair is used to ensure that your control code isn't tampered with.

After you've given your control a strong name, all that's left is running the GAC utility to install the control into the GAC. That task is as simple as running the following command at the command prompt:

```
gacutil -i PictureBox.dll
```

Finally, to use a control that's been registered in the GAC, you need to add a reference to the web.config file using the control's public key that was created with the sn.exe tool. The public key will be different for your control because they're unique for each control:

```
<configuration>
 <system.web>
  <compilation>
   <assemblies>
    <add assembly="PictureBox"
         PublicKeyToken=
         "cad977a98d6645sf" />
   </assemblies>
  <compilation>
 </system.web>
</configuration>
```

Then the Register command at the top of your Web Forms would be the same as if the control's DLL file were in the Web site's bin directory. But now multiple Web sites can reference the same DLL file instead of having to maintain a copy of it in their own bin directories.

Data-Driven Custom Server Controls

So far we've learned that custom server controls can have both dynamic properties and content between their opening and closing tags. We've also learned how to manage JavaScript code blocks so that only one copy of the code is added to the page no matter how many copies of the control the page contains. Now we're going to learn about custom server controls that act as containers for other custom server controls—referred to as *composite controls*.

Composite controls are usually used in more complex scenarios. In a composite control, one control is placed in a Web Form, and then that one control is in charge of creating all the other controls that make up the composite control. Often composite controls are programmed to accept template definitions between their opening and closing tags. The asp:repeater control is an example of a composite control that uses templates. Templates make a control flexible because they give the developer the ability to define how the contents of the control should be displayed. "The asp:repeater Control" sidebar shows an example of how to use templates.

Because the asp:repeater control is so powerful and comes built in to ASP.NET, we're not going to be building another template-driven composite control. Instead we'll build a data-driven composite control. It will consist of one control class that we'll register and use in a Web Form. In that Web Form we'll assign a list of data items to our composite control. Then our control will create an HTML table containing one row for each data item. The rows will have two cells: one to contain our data item as a label, and one to contain a text box mapped to that data item.

Two main differences you'll see between this custom server control and the PictureBox control we created in "To create a custom server control" is that there's no Render method to output HTML to the visitor's browser. Instead we're using the CreateChildControls method. The CreateChildControls method is called by the Web server to signal to a control that it should create its child control. Each child control will be responsible for implementing its own Render method to create its HTML, freeing us from that task.

The asp:repeater Control

The asp:repeater control is a data-driven control that requires the developer to define a template that describes how the data should appear in the browser. Often the developer will want the data to be represented in an HTML table, and the asp:repeater control is the only control that allows a table to be opened in one template, such as the HeaderTemplate, and closed in different template, such as the FooterTemplate.

The following are the five templates that may be defined:

- **ItemTemplate.** This is the only required template. It holds the definition of how the developer wants the items in the bound data source to be displayed.

- **AlternatingItemTemplate.** This template defines how every other item from the data source should be displayed.

- **SeparatorTemplate.** This defines a region that should appear between items.

- **HeaderTemplate.** This defines what the header of the list of items should look like.

- **FooterTemplate.** This defines what the footer of the list of items should look like.

Here's an example of an asp:repeater control definition. The definition of the data source referenced by the asp:repeater control is omitted for simplicity:

```
<asp:Repeater id="rptr" runat="server">
  <HeaderTemplate>
    <table border=1>
      <tr>
        <td><b>Name</b></td>
        <td><b>Value</b></td>
      </tr>
  </HeaderTemplate>
  <ItemTemplate>
      <tr>
        <td>
          <%# DataBinder.Eval( Container.DataItem, "Name") %>
        </td>
        <td>
          <%# DataBinder.Eval( Container.DataItem, "Value") %>
        </td>
      </tr>
  </ItemTemplate>
  <FooterTemplate>
      </table>    ,
  </FooterTemplate>
</asp:Repeater>
```

DATA-DRIVEN CUSTOM SERVER CONTROLS

The WinCV Tool

How do you know if a class already exists that satisfies your needs? Or what if you know about a class but can't remember what methods are available for it? The WinCV tool comes with the .NET Framework SDK and lets you search for classes to get a list of their methods, properties, constructors, events, and any other information that would be useful to you as a developer.

To use the WinCV tool, simply open a command prompt and type "wincv." Then press Enter to open the class viewer tool (**Figure 11.6**). Once the tool is open, you can type words into the search field at the top to find class definitions that match your search string.

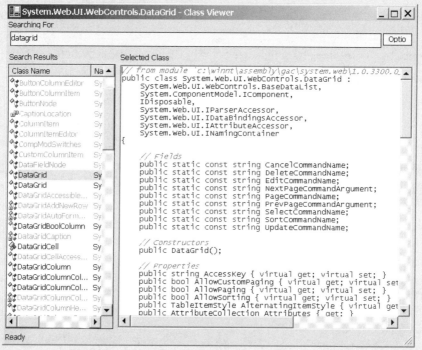

Figure 11.6 Use the WinCV tool to search for class definitions.

To create a composite control:

1. Create a new C# document like we did in Steps 1 and 2 of "To create a custom server control," except save this file as "AutoTable.cs."

2. Now in the file, type the following:

```
using System;
using System.Web.UI;
using System.Web.UI.WebControls;
using System.Collections;
```

   These namespace references will give us access to several classes that we'll need in this class.

3. We'll create a namespace for our class to ensure our class names are unique. Type the following to have our class in the VQP namespace:

```
namespace VQP
{
}
```

4. Within the VQP namespace's opening and closing curly braces, type the following highlighted code:

```
namespace VQP
{
    public class AutoTable : Control,
    INamingContainer
    {
    }
}
```

This creates a publicly available class called AutoTable. Placing a colon and then adding the keyword Control after the class name allows our new class to inherit the functionality of the Control class. So far, this is similar to the PictureBox control we created earlier in this chapter, but here we've included a comma after the Control class followed by INamingContainer. The InamingContainer is a special kind of object component called an *interface*. Although we're only able to inherit from one class at a time, we can implement as many interfaces as we want. In this case, we're inheriting from Control and implementing the InamingContainer interface.

An interface isn't a class because it doesn't define any working methods. It only defines what the methods should be called. Interfaces are used to make developers stick to predefined method names for commonly implemented methods rather than letting developers come up with new names every time. Effectively, it makes classes that implement interfaces easier to work with, because their method names are predictable.

Here we're implementing the INamingContainer interface, which actually doesn't require us to implement any predefined methods, as interfaces usually require. Instead it's a special kind known as a marker interface. It ensures that our child controls have unique names, since they may appear several times and controls can't have duplicate names.

continues on next page

5. Create a private member variable and its matching property method by typing the following within the AutoTable class:

```
private IEnumerable DataSrc;
public IEnumerable DataSource
{
    get { return DataSrc; }
    set { DataSrc = value; }
}
```

You can tell from the I at the beginning of the IEnumerable data type seen here that we're dealing with another interface. This is a more typical use of an interface. Many classes that use data also implement the IEnumerable interface so that we can iterate through variable types that contain multiple elements, such as arrays. Later we'll use some useful functions derived from the IEnumerable interface. This makes our control very flexible, because we can use any class as a data source as long as that class implements the IEnumerable interface.

6. Here we'll override the CreateChildControls method that we inherit from the Control class. However, we won't add code to it, because the code to create the child controls will go into a different method for this unique data-binding scenario:

```
protected override void
CreateChildControls()
{
}
```

7. Because we're binding data to this control, we have to implement the OnDataBinding method. This method will loop through the data items in our DataSrc member variable and create a new AutoTableRow for each item. Then we'll add the method to our AutoTable control, making this control a composite control. Type the following to begin defining our version of the OnDataBinding method:

```
protected override void
OnDataBinding(EventArgs e)
{
    base.OnDataBinding(e);
}
```

As you now know, one principle of object-oriented programming is inheritance—we can inherit functionality from an existing class. We do it for the AutoTable class we're building by inheriting from the Control class. When we inherit functionality, we usually want to customize some methods, which is why we override them. But sometimes, we want to override the base methods from the inherited class. We're doing that here as we override the OnDataBinding method of the Control class, and call the Control class's version of the OnDataBinding method with the base keyword. We'll next add the custom code to the OnDataBinding method.

8. Just after the call to the base class Control's OnDataBinding method, add the following code:

```
if( DataSrc != null )
{
    Controls.Clear();
    Controls.Add( new
        LiteralControl( "<table>" ) );

    IEnumerator item =
            DataSrc.GetEnumerator();
    while( item.MoveNext() )
    {
        AutoTableRow row = new
            AutoTableRow( item.Current );
        Controls.Add( row );
    }
    Controls.Add( new
        LiteralControl( "</table>" ) );
}
```

Script 11.4 You can bind custom server controls to lists of data by using the `OnDataBinding` function, which dynamically adds the HTML that gets sent to the browser.

```
                    script
1  using System;
2  using System.Web.UI;
3  using System.Web.UI.WebControls;
4  using System.Collections;
5
6  namespace VQP
7  {
8    public class AutoTable : Control,
     INamingContainer
9    {
10     private IEnumerable DataSrc;
11
12     public IEnumerable DataSource
13     {
14       get { return DataSrc; }
15       set { DataSrc = value; }
16     }
17
18     protected override void
       CreateChildControls()
19     {
20     }
21
22     protected override void OnDataBinding(
       EventArgs e )
23     {
24       base.OnDataBinding(e);
25
26       if( DataSrc != null )
27       {
28         Controls.Clear();
29         Controls.Add( new LiteralControl(
           "<table>" ) );
30
31         IEnumerator item =
           DataSrc.GetEnumerator();
32         while( item.MoveNext() )
33         {
34           AutoTableRow row = new
             AutoTableRow( item.Current );
35           Controls.Add( row );
36         }
37
38         Controls.Add( new LiteralControl(
           "</table>" ) );
39       }
40     }
41   }
42 }
```

Before we do any work with `DataSrc`, we need to make sure it contains data items by checking to see if it is `null`. Then we clear any child controls to guarantee that we'll begin with an empty list. After that, we define a new HTML table. Since the table definition is HTML text and not a control, we need to define it as a LiteralControl object.

Now that a table's been defined, we need to add rows to it. We do that by iterating through the items in the `DataSrc`. For each item in the DataSrc, we create a new AutoTableRow control and then add it to the AutoTable's list of controls. Finally, we close the HTML table.

9. Compare your AutoTable.cs file to **Script 11.4**. Then save it.

Now we need to create the "AutoTableRow" custom server control that this class depends on before we can use it in a Web Form.

To create the child control:

1. Create a new C# document like we did in Steps 1 and 2 of "To create a custom server control," except save this file as AutoTableRow.cs.

2. Now in the file, type the following:
```
using System;
using System.Web.UI;
using System.Web.UI.WebControls;
```
These namespace references will give us access to server classes that we'll need in this class.

3. We'll place our AutoTableRow class inside the same namespace as the AutoTable class so that we don't need to have a cross-reference for them to find each other. Type the following below the namespace references entered in Step 2:
```
namespace VQP
{
}
```

4. Within the VQP namespace's opening and closing curly braces, type the following:
```
namespace VQP
{
    public class AutoTableRow : Control
    {
    }
}
```
We just need to inherit from the Control class this time.

5. Create two private member variables. They will hold text for the text box's label and the textbox's id attribute. Type the following within the AutoTableRow class:
```
private string lbl;
private string id;
```

We won't be creating property methods for our two member variables this time. Instead, we'll set them in our class constructor method.

A *constructor* is a special method used to initialize a class when it's created. It has the same name as the class it's defined in, and it doesn't have a return type. Constructor methods are called automatically when a new instance of the class is created. That's what the new keyword is doing when we're assigning a new instance of a class to a variable; it's calling the constructor for the class.

The constructor is so important that a default one is created for you if you don't write one yourself. This default constructor doesn't do much but set up the memory space for the class. However, in the next step we're going to create our own constructor to perform custom logic.

6. Type the following to define our constructor:
```
public AutoTableRow(object dataItem)
{
    lbl = (string) dataItem;
    id = "txt" + lbl.Replace(" ", "");
}
```
Our version of the constructor for this class takes a data item, converts it to a string, and stores it in the lbl variable. Referencing the lbl string, we remove all the spaces in the string and append it with "txt" before assigning it to the id member variable.

7. We said in "To create a custom server control" that a composite control doesn't have to implement the Render method because its child controls take care of that. Note that AutoTableRow is itself a composite control, since it creates controls of its own such as "TableRow" and "TableCell." Composite controls can contain other composite controls many layers deep, but in practice it's usually not more than three because after that it starts getting confusing. So, override the Control class's CreateChildControls method in this class by typing the following:

```
protected override void
CreateChildControls()
{
  TableRow tr = new TableRow();
  TableCell td = new TableCell();

  td.Text = lbl;
  tr.Cells.Add( td );

  td = new TableCell();
  TextBox tb = new TextBox();
  tb.ID = id;
  td.Controls.Add( tb );

  tr.Cells.Add( td );
  Controls.Add( tr );
}
```

Since all of our child controls come with ASP.NET, we don't have to create more child controls and implement their Render methods. We don't have to write any more HTML in LiteralControls, because we're using controls instead of literal text.

continues on next page

These controls represent table rows and cells. We set the first cell's text to be the text stored in our `lbl` member variable. Then we create a text box control and set its ID property to the text in our `id` member variable and add it to the second cell. Both cells are added to the row, and the row is added to this control's list of controls.

8. **Script 11.5** contains a copy of the finished code for the AutoTableRow control. Compare your code to it, checking for inconsistencies. Then save the file.

In order to use our custom composite server control, we need to compile both classes into the same DLL file. The following instructions will walk you through the process.

To prepare a composite control for use:

1. Click the Windows taskbar's Start button. Then click Run to open its dialog box. Type "cmd" in the text box and press Enter.

   A new command prompt window will open.

2. In the command prompt window, change to the directory that contains your AutoTable.cs and AutoTableRow.cs files.

   Refer to Step 3 of "To prepare a custom server control for use" earlier in this chapter if you need a reminder of how to do this.

3. Type the following to compile both files into one DLL file called AutoTable.dll:

   ```
   csc /out:AutoTable.dll /t:library
   AutoTable.cs AutoTableRow.cs
   ```

4. Assuming there weren't any errors, you'll now have a file called AutoTable.dll in your directory. Copy that file into your Web site's bin directory.

Now let's use our new custom control in a Web Form.

Script 11.5 Custom server controls overriding the `CreateChildControls` function have the ability to add any number of other server controls.

```
1  using System;
2  using System.Web.UI;
3  using System.Web.UI.WebControls;
4
5  namespace VQP
6  {
7    public class AutoTableRow : Control
8    {
9      private string lbl;
10     private string id;
11
12     public AutoTableRow( object dataItem )
13     {
14       lbl = (string) dataItem;
15       id = "txt" + lbl.Replace( " ", "" );
16     }
17
18     protected override void
         CreateChildControls()
19     {
20       TableRow tr = new TableRow();
21       TableCell td = new TableCell();
22
23       td.Text = lbl;
24       tr.Cells.Add( td );
25
26       td = new TableCell();
27       TextBox tb = new TextBox();
28       tb.ID = id;
29       td.Controls.Add( tb );
30
31       tr.Cells.Add( td );
32
33       Controls.Add( tr );
34     }
35   }
36 }
```

Figure 11.7 Use the Page_Load icon on the ASP.NET tab to insert the default Page_Load function.

To incorporate a composite control into a Web Form:

1. Create a Web Form and make sure the code is visible by clicking the Document toolbar's Show Code View icon.

2. Just after the page declaration command that looks like this:

```
<%@ Page Language="C#" ContentType=
"text/html" ResponseEncoding=
"iso-8859-1" %>
```

Add the following code to register our control with the page:

```
<%@ Register TagPrefix="VQP" Namespace=
"VQP" assembly="AutoTable" %>
```

3. Enter the following just after the `<body>` tag:

```
<form runat="server">
</form>
```

This places our control inside a form, which we needed to do because it contains an asp:textbox control.

4. Inside the form, just before the `</form>` tag, type the following to place the AutoTable control inside the form:

```
<VQP:AutoTable id="at" runat=
"server" />
```

5. We still have to bind data to our control. We'll define and populate an ArrayList object and use it as our data source. To do that, move your cursor up to just before the `</head>` tag. From the Insert bar, click on the ASP.NET tab, and then click the Page_Load icon (**Figure 11.7**). This inserts the default Page_Load function code into the page.

continues on next page

DATA-DRIVEN CUSTOM SERVER CONTROLS

6. Alter the default Page_Load function to look like this:

```
protected void Page_Load( Object Src,
EventArgs E )
{
  ArrayList values = new
ArrayList();
  values.Add("First Name");
  values.Add("Last Name");

  at.DataSource = values;
  at.DataBind();
}
```

This code creates the ArrayList object called values to hold our data and populates it with sample data. Then it sets our AutoTable's DataSource property to it and binds it to our control.

Note: Because we used the IEnumerable interface as our data type for the DataSource property we defined in Step 8 of "To create a composite control," we could just as easily have used another object type, such as a DataSet object filled with data retrieved from a database, rather than an ArrayList.

7. Finally, compare your code to **Script 11.6** to check for errors. Then save the file, and press F12 to open it in the browser.

You'll see two labels and their text boxes (**Figure 11.8**).

This concludes what we'll cover in this chapter on custom server controls, but there's much more to explore. If you want to take it further, a good place to begin is the .NET Framework SDK's documentation.

Script 11.6 The code necessary to bind a custom server control to a data source is the same as the code needed to bind a standard control to a data source.

```
                          script
1  <%@ Page Language="C#" ContentType=
   "text/html" ResponseEncoding="iso-8859-1" %>
2  <%@ Register TagPrefix="VQP" Namespace="VQP"
   assembly="AutoTable" %>
3  <html>
4  <head>
5  <title>Untitled Document</title>
6  <meta http-equiv="Content-Type" content=
   "text/html; charset=iso-8859-1">
7  <script runat="server">
8  protected void Page_Load(Object Src,
   EventArgs E)
9  {
10   ArrayList values = new ArrayList();
11   values.Add("First Name");
12   values.Add("Last Name");
13
14   at.DataSource = values;
15   at.DataBind();
16 }
17 </script>
18 </head>
19 <body>
20 <form runat="server">
21 <VQP:AutoTable id="at" runat="server" />
22 </form>
23 </body>
24 </html>
```

Figure 11.8 Here's the AutoTable control rendered in Internet Explorer.

CREATING AND CONSUMING WEB SERVICES

Developers have worked for years to create a dependable, yet easy way for enterprise applications to work together. An example of such programs might be an automaker's warehouse inventory application exchanging data with the supplier's ordering application. In this scenario, the two programs could do most of the work required to keep the warehouse filled with auto parts. For instance, say the automaker's inventory system noticed that the fan belts were running low. It would then automatically create an order in the supplier's ordering application for more fan belts to be delivered to the warehouse. The only required human effort would be the manual packing, shipping, and receiving of the fan belts.

The problem has always been that there was no good way for two applications at two different companies to work directly together. Among the reasons for this are that the different companies had disparate system architectures, platforms, and development environments, and that, quite simply, some applications just weren't designed to communicate with other applications. Technologies like Distributed Component Object Model (DCOM) and Common Object Request Broker Architecture (CORBA) were developed years ago to accomplish cross-application communication, but both require a great deal of time, effort, and money to make them work. Fortunately, Web services were developed to solve the cross-application communication problem more easily and at a much lower cost.

Web services are a cross-application communication technology based on standard Internet protocols such as HTTP (Hypertext Transfer Protocol) and XML (eXtensible Markup Language). XML, as we learned in Chapter 9, describes data in a completely flexible, customizable way using text. And since all applications can understand and work with textual data, they can all communicate with Web services regardless of differences in platform or development environment. Better yet, unlike DCOM and CORBA, Web services are easy to build and distribute.

We'll see just how easy it is to create a Web service in this chapter. Then we'll use (consume) it in a Web Form by adding a reference to it and invoking its methods. But since the real power of Web services is the ability to reuse functionality that someone else has already built, we'll search the Internet for one that suits our needs and use it in a Web Form instead of creating that functionality ourselves.

About Web Services

A *Web service* is program that's accessible over the network for use by other programs. The accessibility can be to a single application inside a company's private network, or to any program in the world over the Internet. Because Web services use Internet standards like HTTP and XML, they are uniformly accessible. By using the standards, a program written in Java running on a Unix server can call a Web service written in C# running on a Windows 2000 server. Until Web services, there was no easy, inexpensive way to do this.

Speaking a common language

The standards defining Web services must be strictly adhered to so that cross-application communication works consistently. There are three standards that form the basis of Web services: Simple Object Access Protocol (SOAP), Web Service Description Language (WSDL), and Universal Description, Discovery and Integration (UDDI). To use Web services in Dreamweaver, you don't need to know much about these standards, but we'll discuss each of them anyway, to give you a better understanding of how Web services are created and used.

SOAP is a protocol that describes what the format for messages sent back and forth between two applications should look like. However, it's only one of the options available for describing how the messages are to be formatted. In addition to SOAP, two other

options for standardizing the communication between a client and a Web service are HTTP-GET and HTTP-POST. Surely you'll recognize these names, as they are the two options available for passing data back to a Web server from a Web client. However, SOAP is the more common protocol used for Web services and it's what we'll use in this book.

We use SOAP to describe the format of the messages sent, but we use WSDL to describe the content of the messages. The structure of WSDL, like much of Web services, is based on XML. Since Web services are applications with their own functions that are available for you to call, we use WSDL to describe how to call those functions. We'll be providing Dreamweaver with the WSDL for the Web service we're about to create, so Dreamweaver will know what the function names are, what types of parameters the functions take, and what the returning data type format is. What's so easy about building Web services in ASP.NET is that we only have to write the functions. The WSDL document is created for us.

UDDI is a standard that describes how developers should publish a Web service they've created so that other developers can easily find it. We'll discuss UDDI much more in the second half of this chapter, when we find a Web service on the Internet to use in our Web Form.

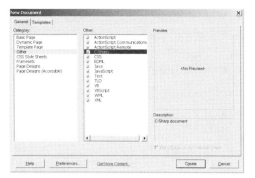

Figure 12.1 Create a new C# file using the New Document dialog box.

Providing a service

As you'll discover, Web services are really quite simple to define and use. Most of the time they're created to access dynamic content from a database and return the content to the Web service's user. Since you learned in Chapters 7 and 8 how to retrieve data from a database, you already know enough to create Web services on a par with the majority of the Web services available today. In the second half of this chapter, we'll learn more about finding the Web services that are available publicly. To begin, we'll clear up some of the mystery behind Web services by creating one.

To create a Web service:

1. From the File drop-down menu at the top of Dreamweaver, choose New.

   This will open the New Document dialog box (**Figure 12.1**).

2. In the list of categories on the left of the New Document dialog box, select Other. Then in the list to the right, select C-Sharp. Click the Create button to close the dialog box and open the file. Save your file as Salutation.asmx.

   Notice that the extension this time is .asmx, not .aspx or .ascx as in other chapters.

3. Delete the contents of the file and then type the following, starting on the first line:

   ```
   <%@ WebService Language="C#"
   Class="VQP.Salutation" %>
   ```

   You'll notice that like the Web Form and user control files, the Web service file has its own page-level directive.

   We need to import some namespaces to gain access to the classes they contain.

   continues on next page

4. Add the following code in the line after the WebService directive in order to import the System and System.Web.Services namespaces:

```
using System;
using System.Web.Services;
```

Let's create our own namespace to ensure our class's name is unique.

5. Type the following to create the VQP namespace:

```
namespace VQP
{
}
```

Now we're ready to create our first Web service. It's simply a class that inherits from the WebService class. In fact, it's similar to the work we did in Chapter 11 when creating custom server controls.

6. Type the following inside the VQP namespace:

```
namespace VQP
{
 public class Salutation :
WebService
  {
  }
}
```

Within our new Salutation class, we'll create a method to return a greeting message. The method will allow the caller to request a regional greeting message.

7. Add the following code for the SaySalutation method inside the Salutation class:

```
public class Salutation: WebService
{
  public String SaySalutation(
  String region )
  {
    String salutation;
    switch( region )
    {
      case "Globe":
        salutation = "Hello World";
        break;
      case "USA":
        salutation = "Hi";
        break;
      case "West":
        salutation = "Howdy";
        break;
      default:
        salutation = "Hello";
        break;
    }
    return salutation;
  }
}
```

There's one last thing we need to do in order for the SaySalutation method to be available over the network as a Web service.

Script 12.1 Web services are easy to create. They're simply classes that inherit from the WebService class. The only extra information can be found in the attributes that designate the class as a Web service and some of its methods as Web methods.

```
                        script
1  <%@ WebService Language="C#" Class=
   "VQP.Salutation" %>
2  using System;
3  using System.Web.Services;
4
5  namespace VQP
6  {
7    [WebService(Namespace="VQP")]
8    public class Salutation : WebService
9    {
10     [WebMethod]
11     public String SaySalutation( String region )
12     {
13       String salutation;
14
15       switch( region )
16       {
17         case "Globe":
18             salutation = "Hello World";
19             break;
20         case "USA":
21             salutation = "Hi";
22             break;
23         case "West":
24             salutation = "Howdy";
25             break;
26         default:
27             salutation = "Hello";
28             break;
29       }
30
31       return salutation;
32     }
33   }
34 }
```

8. Add the WebService and WebMethod attributes like this:

```
[WebService(Namespace="VQP")]
public class Salutation: WebService
{
  [WebMethod]
  public String SaySalutation(
  String region )
  {
    String salutation;
    switch( region )
    {
      case "Globe":
        salutation = "Hello World";
        break;
      case "USA":
        salutation = "Hi";
        break;
      case "West":
        salutation = "Howdy";
        break;
      default:
        salutation = "Hello";
        break;
    }
    return salutation;
  }
}
}
```

9. Compare your page against **Script 12.1** to check for errors and then save it.

As you can see, it doesn't take much effort to create a Web service. First we added the page-level declaration stating that this was a Web service. Then we created a namespace for our class to reside in. Next we created a class that inherited from the class WebService. All of this should be familiar to you, since we covered similar topics in Chapter 11, when we created custom server controls. The only truly new topics are the WebService and WebMethod attributes.

Attributes are used in .NET to add descriptive information to methods, classes, properties, and so on. Here, we added an attribute to our Salutation class so that the VQP namespace will be the namespace used when we publish our Web service. We could have set it to something other than VQP even though that's our class's namespace. While the names aren't required to be the same, it's a good practice to keep them consistent.

We also added the WebMethod attribute to our SaySalutation method to mark it as being available to consumers of our Web service. If we had to define additional methods to support our Salutation class, we could do so. But only those marked with the WebMethod attribute would be available to our Web service's consumers.

Consuming a service

Web services are so simple to create that ours is ready to use "as is." There are two ways we can access the functions inside the Web service. The first is to invoke it directly in a Web browser through its URL. That method is usually reserved for testing purposes. The second method is via an application such as a Web Form. Let's use our Salutation Web service by invoking it directly from the browser first.

To open a Web service in a browser:

1. With your Salutation.asmx file open in Dreamweaver, press F12 to open it in your default browser.

    You'll see a page that looks nothing like what you created in "To create a Web Service." This page is automatically generated by the Web server so that you can test the Web service (**Figure 12.2**).

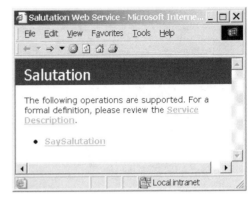

Figure 12.2 Here is the Salutation Web service as seen in Internet Explorer.

Figure 12.3 Test the SaySalutation Web service in Internet Explorer by setting the region parameter and clicking the Invoke button.

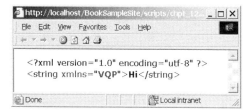

Figure 12.4 The result of invoking the SaySalutation Web service is formatted in XML.

2. Click the hyperlink labeled SaySalutation to go to a page that allows you to call that method of your Web service.

Note: If your class had more methods with the `WebMethod` attribute set, they would be displayed here, too.

The page that you're brought to when you click the SaySalutation link is auto-generated by the Web server as well (**Figure 12.3**). It lets you test your Web service by providing a text box for you to specify a value for the region parameter of your `SaySalutation` method.

Below the testing region is a description of the SOAP, HTTP-GET, and HTTP-POST message-encoding definitions for this method. You would need those if you didn't have a tool like Dreamweaver to help you consume the Web service.

3. In the new page that appears, type "USA" as the region. Then click the Invoke button to call the SaySalution Web service.

A new browser window will open containing XML that describes your Web service's return message (**Figure 12.4**). ASP.NET will change this into a more usable format when we use this Web service in a Web Form, but as you can see, XML is used everywhere in a Web service.

Having successfully tested the Salutation Web service, let's use it in a Web Form. To do so, Dreamweaver will need the WSDL document that describes our Web service in XML format. Fortunately, all you have to do to obtain the WSDL document that describes the Salutation Web service is to add "?WSDL" to the end of the URL. The Web server will automatically generate it for you when it sees this at the end of the URL.

To consume a Web Service:

1. Create a new Web Form as we did in "To create a new Web Form" in Chapter 4. Save it as ConsumeSalutation.aspx.

   Make the Code and Design views visible by clicking the Document toolbar's Show Code and Design Views icon (**Figure 12.5**).

2. In the code of the page, add a form element with its runat attribute set to "server". It'll look like this:

   ```
   <form runat="server">
   </form>
   ```

3. In Design view, click inside of the dotted red box that represents the form. From the Insert bar, click on the ASP.NET tab, and then click the asp:dropdownlist icon (**Figure 12.6**).

   The Tag Editor opens.

4. In the Tag Editor, set the ID to "ddlRegions" and click the Auto Postback check box once so that its checkmark turns from gray to black.

   This will cause the Web Form to post back to itself when the ddlRegion control's selection changes.

5. Click OK to close the dialog box.

6. Back in Design view, click next to the drop-down list, and then on the ASP.NET tab click the asp:label icon abc.

   The Tag Editor will open.

7. In the Tag Editor, set the ID to "lblSalutation" and click OK.

Figure 12.5 Display both code and design by clicking the Show Code and Design Views icon on the Document toolbar.

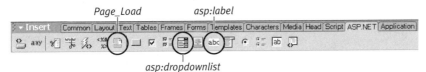

Figure 12.6 Use the icons on the ASP.NET tab to start the Tag Editor for those controls.

8. Now click in the Code view, and add the following list items to the ddlRegions control:

```
<asp:dropdownlist AutoPostBack="true"
ID="ddlRegions" runat="server">
  <asp:listitem>
    Make a Selection
  </asp:listitem>
  <asp:listitem>
    Globe
  </asp:listitem>
  <asp:listitem>
    USA
  </asp:listitem>
  <asp:listitem>
    West
  </asp:listitem>
  <asp:listitem>
    Other
  </asp:listitem>
</asp:dropdownlist>
```

9. Further up in the code, place your cursor just before the </head> tag to set your insertion point for the Page_Load function.

10. From the ASP.NET tab, click the Page_Load icon 🖼 to insert its default code.

11. Change the Page_Load function to read:

```
protected void Page_Load(Object Src,
EventArgs E)
{
  if( IsPostBack )
  {

  }
}
```

We'll only be running the code that we'll place between the curly braces when the page is in Postback mode.

continues on next page

12. From the Application panel group, click on the Components tab, and select Web Services from the drop-down list (**Figure 12.7**).

13. Click the Add a Web Service button 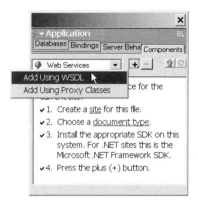 to open a list of available options. Select Add Using WSDL from the list.

The Add Using WSDL dialog box will open.

Figure 12.7 Add a Web service using WSDL from the Components tab of the Application panel group.

14. In the Add Using WSDL dialog box, enter the URL to your Salutation.asmx file (**Figure 12.8**). At the end of the URL, type "?WSDL" so Dreamweaver can access the autogenerated WSDL file for our Web service. In the Proxy Generator drop-down list, select .NET C# and then click OK.

Figure 12.8 Add a reference to the Salutation Web service with the Add Using WSDL dialog box. Your URL may differ from the one shown here.

You'll see that the Components tab in the Application panel group now shows a reference to the Salutation Web service (**Figure 12.9**). What you might not have noticed is that two files were created as well: Salutation.cs and Salutation.dll. The cs file was generated from the WSDL file and then compiled into the DLL file. We need to copy the DLL file up to the bin directory on our testing server.

Figure 12.9 A reference to the Salutation Web service on the Components tab.

15. On the top right of the Components tab, click the Deploy Supporting Files To Testing Server button.

The Deploy Supporting Files To Testing Server dialog box appears.

16. In the dialog box, set the correct access method and path to your testing server's bin directory (**Figure 12.10**). Click Deploy to copy the Salutation.dll file to the testing server's bin directory.

Figure 12.10 Set the access method and bin directory location for your testing server in the Deploy Supporting Files To Testing Server dialog box.

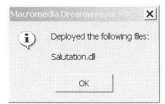

Figure 12.11 Click OK after successfully deploying the Salutation.dll file.

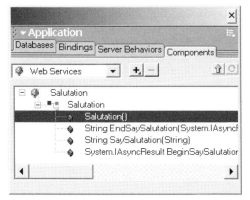

Figure 12.12 Here is the Salutation Web service on the Components tab. You see each of the exposed methods of the service's proxy class.

17. Click OK in the message box that appears upon successful deployment of the Salutation.dll file (**Figure 12.11**).

18. Expand the reference to the Salutation Web service on the Components tab (**Figure 12.12**). Then click and drag the Salutation constructor (`Salutation()`) from that panel to your `Page_Load` function so it reads:

```
protected void Page_Load(Object Src,
EventArgs E)
{
  if( IsPostBack )
  {
    Salutation aSalutation =
    new Salutation();
  }
}
```

This code stores a reference to the Web service in the `aSalutation` variable.

19. Again from the Components tab, click and drag the `String SaySalutation(String)` item to the code just after the line you added in the previous step. The resulting code will look like this:

```
if( ! IsPostBack )
{
  Salutation aSalutation =
  new Salutation();
  String aString =
    aSalutation.SaySalutation(
    /*String*/enter_value_here );
}
```

This new statement calls the `SaySalutation` method on the `aSalutation` object and assigns the returned value to a string called `aString`. We'll replace the `/*String*/enter_value_here` placeholder with text of the ddlRegions control's selected item.

continues on next page

ABOUT WEB SERVICES

20. Change the parameter for the SaySalutation method to the following:

```
String aString =
    aSalutation.SaySalutation(
    ddlRegions.SelectedItem.Text );
```

21. Finally, add the following code to assign the method's return value to the **Text** property of our lblSalutation control:

```
String aString =
    aSalutation.SaySalutation(
    ddlRegions.SelectedItem.Text );
lblSalutation.Text = aString;
```

22. Compare your code against **Script 12.2**. Then press F12 to test it in your default browser.

You should get a different Salutation every time you change the selection in the drop-down list.

You saw in Step 14 how Dreamweaver used the Salutation Web service's WSDL document to create a C# file, which it compiled into a DLL file. The DLL file is referred to as a Web service proxy.

A *proxy* is something that acts as a substitute for something else. A Web service proxy is an object that looks just like the Web service but resides locally, like in the bin directory. We call the proxy's methods rather than directly calling the Web service's methods because, as we said before, Web services need to communicate with specially encoded and formatted messages, like SOAP messages. If we called the Web service directly from the Web Form, we'd have to do all that encoding and formatting ourselves. Dreamweaver relieves us of that work by creating the proxy for us. That way we can call the proxy's methods and concentrate on what the Web Form is supposed to do, like display regional salutations, instead of worrying about sending and receiving SOAP messages.

Script 12.2 Here we use the Web service to determine which salutation to display each time the drop-down list's selection changes.

```
1  <%@ Page Language="C#" ContentType=
   "text/html" ResponseEncoding="iso-8859-1" %>
2  <html>
3  <head>
4  <title>Untitled Document</title>
5  <meta http-equiv="Content-Type" content=
   "text/html; charset=iso-8859-1">
6  <script runat="server">
7  protected void Page_Load(Object Src,
   EventArgs E)
8  {
9    if( IsPostBack )
10   {
11     Salutation aSalutation = new Salutation();
12     String aString = aSalutation.SaySaluta
       tion( ddlRegions.SelectedItem.Text );
13     lblSalutation.Text = aString;
14   }
15 }
16 </script>
17 </head>
18 <body>
19 <form runat="server">
20   <asp:dropdownlist AutoPostBack="true" ID=
     "ddlRegions" runat="server">
21     <asp:listitem>Make a Selection</asp:
       listitem>
22     <asp:listitem>Globe</asp:listitem>
23     <asp:listitem>USA</asp:listitem>
24     <asp:listitem>West</asp:listitem>
25     <asp:listitem>Other</asp:listitem>
26   </asp:dropdownlist>
27   <asp:label ID="lblSalutation" runat=
     "server"></asp:label>
28 </form>
29 </body>
30 </html>
```

Finding the Right Web Service

The true power of Web services comes from their ability to let one developer use another developer's program, regardless of which language or platform either developer uses. You could write a program on Windows using C# but use a service running on Unix written in Java without even knowing it.

Looking for help

Finding the right Web service to fit your needs is possible because of UDDI. UDDI is a standard definition for how developers describe the Web services they're providing so that those services can be made available publicly to anyone who wants to use them. If it weren't for this standard definition, finding a Web service would be difficult, because every developer would provide different levels of detail—and in different formats. You'd have to carefully read through every description to learn about a Web service, rather than quickly scanning for keywords in a fixed section of the description.

Having a standard definition also lays the groundwork for having UDDI registries. UDDI registries are searchable by category of service, by keyword in a service name or description, or by the provider of the service, and so on, because these are all fixed sections of the description available in the UDDI registry. And it doesn't matter whether you look for your potential Web service in Microsoft's UDDI registry, IBM's registry, or any of the other official registries. They all share information with each other, so you'll be able to find the same Web services in all of them.

In Chapter 1 we introduced the scenario in which the U.S. Postal Service could provide a Web service to list all zip codes. Then from within your Web page you could call that Web service to get the list of zip codes and add that data to a drop-down list box for your users to select from. If the list changed, by maybe including a few more zip codes, you wouldn't even need to know about the change for your page to be up-to-date, because you wouldn't be storing that information locally.

Unfortunately, the U.S. Postal Service doesn't have a Web service registered to list zip codes, at least not at the time of this writing when we searched for it. However, there are other developers in the world who do provide this sort of functionality in their Web services. The following instructions show you how to find them in Microsoft's UDDI registry. We could have used any other registry, but we thought that since we're dealing with ASP.NET in this book we'd use Microsoft's.

To find a service in Microsoft's UDDI registry:

1. Open your Web browser and browse to http://uddi.microsoft.com/.

   The home page of Microsoft's UDDI registry will appear (**Figure 12.13**).

2. Click the Search link on the left of the page to go to the site's search page.

3. In the Search Criteria section of the search page, click the Services tab (**Figure 12.14**).

   We'll be searching for a service that lists zip codes.

4. With the Search Criteria set to search by the service name, type "zipcode" in the Service Name field and press Enter.

   On the left side of the page, the Search section's Results tab lists the search results (**Figure 12.15**).

5. Click the service titled ZipCodes, with the description of Zip Code Utility Service.

   The screen will update to show more information about this Web service.

Figure 12.13 From the home page of Microsoft's UDDI registry, click Search to go to the search page.

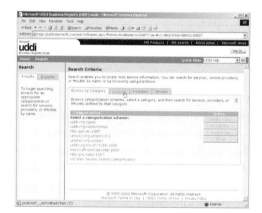

Figure 12.14 Search for a service by switching to the Services tab on the default search page.

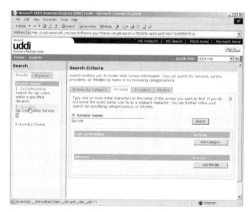

Figure 12.15 Search for and find Web services named "zipcode."

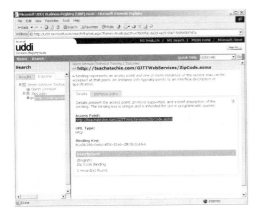

Figure 12.16 Find the Access Point URL of the ZipCode Web service.

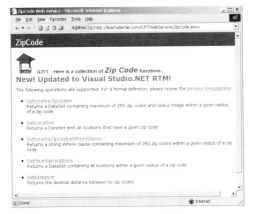

Figure 12.17 Test the ZipCode.asmx file in Internet Explorer.

6. Click the plus sign next to the ZipCodes link on the left side of the page to expand it. Then click the URL that appears below the ZipCodes link (**Figure 12.16**).

The right part of the page will update to show the details about the URL you just clicked. That URL is what's referred to as the Web service's access point. We can see that the page ends in .asmx, so we know that we'll be able to get its WSDL file by adding "?WSDL" to the end of the URL (adding this causes the Web server to automatically return the WSDL document describing the Web service).

7. From the main section of the page, highlight and copy the URL under the Access Point heading.

8. Paste the copied URL into your Web browser's address field and press Enter.

The main page for the ZipCode Web service will appear (**Figure 12.17**). Notice that the GetNearbyZipCodes, GetLocation, and GetNearbyLocations methods say they return DataSets in their descriptions, which means we can easily assign their results to ASP.NET controls later on when we consume this service in a Web Form.

9. To make sure the Web service provides what we want, click the GetNearbyZipCodes link.

continues on next page

FINDING THE RIGHT WEB SERVICE

10. To test the page that appears, in the ZipCode field type "32765" and in the RadiusMiles field type "10" (**Figure 12.18**). Click the Invoke button to run the test.

If the Web service works, it will return a list of all the zip codes within a 10-mile radius of the 32765 zip code.

Just like the test we ran in "To open a Web Service in a browser" on the Salutation Web service we created, the result is returned in XML format (**Figure 12.19**). While the result is somewhat overwhelming, we learn something important: Each Location row has a ZIP_CODE field and a RADIUS_MILES field. This information will be useful when we consume this Web service in a Web Form.

Consuming other's services

Having found a working Web service that'll give us a list of zip codes, we can consume it in a Web Form. When testing this Web service, we learned that it also provides a method called GetLocation that returns the city, county, and state information for a given zip code. If we wanted to help our Web site's users fill out their address information, we could let them choose from a list of zip codes, like we had planned, but then use the selected zip code to automatically populate the city and state fields. Let's build a Web Form to do that. We've divided the instructions into two sets. The first set is for creating the design of the page. The second is for writing the code that will consume the Web service.

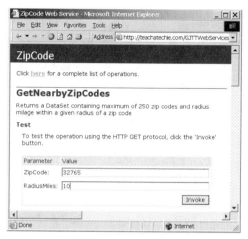

Figure 12.18 Test the GetNearbyZipCodes Web method by entering values for its parameters and clicking Invoke.

Table name   Field names

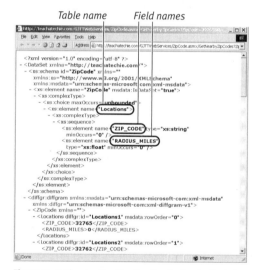

Figure 12.19 The results of testing the GetNearbyZipCodes Web method are in XML. We can learn the names of the table and its columns from it.

Figure 12.20 Start the Insert Table dialog box by clicking its icon on the Common tab.

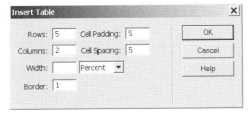

Figure 12.21 Use the Insert Table dialog box to define the table you want to create.

Figure 12.22 Start the Tag Editor by clicking the asp:textbox icon on the ASP.NET tab.

To create the design of the Web Form:

1. Create a new Web Form and make the Code and Design views visible by clicking the Document toolbar's Show Code and Design Views icon.

2. In the code of the page, add a form element with its runat attribute set to "server". It'll look like this:

```
<form runat="server">
</form>
```

3. In Design view, click inside the dotted red box that represents the form. From the Insert bar, click on the Common tab, and then click on the Insert Table icon (**Figure 12.20**).

   This opens a dialog box of the same name (**Figure 12.21**).

4. In the Insert Table dialog box, set Rows to 5 and Columns to 2. Clear the Width field. Then set Border to 1 and both Cell Padding and Cell Spacing to 5. Click OK.

   This creates the table and closes the dialog box.

5. In Design view, click in the table's first column in the first row, and type "Name."

6. Click in the second column of the first row. From the Insert bar, click on the ASP.NET tab, and then click the asp:textbox icon (**Figure 12.22**).

   This opens its Tag Editor.

7. In the Tag Editor, set the ID to "txtName" and click OK.

8. Back in Design view, click in the table's first column in the second row and type "Street."

9. Click in the table's second column in the second row. Then from the ASP.NET tab, click the asp:textbox icon to open its Tag Editor.

continues on next page

FINDING THE RIGHT WEB SERVICE

10. In the Tag Editor, set the ID to "txtStreet" and click OK.

11. Back in Design view, click in the table's first column in the third row, and type "ZIP."

12. Click in the table's second column in the third row. Then from the ASP.NET tab, click the asp:dropdownlist icon .

Its Tag Editor opens.

13. In the Tag Editor, set the ID to "ddlZIP." Then click the Auto Postback check box once to change the checkmark from gray to black.

This will cause the form to automatically post back to the server, just like it did in "To consume a Web Service" earlier in this chapter.

14. Back in Design view, click in the table's first column in the fourth row, and type "City."

15. Click in the table's second column in the fourth row. Then from the ASP.NET tab, click the asp:textbox icon.

This opens its Tag Editor.

16. In the Tag Editor, set the ID to "txtCity" and click OK.

17. Back in Design view, click in the table's first column in the fifth row and type "State."

18. Click in the table's second column in the fifth row. Then from the ASP.NET tab, click the asp:textbox icon.

This opens the Tag Editor.

19. In the Tag Editor, set the ID to "txtState" and click OK.

20. Save the page as "webServiceForm.aspx" (**Figure 12.23**).

Figure 12.23 This is the final Design view for the address form.

To consume a real-world Web service:

1. In the Web Form you were just working in, move into the Code view of the page.

2. Click just in front of the </head> tag to set your insertion point. From the Insert bar, click on the ASP.NET tab, and then click on the Page_Load icon 🖺 to insert Dreamweaver's default Page_Load function.

3. Change the Page_Load function to look like this:

```
protected void Page_Load(Object Src,
EventArgs E)
{
  if( ! IsPostBack )
  {

  }
  else
  {

  }
}
```

This will allow us to have different code run when the page loads for the first time than when the page posts back to the server.

Now it's time add a reference to the ZipCode Web service we discovered in "To find a service in Microsoft's UDDI registry."

4. From the Application panel group, click on the Components tab, and then select Web Services from the drop-down list.

5. Then click the Add a Web Service button ⊞ to open a list of available options. Select Add Using WSDL from the list to open a dialog box with that name.

continues on next page

FINDING THE RIGHT WEB SERVICE

6. In the Add Using WSDL dialog box, enter the URL to the ZipCode Web service with "?WSDL" appended to the end like this:

```
http://teachatechie.com/GJTTWebservi
ces/ZipCode.asmx?WSDL
```

Notice that we have a list of common UDDI registries available here under the globe icon (**Figure 12.24**). Unfortunately, opening a registry from here will not automatically populate the "URL of the WSDL file" field once we've found a Web service we want to use, so we'd still have to manually enter it.

7. Click OK to close this dialog box and create a reference to the Web service in the Components tab of the Application Panel group.

8. In the Components tab, click the Deploy Supporting Files To Testing Server button 🗟.

The Deploy Supporting Files To Testing Server dialog box appears (**Figure 12.25**).

9. In the dialog box, set the correct access method and path to your testing server's bin directory. Then click OK.

This copies the ZipCode.dll file to the testing server's bin directory.

10. Click OK in the message box that appears upon successful deployment of the ZipCode.dll file (**Figure 12.26**).

11. Expand the reference to the ZipCode Web Service on the Components tab (**Figure 12.27**). Then click on the ZipCode constructor (`ZipCode()`) located at the bottom of the list in that panel, and drag it to just before your `if( ! IsPostBack )` statement so that it reads:

Figure 12.24 You can open a UDDI registry from the available list in the Add Using WSDL dialog box.

Figure 12.25 Set the access method and bin directory location for your testing server in the Deploy Supporting Files To Testing Server dialog box.

Figure 12.26 Click OK after successfully deploying the ZipCode.dll file.

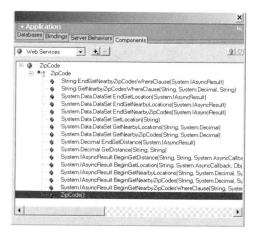

Figure 12.27 The ZipCode Web service expanded on the Components tab shows all available methods.

```
protected void Page_Load(Object Src,
EventArgs E)
{
  ZipCode aZipCode = new
ZipCode();
  if( ! IsPostBack )
```

We created a reference to the ZipCode Web Service here because we're going to need it in both the `if` and the `else` code blocks.

12. Again from the Components tab, click and drag the item in the middle of the list that reads `System.Data.DataSet GetNearbyZipCodes( String, System.Decimal )` to within the `if` code block. The resulting code will look like this:

```
if( ! IsPostBack )
{
  System.Data.DataSet aDataSet =
  aZipCode.GetNearbyZipCodes( /*St
ring*/enter_value_here, /*System
.Decimal*/enter_value_here );
}
```

We'll need to replace the parameter placeholders before the DataSet will be populated with data.

13. Change the first parameter from the following:

```
/*String*/enter_value_here
```

to:

```
"32765"
```

14. Then change the second parameter from the following:

```
/*System.Decimal*/enter_value_here
```

to:

```
10
```

15. Add the following code into the `if` code block as well, so that our ddlZIP control will be populated with the result of the call to the ZipCode Web service:

```
if( ! IsPostBack )
{
  System.Data.DataSet aDataSet =
    aZipCode.GetNearbyZipCodes(
    "32765", 10 );
  ddlZIP.DataSource = aDataSet;
  ddlZIP.DataTextField = "ZIP_CODE";
}
```

Remember that we learned what the DataSet's field names were in Step 10 of "To find a service in Microsoft's UDDI registry."

16. Below the code you just added, type the following:

```
ddlZIP.DataTextField = "ZIP_CODE";
DataBind();
ddlZIP.Items.Insert( 0,
new ListItem("Select a ZIP","") );
```

This extra code will bind the data in the DataSet to the ddlZIP control. Then a new non-ZIP list item will be placed into the control as its new first item. This will force our users to make a selection instead of potentially just leaving the first zip code in the list as their selection. In that case, the page wouldn't post back to the server, and the code we're about to add to the `else` code block wouldn't be executed, forcing our users to manually type in their city and state.

17. Now from the Components tab, click and drag the item that reads `System.Data.DataSet GetLocation (String)` to within the `else` code block. The result will look like this:

```
else
{
  System.Data.DataSet aDataSet =
    aZipCode.GetLocation(
    /*String*/enter_value_here );
}
```

continues on next page

FINDING THE RIGHT WEB SERVICE

18. Change the parameter from:

```
/*String*/enter_value_here
```

to:

```
ddlZIP.SelectedItem.Text
```

19. Then set the Text properties of the txtCity and txtState controls to the correct fields of the Locations table in the returned DataSet:

```
else
{
    System.Data.DataSet aDataSet =
        aZipCode.GetLocation(
        ddlZIP.SelectedItem.Text );
    txtCity.Text  = aDataSet.Tables[
    "Locations" ].Rows[0][
    "CITYSTNAME" ].ToString();
    txtState.Text = aDataSet.Tables[
    "Locations" ].Rows[0][ "STATE" ]
    .ToString();
}
```

We obtained the table and field names from running the GetLocations Web method in the browser like we did the GetNearbyZipCodes Web method in "To find a service in Microsoft's UDDI registry."

20. Make sure to add the DataBind method as the last line of the else code block to make the data we retrieved in our Web service call bind to the controls. It will look like this:

```
else
{
    System.Data.DataSet aDataSet =
        aZipCode.GetLocation(
        ddlZIP.SelectedItem.Text );
    txtCity.Text  = aDataSet.Tables[
    "Locations" ].Rows[0][ "CITYSTNAME"
    ].ToString();
    txtState.Text = aDataSet.Tables[
    "Locations" ].Rows[0][ "STATE"
    ].ToString();
    DataBind();
}
```

Script 12.3 Using a Web service built by another developer is no harder than using one you create yourself. Here we look up a list of zip codes and display them to the user. Then when the user picks one, the city and state fields are automatically populated with more data retrieved from the service.

```
1  <%@ Page Language="C#" ContentType=
   "text/html" ResponseEncoding="iso-8859-1" %>
2  <html>
3  <head>
4  <title>Untitled Document</title>
5  <meta http-equiv="Content-Type" content=
   "text/html; charset=iso-8859-1">
6  <script runat="server">
7  protected void Page_Load(Object Src,
   EventArgs E)
8  {
9    ZipCode aZipCode = new ZipCode();
10   if( ! IsPostBack )
11   {
12     System.Data.DataSet aDataSet =
       aZipCode.GetNearbyZipCodes("32765", 10);
13     ddlZIP.DataSource = aDataSet;
14     ddlZIP.DataTextField = "ZIP_CODE";
15     DataBind();
16     ddlZIP.Items.Insert( 0, new
       ListItem("Select a ZIP","") );
17   }
18   else
19   {
20     System.Data.DataSet aDataSet =
       aZipCode.GetLocation( ddlZIP.Selec
       tedItem.Text );
21     txtCity.Text  = aDataSet.Tables[
       "Locations" ].Rows[0][ "CITYSTNAME" ]
       .ToString();
22     txtState.Text = aDataSet.Tables[
       "Locations" ].Rows[0][ "STATE" ]
       .ToString();
23     DataBind();
24   }
25 }
26 </script>
27 </head>
28 <body>
29 <form runat="server">
30 <table border="1" cellspacing="5"
   cellpadding="5">
31   <tr>
32     <td>Name</td>
33     <td><asp:textbox ID="txtName" runat=
       "server" /></td>
```

(script continues)

Script 12.3 *continued*

```
 _____
|▓▓▓▓▓▓▓▓▓▓▓ script ▓▓▓▓▓▓▓▓▓▓▓|
|─────────────────────────────|
|34   </tr>
|35   <tr>
|36    <td>Street</td>
|37    <td><asp:textbox ID="txtStreet" runat=
|      "server" /></td>
|38   </tr>
|39   <tr>
|40    <td>ZIP</td>
|41    <td>
|42      <asp:dropdownlist AutoPostBack=
|        "true" ID="ddlZIP" runat=
|        "server"></asp:dropdownlist>
|43    </td>
|44   </tr>
|45   <tr>
|46    <td>City</td>
|47    <td><asp:textbox ID="txtCity" runat=
|      "server" /></td>
|48   </tr>
|49   <tr>
|50    <td>State</td>
|51    <td><asp:textbox ID="txtState" runat=
|      "server" /></td>
|52   </tr>
|53  </table>
|54  </form>
|55  </html>
```

21. Compare the file against **Script 12.3** to check for errors, and then save it.

22. To test, open the page in your default browser by pressing F12. Change the drop-down list's selection, and your page will update with the newly selected zip code's correct city and state.

It sure is nice to know that we can use zip code data in our Web Form without having to maintain that data. And think of all the time we saved not having to write all the code needed to make this zip code lookup work.

Web services are going to become more and more valuable to Web developers, because they let us reuse functionality created by someone else, rather than just the functionality we ourselves created in previous projects. So in your next project, look around a UDDI registry for Web services that will meet your needs. You could save yourself hours of development time.

FINDING THE RIGHT WEB SERVICE

EXTENDING DREAMWEAVER MX

Dreamweaver is designed to be completely extensible, meaning that you can extend it and customize it in countless ways. No two developers need work from the same Dreamweaver development environment, even if they share the same version of Dreamweaver. That's because Dreamweaver MX is not only extensible, but it can also store configuration settings for each user of a multiuser operating system such as Windows 2000. And because all of Dreamweaver's components are built with HTML, JavaScript, and XML, you already possess the basic skills to extend Dreamweaver.

In this chapter, you'll learn how to add extensions that have been built by Dreamweaver developers around the world. Then we'll show you how to create two types of extensions on your own. This first type of extension adds often-used ASP.NET code to a Web Form with the click of a button. It's a custom server behavior that Dreamweaver helps you create. The second extension adds a new tab to the Insert bar. We'll also show you how to package it so that it's ready for other developers to install in their copies of Dreamweaver, too.

Dreamweaver Extensions

Developers have been creating extensions for Dreamweaver since version 3. To help them manage their extensions, Macromedia provides a free add-on tool called the Extension Manager. We'll install the Extension Manager and then use it to install an extension we'll find and load via the Internet.

The Extension Manager

With the explosion of developers creating their own extensions for Dreamweaver, Macromedia added the capability to create extensions into most of their development products, including most recently Dreamweaver MX, Fireworks MX, and Macromedia Flash MX. Then as developers increasingly created and shared their extensions with other developers, Macromedia created the Extension Manager to help developers install and track the extensions they had installed, as well as package new ones for distribution. The Extension Manager runs as an add-on to the development tools from Macromedia, so it will work with all of them concurrently.

The Extension Manager can be downloaded for free directly from Macromedia's Web site. The following instructions detail how to install it.

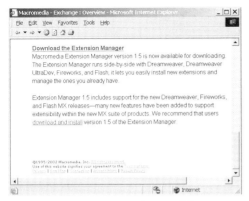

Figure 13.1 Click the link at the bottom of the Macromedia Exchange's home page to download the Extension Manager.

Figure 13.2 Click the link for the Windows download at the bottom of the page.

Figure 13.3 Save the em_install.exe file to your computer.

To install the Extension Manager:

1. Open your browser to http://exchange.macromedia.com/.

2. Scroll to the bottom of the page, and click the link that says Download the Extension Manager (**Figure 13.1**).

   The Extension Manager download page appears. The current release is version 1.5—the version recommended for Dreamweaver MX.

3. On the download page, scroll to the bottom and click on the link for the Windows version (**Figure 13.2**).

   A File Download dialog box will open, prompting you to save the file called em_install.exe.

4. In the File Download dialog box, click the Save button (**Figure 13.3**). In the resulting Save As dialog box, specify where you want the file saved and click Save.

continues on next page

DREAMWEAVER EXTENSIONS

5. Now double-click the em_install.exe file you just saved.

The file will run a system check. When it's done you'll see the first screen of the Macromedia Extension Manager Installation program (**Figure 13.4**).

6. Click Next to move from the installation program's introductory screen to the license agreement (**Figure 13.5**).

7. After reading the license agreement, click Yes to agree and continue.

You will then be asked where you want to install the Extension Manager (**Figure 13.6**).

8. Click Next to accept the default location, or use the Browse button before clicking Next to customize where you want to install the Extension Manager.

Clicking Next saves the files to your system. Then a new page will open in your default Web browser giving an overview of the Extension Manager (**Figure 13.7**).

Note: You can reopen this overview page by clicking the Start button and navigating to the Macromedia folder. The file is called Macromedia Extension Manager Readme.

Figure 13.4 The Macromedia Extension Manager has a wizard to help you through its installation process.

Figure 13.5 Read and accept the the Extension Manager's license agreement.

Figure 13.6 Set the Extension Manager's installation folder and click Next.

Figure 13.7 The Extension Manager's read-me file has useful links, like one that leads to the Macromedia (Dreamweaver) Exchange and one that opens a document describing the MXI file format.

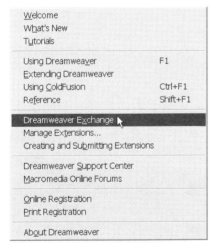

Figure 13.8 Open the Dreamweaver Exchange from Dreamweaver's Help menu.

Adding extensions

In Chapter 12 we talked about using Web services written by other developers in our Web pages. Web services are programs distributed over the Internet that provide reusable, useful functionality so that you don't have to write the code for that function yourself.

While Web services add functionality to Web Forms, with extensions you can insert functionality written by another developer directly into Dreamweaver. And Dreamweaver makes it easy for you to use them—just find the right one for your needs, download and install it.

You'll find extensions in several places. First, look in the Dreamweaver Exchange. It's a repository for extensions that have been reviewed by Macromedia technicians for security, quality, and stability. You can get there from Dreamweaver's Help menu (**Figure 13.8**). Just click Dreamweaver Exchange to open the site. Once there, you'll be able to search for extensions by any number of parameters, such as category, type, author, and so on.

The Dreamweaver Exchange isn't the only place to look for extensions, however. Many sites have extensions you can download. At one such site, for example, we found a useful extension, Live Preview, that lets you preview a page in Dreamweaver without having to leave Dreamweaver to see it in a browser, like we do when we press the F12 key. In the stepped list that follows, we show you how to download this extension from the Dreamweaver Team Web site.

To download the Live Preview extension:

1. Open your browser to www.dwteam.com/. The Dreamweaver Team home page appears (**Figure 13.9**).

2. Click on the Extensions link in the main navigation bar at the top of the home page. The Extensions page opens (**Figure 13.10**).

3. Click the Toolbars link just below the main navigation bar to jump down to that section of the page.

4. Click the Live Preview link to download the extension (**Figure 13.11**).

5. Save the file to your computer when prompted to do so.

Now that you have the preview extension downloaded, you need to install it. To do this, you can do one of two things: simply double-click the file in Windows Explorer, or use the Extension Manager. Whichever method you choose, the extension will end up being listed in the Extension Manager. We'll show you how to use the Extension Manager to install the Live Preview extension.

Figure 13.9 The Dreamweaver Team has a Web site with useful extensions available for download.

Figure 13.10 The extension we want is available under the Toolbars section.

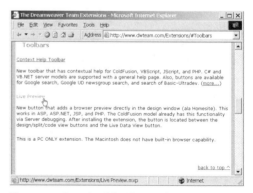

Figure 13.11 Download the Live Preview extension.

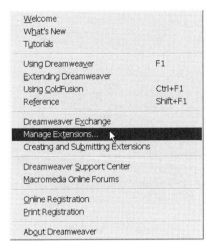

Figure 13.12 Open the Exchange Manager from Dreamweaver's Help menu.

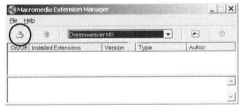

Figure 13.13 The Exchange Manager has no installed extensions by default.

Figure 13.14 Select the Live Preview.mxp file to install the Live Preview extension.

To install an extension using the Extension Manager:

1. From Dreamweaver's Help menu, click Manage Extensions (**Figure 13.12**).

   The Macromedia Extension Manager opens (**Figure 13.13**).

2. From the Extension Manager, click the Install New Extension icon ⬛ at the top left of the page.

   This opens the Select Extension to Install dialog box, in which you can select the extension you want to install.

3. In the dialog box, select the Live Preview.mxp file that you saved to your computer in the previous set of instructions, and click the Install button (**Figure 13.14**).

continues on next page

4. Read the disclaimer that opens, and then click Accept (**Figure 13.15**).

After accepting the disclaimer, the extension will install. When the extension has finished installing, you'll be prompted to restart Dreamweaver (**Figure 13.16**).

5. Click OK. Then restart Dreamweaver.

✔ Tip

■ While you're often informed that you must close and reopen Dreamweaver after installing an extension, sometimes just reloading the extensions will suffice. To do that, hold down the Ctrl key while clicking the Insert bar's Options icon  and selecting Reload Extensions from the menu (**Figure 13.17**).

You can now see the entry for the Live Preview extension in the Extension Manager (**Figure 13.18**). When you click on it in the upper window, you'll get a description of what it does and how to use it in the lower window.

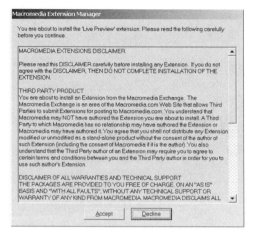

Figure 13.15 All extensions will require that you accept the disclaimer that Macromedia is not responsible for the extension you're installing.

Figure 13.16 The Live Preview extension requires that Dreamweaver be restarted before it will work properly.

Figure 13.17 Sometimes you can reload the extensions rather than having to restart Dreamweaver: Hold down the Ctrl key while clicking the Insert bar's Option icon and selecting Reload Extensions.

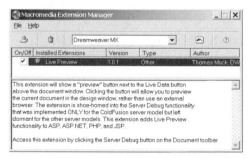

Figure 13.18 Selecting an extension in the Extension Manager will display the extension's description in the text area below.

DREAMWEAVER EXTENSIONS

To use the Live Preview extension:

1. Create a new Web Form. (See "To create a Web Form" in Chapter 4 if you need help.) Make sure it shows both code and design by clicking the Document toolbar's Show Code and Design Views icon (**Figure 13.19**).

2. Click in the Design view. Then from the Insert bar, click on the ASP.NET tab, and then click the asp:label icon (**Figure 13.20**).
   This will start its Tag Editor.

3. In the Tag Editor, set the ID to "lblTestPreview" and click OK.

4. In Code view, click just before the </head> tag. Then from the ASP.NET tab, click the Page_Load icon 📄. This will insert the default Page_Load function's code.

5. Change the Page_Load function to read:

```
protected void Page_Load(Object Src,
EventArgs E)
{
  if (!IsPostBack)
    lblTestPreview.Text =
    "Preview Works!";
}
```

This will set the lblTestPreview control's text to "Preview Works!" when the page is loaded for the first time.

6. Now to test the Live Preview functionality, click the Document toolbar's new Live Preview icon (**Figure 13.21**). Then save your Web Form when prompted.

   Your page will appear in a Web browser within Dreamweaver (**Figure 13.22**).

No more pressing F12 to browse the page in your default browser! Now you can switch to preview mode in the same way you switch from Code view to Design view.

Figure 13.19 Click the Show Code and Design Views icon to split the display.

Figure 13.20 The ASP.NET tab has icons for inserting the Page_Load function and asp:label control.

Figure 13.21 The Live Preview extension adds an icon to the Document toolbar.

Figure 13.22 Previewing a document effectively opens a Web browser in Dreamweaver.

Personal Extensions

Now and then you'll think of a way that you'd like to personalize Dreamweaver that won't be satisfied by extensions created by other developers. Usually the kind of extension you're searching for involves automating a procedure that you often repeat.

One way to do this is to use Dreamweaver's code snippets, which you'll find in the Code panel group under the Snippets tab (**Figure 13.23**). Dreamweaver's default snippets are HTML, JavaScript, or a mix of the two. If you wanted, for instance, you could add snippets of C# code that you use often.

But another, and better, method for adding server-side code is to create your own server behavior like the Insert Record behavior we worked with in Chapter 8.

Creating custom server behaviors

Custom server behaviors can be used to insert markup and code into a page with a single click of a button. This makes it easy for you to insert commonly used code into your Web Forms. For example, you might place a text box with a required field validation control and an email validation control all at once with one click.

Dreamweaver's Server Behavior Builder tool makes the job of creating a custom behavior simple. It involves two tasks: You must first define the markup code for the server behavior and then define the behavior's event handler.

The following two sets of stepped lists walk you through this process, detailing how to use the Server Behavior Builder tool to create an asp:button control with its matching Click event-handling function. (We discussed handlers and events in Chapter 5.)

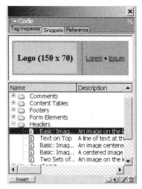

Figure 13.23 Code snippets are helpful for adding predefined sections of code to your pages.

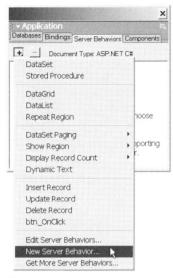

Figure 13.24 Create a new server behavior from the menu on the Server Behaviors panel.

Figure 13.25 The New Server Behavior dialog box.

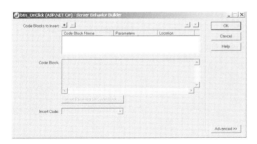

Figure 13.26 The Server Behavior Builder makes creating new server behaviors a snap.

Figure 13.27 Create a code block called btn_OnClick_Markup.

To define the markup code for a custom server behavior:

1. Create a new Web Form.

2. From the Application panel group, click on the Server Behaviors panel, and then click New Server Behavior (**Figure 13.24**).

   The New Server Behavior dialog box opens (**Figure 13.25**).

3. In the New Server Behavior dialog box, select ASP.NET C# as the Document Type and set Name to "btn_OnClick." Click OK.

   The dialog box closes, and the Server Behavior Builder opens (**Figure 13.26**).

   If we already had a custom server behavior that we wanted to use as a base on which to build, we could have checked the box in the New Server Behavior dialog box that was labeled "Copy existing server behavior." Then we would have selected the custom server behavior to copy in the "Behavior to copy" select box.

4. In the Server Behavior Builder, click the + (plus) sign button.

   This will open the Create a New Code Block dialog box (**Figure 13.27**).

continues on next page

5. In the dialog box, set Name to "btn_OnClick_Markup" and click OK.

The dialog box will close and the Server Behavior Builder tool will now list the new code block (**Figure 13.28**).

6. In the Code Block text area, change the default code block from:

```
<% Replace this text with the code to
insert when the server behavior is
applied %>
```

to:

```
<asp:button ID="" runat="server"
Text="" OnClick="" />
```

Next, we'll need to define parameters for the ID, Text, and OnClick attributes for the dynamic data we'll pass to the server behavior.

7. Click in between the quotes for the ID attribute and then click the Insert Parameter In Code Block button.

The Insert Parameter In Code Block dialog box will open (**Figure 13.29**).

8. Set the name of the new parameter to "Name," and click OK.

This closes the dialog box and creates the parameter. Notice that "@@Name@@" is now the value of the ID attribute in the Code Block text area.

9. Back in the Server Behavior Builder tool, click between the Text attribute's quotes in the Code Block text area. Then click the Insert Parameter In Code Block button to add another new parameter.

The Insert Parameter In Code Block dialog box opens again.

Figure 13.28 The contents of the new code block you added appear in the Code Block text area.

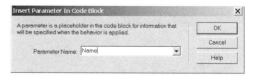

Figure 13.29 Create a parameter called Name.

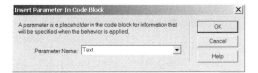

Figure 13.30 Create a parameter called Text.

Figure 13.31 These are the final settings of the btn_OnClick_Markup code block.

10. Set the name of the new parameter to "Text" (**Figure 13.30**). Click OK to close this dialog box and create the parameter.

11. In the Code Block text area, click between the quotes of the OnClick parameter and click the Insert Parameter In Code Block button.

12. From the Parameter Name drop-down list, select Name, because we want to reuse this parameter. Click OK to close this dialog box.

13. Back in the Code Block text area, beside the "@@Name@@" in the OnClick attribute, add _OnClick.

    The code in the Code Block text area should now read:

    ```
    <asp:button ID="@@Name@@"
    runat="server" Text="@@Text@@"
    OnClick="@@Name@@_OnClick" />
    ```

14. Set the value of the Insert Code drop-down list to read Relative to the Selection (**Figure 13.31**).

    When adding the btn_OnClick server behavior to your page, this setting will cause the code to be inserted where your cursor is placed.

15. Set the value of the Relative Position drop-down list to Replace the Selection.

    Your cursor may be highlighting some text when you add this server behavior. This setting will cause that highlighted text to be replaced with the contents of the server behavior.

Now we've completed the first part of the process for creating a custom server behavior—defining the markup code. On to the event handler.

To define the an event handler for a custom server behavior:

1. From the top of the Server Behavior Builder, once again click the + (plus) sign button to create a new code block.

   This opens the Create a New Code Block dialog box.

2. Set the name of the new code block to "btn_OnClick_Handler" and click OK.

3. Back in the Server Behavior Builder, replace the text in the Code Block text area with the following:

   ```
   <script language="C#" runat="server">
   void _OnClick(Object Src, EventArgs E)
   {

   }
   </script>
   ```

   This is the default code necessary to handle a button's Click event.

4. Click just before the underscore (_) in the text _OnClick from the last step. Then click the Insert Parameter In Code Block button to add a parameter to this code block.

   Its dialog box will open (**Figure 13.32**).

5. In the Insert Parameter In Code Block dialog box, select Name from the drop-down list and click OK.

   This will cause the function name to start with the value entered for the Name parameter—the same value that will appear in the btn_OnClick_Markup code block.

6. From the Insert Code drop-down list, select Relative to a Specific Tag (**Figure 13.33**).

   Because it's a good practice to have server-side code display in the same place on every page, we're going to specify that next.

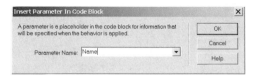

Figure 13.32 Reuse the Name parameter.

Figure 13.33 These are the final settings of the btn_OnClick_Handler code block.

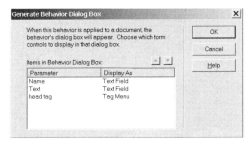

Figure 13.34 Use the dialog box called Generate Behavior Dialog Box to define how the parameters should be collected.

7. From the Tag drop-down list, select "head."

We'll place this server-side code in the same place we've placed all the other code: just before the </head> tag.

8. From the Relative Position drop-down list, select Before the Closing Tag.

9. Click Next.

We're done writing the code that defines our server behavior. However, we still have to define the dialog box that we'll use when creating new instances of the behavior in our pages. And to define that dialog box, we need to invoke the Generate Behavior Dialog Box dialog box. (Don't worry, that's not an echo you're hearing—we're talking about a dialog box for creating a dialog box!) The dialog box should now be open (**Figure 13.34**).

10. In the Generate Behavior Dialog Box dialog box, review the default settings and click OK.

The defaults are what we want. However, if we didn't like the default values, we could have reordered the items in the list, or changed the fields from Text Field to some other type of field like a list menu.

That completes the creation of our btn_OnClick server behavior. Now we can add it to our pages in the same way as the Insert Record and Update Record behaviors we used in Chapter 8.

To use a custom server behavior:

1. Open the Web Form you created in Step 1 of "To define the markup code for a custom server behavior." Make sure it shows both code and design by clicking the Document toolbar's Show Code and Design Views icon .

2. Click in the code just after the <body> tag, and add a form by typing the following:

   ```
   <form runat="server">
   </form>
   ```

3. In Design view, click inside the dotted red lined box that represents the form you just created. Then from the Insert bar, click on the ASP.NET tab, and then click the asp:label icon abc to open the Tag Editor.

4. In the Tag Editor, set the ID to "lblMessage" and click OK.

5. In Design view, click beside the new lblMessage control. This sets the insertion point for our btn_OnClick server behavior.

6. From the Application panel group, click on the Server Behaviors panel, and then open the drop-down menu and select btn_OnClick (**Figure 13.35**).

   This will open the dialog box we defined in Step 10 of "To define an event handler for a custom server behavior." We'll use it to create this instance of our btn_onClick server behavior.

7. In the btn_OnClick dialog box, set the Name to "btnTest" and Text to "Test the Code" (**Figure 13.36**). Then click OK to have the markup and handler written to the page.

Figure 13.35 Use the new btn_OnClick server behavior from the menu on the Server Behaviors panel.

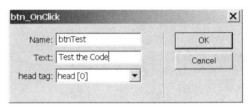

Figure 13.36 Set the parameters for the server behavior you're adding to your page.

Script 13.1 Test the btn_OnClick server behavior by adding a text label that changes when the button is clicked.

```
                        script
 1  <%@ Page Language="C#" ContentType=
    "text/html" ResponseEncoding=
    "iso-8859-1" %>
 2  <html>
 3  <head>
 4  <title>Untitled Document</title>
 5  <meta http-equiv="Content-Type" content=
    "text/html; charset=iso-8859-1">
 6  <script language="C#" runat="server">
 7  void btnTest_OnClick(Object Src, EventArgs E)
 8  {
 9    lblMessage.Text = "It Works!";
10  }
11  </script>

12  </head>
13  <body>
14  <form runat="server">
15    <asp:label ID="lblMessage" runat=
      "server"></asp:label>
16    <asp:button ID="btnTest" runat=
      "server" Text="Test the Code"
      OnClick="btnTest_OnClick" />
17  </form>
18  </body>
19  </html>
```

8. Add the following to the body of the btnTest_OnClick function:

```
void btnTest_OnClick(Object Src,
EventArgs E)
{
   lblMessage.Text = "It Works!";
}
```

The resulting code should look like **Script 13.1**.

9. Save the document and then preview the page using the Live Preview extension we downloaded and installed earlier in this chapter by clicking the Live Preview icon on the Document toolbar 🔲 .

You'll first see just the button, but when you click it, the message "It Works!" will appear.

See how easy it is to use custom server behaviors? All server behaviors you create this way will appear under the Server Behaviors panel's menu. If you want a handy icon that achieves this functionality to appear on the Insert bar instead, just keep reading.

Creating extensions

In the same way that we added an icon to the Document toolbar for the Live Preview extension, you can also add other Dreamweaver extension icons—and not just to the Document toolbar, but to any toolbar or panel group, including the Insert bar. You can even add an entry to one of the drop-down menus at the top of Dreamweaver—or create your own if you like. The secret to doing it is to create a special file called the Macromedia eXtension Installation (MXI) file.

MXI files are XML-formatted files that describe an extension's name, version number, and type; the files that make up the extension; and information about how to use it. An MXI file can describe changes to make to the menus at the top of Dreamweaver or to the Insert bar tabs. And because Dreamweaver is designed to let every developer have a unique configuration, the altered menu and Insert bar definition files can be saved to the extension user's personal configuration folder so that just one developer's environment will change.

Before we define the MXI file, though, we'll create an extension. It will be an *object extension,* which means that it will appear on a tab of the Insert bar. To keep our extension separate from the ones that come with Dreamweaver, we'll create our own custom tab called VQP, although if we preferred we could add it to one of the preexisting tabs.

Our object extension will have the same functionality as the custom server behavior we created earlier in the chapter; but because we'll define an MXI file for it and eventually package it for distribution, other developers will be able to use our extension as well.

Object extensions consist of HTML and JavaScript and utilize special API functions provided by Dreamweaver to accomplish their task. All object extension definition files that come with Dreamweaver will be found in their default location: C:\Program Files\Macromedia\Dreamweaver MX\ Configuration\Objects.

In that directory, you'll find subdirectories for each tab of the Insert bar, along with a file called insertbar.xml. The insertbar.xml file describes the layout of the Insert bar, so we'll have to alter it for our new VQP tab to appear.

Once a subdirectory is defined to appear as a tab on the Insert bar, it's easy to add an object extension to it. All we have to do is copy the object extension's definition files (HTML, Javascript, and XML) to the subdirectory to activate them. An icon that represents the object extension will automatically appear on that tab when Dreamweaver starts.

While it's nice to be able to easily add extensions to the Insert bar's preexisting tabs, this method of adding an object extension has some limitations if you're considering publishing it. Instead, we'll use an alternative that will allow us to package and distribute the custom object extension. We'll create the btn_OnClick object extension, then define the MXI file to describe the extension and its special settings. Then we'll use the Extension Manager to package the extension's definition and MXI files into a single file for easier deployment to other computers.

The following instructions walk you through the creation of the interface that Dreamweaver will present for you to set the Name and Text properties of the btn_OnClick extension. Then in a second set of instructions we'll add the JavaScript code our extension will need to function.

Figure 13.37 Create a new HTML file in the New Document dialog box.

Figure 13.38 Click the Insert Table icon to start its dialog box.

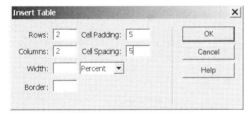

Figure 13.39 Create a new table with two rows and two columns.

To create an object extension's interface:

1. From Dreamweaver's File drop-down menu, select New.

This opens the New Document dialog box (**Figure 13.37**).

2. In the New Document dialog box's list of categories on the left, click Basic Page. Then from the list of page types on the right, click HTML. Then click Create.

This opens a new HTML file. Make sure it shows both code and design by clicking the Document toolbar's Show Code and Design Views icon ![icon].

3. Click in the page's code just after the <body> tag. Then type the following to create a form:

```
<form id="frmButton">
</form>
```

This time we don't want it to have the runat attribute set to "server" since we want the form to execute on the client rather than on the server; but we do need to give it an ID.

4. Click in the design area inside the red box that represents the form we just created. From the Insert bar, click on the Common tab, and then click on the Insert Table icon (**Figure 13.38**).

The Insert Table dialog box opens (**Figure 13.39**)

5. In the Insert Table dialog box, set Rows and Columns to 2. Clear the Width and Border fields, and set Cell Padding and Cell Spacing to 5. Click OK to create the table.

6. Back in Design view, click in the top left cell of the table and type "Name."

continues on next page

7. Move to the top right cell, and from the Insert bar, click on the Forms tab, and then click the Text Field icon to insert a text form field (**Figure 13.40**).

8. Click in the Property inspector's name field and set it to "txtName" (**Figure 13.41**).

9. Click in the bottom left cell of the table and type "Text."

10. Move to the bottom right cell, and from the Forms tab, click the Text Field icon ▯ to add a text form field to that cell.

11. Click in the Property inspector's name field and set it to "txtText" (**Figure 13.42**).

Now that we've defined these form fields, when we add our object extension to a page, Dreamweaver will automatically change this HTML into a dialog box. However, we still have to define the JavaScript functions that are called by Dreamweaver when an icon on the Insert bar is clicked. For simple object extensions like one that adds a Page_Load object, we'd only have to define the `objectTag` function, which returns a string that defines the code or markup to insert where the cursor is located. However, since we'll be inserting code and markup in a few different places, we need to implement a more complex function called `insertObject`.

Use the following instructions to define what will be done with the values entered into our txtName and txtText form fields.

Figure 13.40 The ASP.NET tab has an icon for inserting the asp:textbox control.

Figure 13.41 Use the Property inspector to change the name of the text box to "txtName."

Figure 13.42 Use the Property inspector to change the name of the text box to "txtText."

To write an object extension's JavaScript:

1. In the HTML document we were just working in, switch to Code view by clicking the Document toolbar's Show Code View icon ⬦.

2. Change the text between the `<title>` and `</title>` tags to `btn_OnClick`. The title is what gets displayed when the user's mouse rests over the extension's icon.

3. Click just before the `</head>` tag, and add the following JavaScript code block:

```
<script language="JavaScript">
function insertObject()
{
  var Name = document.frmBut
  ton.txtName.value;
  var Text = document.frmBut
  ton.txtText.value;
}
</script>
```

   Here we're setting variables for the values of the two form fields we created in the "To create an object extension's interface."

4. Now add some more code to that function to make sure the Name and Text variables have their values set:

```
if( Name != "" && Text != "" )
{
}
else
{
  return "The button must be have a
name and text.";
}
```

The `insertObject` function doesn't return anything if all is well. That's why we only return a message when either the Name or Text variable is empty. In the event that an error occurred, this message would pop up, and the dialog box that Dreamweaver generates from the form we defined in "To create an object extension's interface" would remain open so that the values could be updated. If no errors occurred, no message would pop up and the dialog box would close when OK is clicked.

5. Inside the `if` code block between the opening and closing curly braces, add the following code:

```
if( Name != "" && Text != "" )
{
var b = '<asp:button '
+ 'id="' + Name + '" '
+ 'Text="' + Text  + '" '
+ 'OnClick="' + Name + '_OnClick" '
+ 'runat="server" />';
}
```

   This code adds the markup for an asp:button control to a variable named b. We'll write it to the page our object extension is being added to next.

6. Add the following code to get a reference to the user's document and insert the contents of the b variable into it:

```
var userDOM = dw.getDocumentDOM(
'document' );
userDOM.insertHTML( b );
```

   The `dw.getDocumentDOM` function here returns the contents of the document to which we're adding this extension. Then the `insertHTML` function adds the contents of the b variable to the document where the user's cursor is currently located.

continues on next page

PERSONAL EXTENSIONS

7. Still inside the `if` condition code block, we'll create a variable to hold the Click event-handling function.

```
var f = '<script language="c#"
runat="server">\n'+ 'void ' + Name +
'_OnClick( Object Src, EventArgs E
)\n'
+ '{\n'
+ '\t\n'
+ '}\n'
+ '<' + '/script>';
```

Because we have to define the event handler as a string, we need to use the newline '\n' and tab '\t' special characters to have the right formatting when it's written out to the page.

8. We now need to output this function to just before the </head> tag. In order to do that, we need to find the </head> tag:

```
var headTag =
userDOM.getElementsByTagName( 'head'
)[0];
headTag.innerHTML = headTag.innerHTML
+ f;
```

You see here that we use `getElementsByTagName` to find all elements named head. Since we know there's only one, we grab the first element in the array. Then we append our event handler to its contents.

9. Compare your file against **Script 13.2** and save it as btn_OnClick.html.

Now we could save this file to an object extension directory such as the common directory. Its default location is C:\Program Files\Macromedia\Dreamweaver MX\Configuration\Objects\Common. This would make this extension accessible from the Common tab of Insert bar. However, instead we'll create an MXI file to make it more easily reusable by other developers.

Script 13.2 Implement the special `insertObject` function to insert code into a page at several locations.

```
1  <!DOCTYPE HTML PUBLIC "-//W3C//DTD HTML 4.01
   Transitional//EN">
2  <html>
3  <head>
4  <title>btn_OnClick</title>
5  <meta http-equiv="Content-Type" content=
   "text/html; charset=iso-8859-1">
6  <script language="JavaScript">
7  function insertObject()
8  {
9    var Name =
     document.frmButton.txtName.value;
10   var Text =
     document.frmButton.txtText.value;

11   if( Name != "" && Text != "" )
12   {
13     var b = '<asp:button '
14       + 'id="' + Name + '" '
15       + 'Text="' + Text  + '" '
16       + 'OnClick="' + Name + '_OnClick" '
17       + 'runat="server" />';

18     var userDOM = dw.getDocumentDOM(
       'document' );
19     userDOM.insertHTML( b );

20     var f = '<script language="c#" runat=
       "server">\n'
21       + 'void ' + Name + '_OnClick( Object
       Src, EventArgs E )\n'
22       + '{\n'
23       + '\t\n'
24       + '}\n'
25       + '<' + '/script>';
26
27     var headTag = userDOM.getElementsByTagNa
       me( 'head' )[0];
28     headTag.innerHTML = headTag.innerHTML + f;
29   }
30   else
31   {
32     return "The button must be have a name
       and text.";
33   }
34 }
```

(script continues on next page)

Script 13.2 *continued*

```
                    script
35  </script>
36  </head>
37  <body>
38  <form id="frmButton">
39  <table cellspacing="5" cellpadding="5">
40    <tr>
41      <td>Name</td>
42      <td><input name="txtName" type="text" id=
        "txtName"></td>
43    </tr>
44    <tr>
45      <td>Text</td>
46      <td><input name="txtText" type="text" id=
        "txtText"></td>
47    </tr>
48  </table>
49  </form>
50  </body>
51  </html>
```

To define an extension with an MXI file:

1. Create a new HTML document, delete all contents in the file, and save it as btn_OnClick.mxi.

2. In the first line of the document, add the following to define this document as an MXI file for version 1 of the btn_OnClick object extension:

    ```
    <macromedia-extension
    name="btn_OnClick"
    version="1.0"
    type="Object"
    requires-restart="true" >
    ```

    We're also stating that this extension requires that Dreamweaver be restarted before the extension can be used.

3. Next, add the code that limits this extension to the MX version of Dreamweaver:

    ```
    <products>
      <product name="Dreamweaver"
          version="6" required="true" />
    </products>
    ```

    Though you can make extensions for Dreamweaver all the way back to version 3, only MX can work with ASP.NET. And because MX's version number is 6, we set version 6 to be required.

    continues on next page

PERSONAL EXTENSIONS

4. Now we'll define the author and description of this extension:

```
<author name="Ryan Parnell
             and Joel Martinez" />
<description>
  <![CDATA[ This object extension is
  meant to add an asp:button control
  and its empty Click event handler. ]]>
</description>
```

The `<![CDATA[]]>` is an XML statement that marks the text it contains as plain text that should not be processed as XML content. It makes it easier to write English sentences in XML without worrying about accidentally using a specialized XML character or keyword.

5. Now add the `ui-access` element that is similar to the description element.

```
<ui-access>
  <![CDATA[ Start this extension from
  the VQP tab of the Insert bar. ]]>
</ui-access>
```

The `ui-access` element differs from the description element in that it's meant to describe the way the object extension is used, not what it does.

Now that we've described this extension, it's time to define how Dreamweaver will change when the object extension is installed.

6. List the files that make up this extension:

```
<files>
  <file name=" btn_OnClick.html"
  destination="$dreamweaver/
  configuration/objects/VQP" />
</files>
```

We only have one file—the btn_OnClick.html file—but we could have also had an icon to go along with it. Without one defined, Dreamweaver will just use its default icon ▣ .

If you do make one, it should be 18 by 18 pixels; any bigger, and Dreamweaver will resize it for you. You must also give it the same name as your html file, but of course with the .gif extension.

The `$dreamweaver` that you see in the `destination` attribute setting is a Dreamweaver variable that signifies its installation directory. That way, if the person who installs this extension put Dreamweaver in a custom directory, you don't have to do anything special for the installation to work.

Here, we're installing the extension into a new directory called VQP. If we had an icon, it would have to go there, too.

We'll alter the Insert bar soon to account for the new directory.

7. Now add the following element, which will contain all the elements that alter Dreamweaver:

```
<configuration-changes>
</configuration-changes>
```

8. Add the following to describe how we want to alter the Insert bar:

```
<configuration-changes>
  <insertbar-changes>
    <insertbar-insert
insertBefore="DW_Insertbar_ASPNET">
    </insertbar-insert>
  </insertbar-changes>
</configuration-changes>
```

All changes to the Insert bar must be enclosed in the `<insertbar-changes>` element as we've done here. The change we want to make is the insertion of a new tab before the ASP.NET tab.

The `DW_Insertbar_ASPNET` is the unique identifier for the ASP.NET tab. We learned its unique identifier by looking in the insertbar.xml file we talked about earlier.

Script 13.3 Creating an MXI file for an object extension gives the developer more control over how that extension adds to and customizes Dreamweaver.

```
                      script

1  <macromedia-extension name=
   "btn_OnClick" version=
   "1.0" type="Object" requires-restart="true">

2    <products>
3      <product name="Dreamweaver" version=
       "6" required="true" />
4    </products>

5    <author name="Ryan Parnell and Joel
     Martinez" />

6    <description>
7    <![CDATA[ This object extension is meant
     to add an asp:button control
8    and it's empty Click event handler.
9    ]]>
10   </description>

11   <ui access>
12   <![CDATA[ Start this extension from the
     VQP tab of the Insert bar. ]]>
13   </ui-access>

14   <files>
15     <file name="btn_OnClick.html" destination=
       "$dreamweaver/configuration/objects/VQP" />
16   </files>

17   <configuration-changes>
18     <insertbar-changes>
19       <insertbar-insert insertBefore=
         "DW_Insertbar_ASPNET">
20         <category folder="VQP" id=
           "VQP_Insertbar_VQP" showIf=
           "_SERVERMODEL_ASPNET">
21           <button id=
             "VQP_ASPNET_btn_OnClick" />
22         </category>
23       </insertbar-insert>
24     </insertbar-changes>
25   </configuration-changes>

26 </macromedia-extension>
```

9. We still have to define what we want to insert, so add the following:

```
<insertbar-insert insertBefore=
"DW_Insertbar_ASPNET">
  <category folder="VQP" id=
  "VQP_Insertbar_VQP" showIf=
  "_SERVERMODEL_ASPNET">
    <button id="VQP_ASPNET_btn
    _OnClick" />
  </category>
</insertbar-insert>
```

Here we're stating that we want to add a new tab called VQP by setting the category element's folder attribute. And since we plan to only put ASP.NET-relevant extensions on that tab, we only show it if the document that's currently open is an ASP.NET document (in other words, showif="SERVERMODEL_ASPNET").

Then on the VQP tab, we'll have an icon (button) linked to our btn_OnClick file. Remember that since we aren't providing an icon ourselves, Dreamweaver will show its default icon.

10. The last thing to do is close out our element with the following:

```
</macromedia-extension>
```

11. Compare your document to **Script 13.3** and save it as btn_OnClick.mxi.

We could install our extension with the Extension Manager, as it's now using our MXI file. However, if we want others to be able to use it on other computers, we have to distribute the MXI and HTML files together. We can make distribution even easier by grouping these files within a single Macromedia eXtension Package (MXP) file.

To package an extension for distribution:

1. Open the Extension Manager.

2. From the File drop-down menu, select Package Extension (**Figure 13.43**).

   This will open the Select Extension to Package dialog box.

3. In the dialog box, select the btn_OnClick.mxi file and click OK.

4. The Extension Manager will automatically package all the relevant files together into a file called btn_OnClick.mxp and save that file to the same directory as your MXI file.

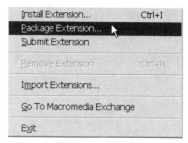

Figure 13.43 Use the Extension Manager to package all the files that make up a custom extension into one file.

Now that you have your extension packaged into the btn_OnClick mxp file, you can email it to your friends, copy it onto other computers, or publish it to the Dreamweaver Exchange library. To install your extension, you just have to double-click it or use the Extension Manager as we did in "To install an extension using the Extension Manager" earlier in this chapter. We'll do that now for practice.

With the package installed and Dreamweaver restarted, follow these instructions to use your new extension. You'll find that these steps are similar to the "To use a custom server behavior" instructions.

To use the btn_OnClick object extension:

1. Create a new Web Form and set it to show both code and design by clicking the Document toolbar's Show Code and Design Views icon ![icon].

2. Click in the code just after the <body> tag, and add a form by typing the following:

```
<form runat="server">
</form>
```

3. In Design view, click inside the dotted red lined box that represents the form you just created. From the Insert bar, click on the ASP.NET tab, and then click on the asp:label icon ![icon] to open the Tag Editor.

4. In the Tag Editor, set the ID to "lblMessage" and click OK.

5. In Design view, click beside the new lblMessage control. This sets the insertion point for our btn_OnClick extension.

6. From the Insert bar, click on the new VQP tab, and then click on the btn_OnClick icon (**Figure 13.44**). This will open the dialog box you defined (**Figure 13.45**).

7. In the btn_OnClick dialog box, set the Name to "btnTest" and Text to "Test the Code." Then click OK. This will cause the markup and handler to be written to the code of the page.

8. Add the following to the body of the btnTest_OnClick function:

```
void btnTest_OnClick(Object Src,
EventArgs E)
{
    lblMessage.Text = "It Works!";
}
```

The resulting code should look like **Script 13.4** on the next page.

continues on next page

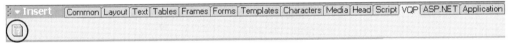

Figure 13.44 The btn_OnClick object extension is available from our custom VQP tab on the Insert bar.

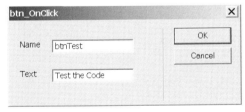

Figure 13.45 The object extension version of btn_OnClick is much prettier than that of the server behavior.

9. Save the document and then preview the page using the Live Preview extension we downloaded and installed in the first half of this chapter by clicking the Live Preview icon 🎯 (its tip will say "Server Debug").

You'll first see just the button; but when you click it, the message "It Works!" will appear.

Now you know how to customize Dreamweaver and distribute your customization to others. We challenge you to come up with your own ideas on how to improve Dreamweaver's ASP.NET functionality and post them on the Dreamweaver Exchange. We'll be watching for them!

Script 13.4 Test the code of the btn_OnClick object extension in the same way you would test the server behavior's code.

```
1  <%@ Page Language="C#" ContentType=
   "text/html" ResponseEncoding="iso-8859-1" %>
2  <html>
3  <head>
4  <title>Untitled Document</title>
5  <meta http-equiv="Content-Type" content=
   "text/html; charset=iso-8859-1">
6  <script language="C#" runat="server">
7  void btnTest_OnClick(Object Src, EventArgs E)
8  {
9    lblMessage.Text = "It Works!";
10 }
11 </script>

12 </head>
13 <body>
14 <form runat="server">
15   <asp:label ID="lblMessage" runat=
   "server"></asp:label>
16   <asp:button ID="btnTest" runat="server" Text=
   "Test the Code" OnClick="btnTest_OnClick" />
17 </form>
18 </body>
19 </html>
```

ONLINE RESOURCES

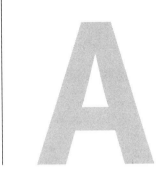

We've covered many topics in this book—some we've explored in depth, and others we've merely touched upon. Because ASP.NET is such a complex topic, this appendix provides some suggestions of where to turn to get more information, not only about ASP.NET and Dreamweaver, but also about other Web development topics.

In addition to the links provided below, this book also has a companion Web site to which you can refer to obtain downloadable versions of the code found within the book, as well as links to other useful sites and added information spawned by reader requests. You can visit the companion site at http://www.peachpit.com/vqp/asp.net/dreamweaver.

The combination of the information available from our companion Web site and the links listed in this appendix should give you endless hours of additional ASP.NET and Dreamweaver reading. Enjoy!

Dreamweaver Sites

There are far too many Web sites dedicated to Dreamweaver to name here. Below are some of the best, in our opinion.

http://www.dreamweaver.com

Macromedia's official Dreamweaver site is the first Dreamweaver-specific site you should look at—it's loaded with valuable information. From the site's navigation menu, you'll of course have access to samples and tutorials, but even better is the fact that you can link to the Application Development Center and access in-depth articles about developing applications with Dreamweaver MX. You can also link to the Support Center to learn about the most recent issues and updates concerning Dreamweaver MX. Also available are the Dreamweaver Online Forums, where you can converse with other developers about issues and topics most interesting to you.

http://www.dwfaq.com

The group at **DreamweaverFAQ.com** is dedicated to providing answers to frequently asked questions about Dreamweaver, helpful tutorials, additional code snippets, and a store where you can find some useful Dreamweaver extensions.

http://www.dwteam.com

The Dreamweaver Team at www.dwteam.com comprises a group of top Dreamweaver professionals focused on helping people learn about Dreamweaver development. The site provides relevant articles, tutorials, and extensions.

ASP.NET Sites

http://msdn.microsoft.com

Microsoft's MSDN site, which is Microsoft's official library for technical information concerning all of its technologies, is the best Web site to go to for first-hand information about ASP.NET. Here you can link to many .NET articles and Web pages assembled by the makers of this technology.

http://www.gotdotnet.com

GotDotNet, maintained by the Microsoft engineers who built .NET, is regularly updated with cutting-edge news and information straight from the source. Users also contribute to site content, so you'll have access to all sorts of information, tutorials, components, and even coding contests.

There are still more sites that are good sources of information for ASP.NET, but most of them you can link to directly from www.gotdotnet.com's home page:

◆ http://www.aspalliance.com

◆ http://www.4guysfromrolla.com

◆ http://www.dotnetjunkies.com

Other Resources

There are many facets of Web development with which it pays to be familiar when working on ASP.NET and Dreamweaver projects. Below we've listed some sites that touch on a few of these topics, including Web development in general, interface design, XML, and so on.

General Web Development

Sites abound that are dedicated to presenting articles and tutorials on the topics related to Web development in general.

Webmonkey, at **http://www.webmonkey .com**, has a long history of providing quality articles that teach people how to do everything from working with Cascading Style Sheets to getting a higher ranking in search engines.

Another site that covers a broad range of topics is DevGuru, at **http://www.devguru.com**. This site is better than Webmonkey for referencing the syntax of different languages, both online and in a downloadable Adobe Acrobat PDF file. But it also has good tutorials and even a knowledge base for determining how to solve errors based on error codes.

For developers that focus entirely on Macromedia products, MX inSite Magazine at **http://www.mxinsite.com** is a relatively new Web site dedicated to Macromedia products and related technologies. It has articles on Dreamweaver, UltraDev, Flash, Fireworks, Director, Cold Fusion, and more.

Interface Design

When it comes to interface design, Create-Online at **http://www.createonline.com** is a fantastic place to learn more. The sleek and attractive design of this online zine is also published as a printed magazine, usually available in larger bookstores like Borders and Barnes & Noble.

On the flip side, you could go to **http://www.webpagesthatsuck.com** to learn how *not* to design your site. It is an entertaining way to learn interface design because it shows badly designed pages and discusses why the pages are bad. By learning the negatives, hopefully you'll be able to avoid repeating the same mistakes that others have made.

For those interested in keeping up with standards-compliant designs, you can visit A List Apart at **http://www.alistapart.com**. This site focuses on providing articles that guide developers on how to make top-notch sites that stay compliant with the standards, in addition to how to deal with Web browsers that don't follow the standards.

HTML Validation

Validation is important because of all the different browsers and assorted technologies that rely on the consistency of code. By validating the pages in your Web site, you can rest assured, knowing that your pages work well with most any other technology.

The best place to validate your code is the W3C Validation Service at **validator.w3.org**. This site is run by the World Wide Web Consortium (W3C), the standards body that actually creates and approves most of the standards used on the Web, so it's obviously the most trustworthy place to verify you are compliant with the standards.

OTHER RESOURCES

XML

Speaking of the W3C, this is the standards body that created the eXtensible Markup Language (XML). While you could go to the W3C Web site for XML information (www.w3.org/XML), it's pretty cryptic, unless you're an engineer. Instead, O'Reilly's XML-specific site at **http://www.xml.com** or ZVON's guide to the XML galaxy at **http://www.zvon.org** are better choices.

On O'Reilly's Web site you'll find simplified articles that explain the complexities of XML, as well as in-depth articles discussing XML at its most advanced levels.

If you want a resource that's more of a simple XML reference tool, the ZVON site is a good alternative. In addition to providing easy-to-use references for XML syntax, the site also provides references for things like Cascading Style Sheets, HTML, and so on. Most topics have tutorials available as well, so if you feel like you need more than a simple reference, the tutorials can help you get to the next level.

INDEX